Choudhury - Sinha's Art Reference Series; 6

ENCYCLOPAEDIA OF INDIAN THEATRE

Books by the Same Authors:

1. Triune System of Classification (1994).
2. All-India Directory of Art, Culture & Allied Centres (1995).
3. Encyclopaedia of Indian Writers: Akademi Laurels Vol.1. Sanskrit (1996).
4. Afro-Asian Directory of Art & Cultures Centres (1997).
5. Encyclopaedia of Indian Writers: Akademi Laurels Vol.2: Bengali (1999).
6. — Vol. 3: Oriya [In Press]
7. International Guide to Art Research Materials: [In Press]
   — Vol. 1: Indian Languages & Literature,
   — Vol. 2: Indian Fine Arts,
   — Vol. 3: Worldwide.
8. Encyclopaedia of Indian Theatre Vol. 2: Kalidasa. [In Press]

Encyclopaedia of Indian Theatre -1

BHASA

Biswajit Sinha

Ashok K. Chaudhary

Raj Publications

New Delhi-110002

Encyclopaedia of Indian Theatre-1: Bhasa

First Published in 2021

Series- 978-81-86208-18-6

978-81-86208-11-3

Rs. 1195

Published by : **Raj Publications**
108, 4855/24, Ansari Road,
Daryaganj, New Delhi - 110002
Tel. : 011- 23250939, 09811010939
E-Mail: rajpublications@yahoo.co.in

Laser Typesetting : Aarati Computers, Delhi-110 009

Printed at : Balaji Offset, Delhi

In
Fond Memory of Our Sister
Deepali Bose

Contents

Dr. K. P. A. Menon, I.A.S. (Retd.)
Chancellor
Shri Lal Bahadur Shastri
Rashtriya Sanskrit Vidyapeeth
(Deemed University)
Katwaria Sarai, New Delhi-110016
Phones . 6851253, 6564003
Fax . 011-6851253

Res . "Panchavati"
215, Kailash Hills,
East of Kailash,
New Delhi-110 065
Phones : 6840374, 6834877
Fax : 011-6922366
Email : kpamenon@hotmail.com

Foreword

The plays of Bhasa have always held a special charm for me ever after I had my first hand acquaintance with them. Is it not but natural that one feels excited about the discovery of a long lost child? Though the great poet's name had been inscribed in golden letters by such great figures like Kalidasa, Dandin, Banabhatta, Vakpatiraja, Jayadeva and Rajasekhara, the plays including the "dream play" had been out of circulation for centuries. There-discovery of the 13 plays ascribed to Bhasa has indeed been one of the most sensational events in the history of Sanskrit literature during the 20th century. Our homage to the rulers of the Travancore royal family for having carefully nursed and preserved our cultural heritage and for the great scholar Ganapati Sastri who, as the first curator of the manuscript library of Trivandrum donated it to the Sanskrit world.

An attempt that has been made by the two young scholars to throw more light on the subject. Interest on the great playwright is definitely on the increase within and outside the country. With a publication of this nature, scholars and researchers might get an idea of where to search for more materials.

Dating of Bhasa, if it could be done with a fair degree of precision will indeed be an important event in the history of Sanskrit literature. One could almost compare it to the dating of invasion which enabled us to reconstruct the history of ancient India for a period spreading to a few centuries before and after that event. Many historians have not unfortunately given adequate attention to the literary sources about which, in many cases they have only an indirect knowledge. Some of them talk about Valmiki's Ramayana as the composition of the closing centuries before Christ. If Bhasa could be dated to 4th century Valmiki should go back to 6th or 7th century B.C. if not earlier. It even appears that a version different from that of Valmiki might have been current during the periods of Bhasa and Kalidasa. Admittedly, Valmiki is the earliest composer of the great epic and if more than one version had been current during the 4th century B.C. it becomes helpful in guaging the antiquity of the poet described as the primeval one.

The present authors have taken a good deal of pains in identifying the voluminous literature on the earliest known among the playwrights of India in different languages. It is only quite appropriate that they should have dealt with the stage presentation of the play in the form of Kutiyattam in Kerala. It could be asserted without any serious fear of contradiction that it was the Kerala stage that kept Bhasa plays alive leading to the final discovery of the manuscripts in Trivandrum. It is my fervent hope that the present work by the two learned research scholars Shri Biswajit Sinha and Shri Ashok K. Choudhury would create an awareness in the coming generation of scholars of the need for paying greater attention to the works of this great playwright and throwing more light on his life and times.

Panchavati,
215, Kailash Hills,
New Delhi.

25.9.99

Dr. K.P.A. MENON
Chancellor,
Shri Lal Bahadur Shastry Rashtirya
Sanskrit Vidyapeeth,
Katwaria Sarai, New Delhi.

Preface

When 'Padmabhusan' was to bestow on Natyacharya Sisir Kumar Bhaduri, in a letter to the Government of India, he stated: "I have a personal reason, besides the one of Principle, for not wishing to be conferred the honour. But by its acceptance I shall mislead the lovers of the theatre into believing that the Government are aware of the importance of drama in the life of the nation." This was the year 1952. And in the same year, by a Resolution dated 31st May 1952 of the Ministry of Education, Government of India constituted 'Sangeet Natak Akademi', India's apex Performing Art Centre. It had sundry objectives ranging from giving recognition to individual artists and organisations. publishing scholarly books, boosting research pursuits, fostering cultural contacts to inculcate theatre consciousness among the Indian masses. In 1959, Sangeet Natak Akademi set up the 'National School of Drama and Asian Theatre Institute' to provide training in the art. Thereafter, scores of similar academies, schools, institutes and organisations sprang up in the post-independent phase with the same mission of the revival, restoration and enrichment of indigenous theatre and to stir up theatre movement throughout the length and breadth of the country. But after celebrating fifty years of independence and when we are about to enter into another millenium, theatre personalities like Satya Dev Dubey outbursts: "Theatre is dying and should be allowed to die a respectable death."

Once in this vast subcontinent this art form identified itself with sacred events and which still enjoys a rich and unprecedented theatrical traditions of diverse nature. But can we barefacedly say that our precious past artistic treasures are well preserved and disseminated? It so, then why many ancient dramatists have gone into oblivion? The gloom and obscurity encompasses many litteratures due to dearth of documentation, why invaluable shastras, art forms and techniques are no more extant? Inspite of colossal efforts, we have failed to trace many important classical works on art and aesthetics. Asvaghosa's plays are available only in fragments today. The play 'Charudatta' of Bhasa ends abruptly in the middle. It is said that the pre-occupation of the Hindus with foreign invasions and internal disturbances left little time for the rulers to read or preserve our glorious literary and other art heritages. Bhasa, the first regular dramatist in India (on whom the present work rests) had written his dramas long before Kalidasa who is belived to be flourished in the second half of the 4th century B.C. But it was only in the year 1909 that due to sedulous quest of a single man that the lost plays of Bhasa were recovered. The great Ganapati Sastri found them in palm leave manuscripts that appeared to be some 300 years old. The play were in old Malayalam characters. Scholars opine that its Devanagari scripts were perhaps destroyed by Muslim invaders. Here our intension is not to unravel any mystery regarding irrepressible loss of the past legacies. Those were the days of suppression, political uncertainty and ineffectual leadership. But our point is that why in a free and developed nation, our indigenous artists still here to brook government's apathy towards the discipline? There is no cultural policy till date. Most of the cultural organisations setup by the Government of free India are staggering. Functioning in the name of autonomy, institutes under government's aegis have worsen the situation. Today everywhere, blind neglect has been endemic. The government has failed to focus national attention on theatre. To quote Sisir Bhaduri again. "A nation is known by its stage". Is it so? Then why no government sponsored theatrical organisations or research bodies could bring out a single encyclopaedia on their most productive areas of research? Here we can add one of the objects for which Sangeet Natak Akademi came into being. It is to publish literature on Indian music, dance and drama including reference works. Then, why not a single comprehensive reference book of international stature could see the light of the day after more than four decades of its existence? There is a real need for a truly accessible drama encyclopaedia. To fill the void, we have ventured into writing an encyclopaedia which is not an easy task. None helped us in writing, compiling, editing, copyediting, proof reading and other stages of production. Inspite of insuperable hindrances, we have succeeded in bringing out the first volumes of this individual endeavour.

Realizing the magnitude of the task that involves in creating a singular or singularly useful encyclopaedia that caters to such a wider subject field like Indian Theatre, we have decided to publish fourty-five handy volumes.

The first few of which would deals with the ancient and medieval Sanskrit dramatists. Eventually the present work and the ensuing volumes become an innovative reference tools that combines the unique features of two traditional reference sources: the encyclopaedia and the biographical dictionary.

In good heart, we aspitre that this encyclopaedia will help direct attention to the appaling and neglected state of the documentation of dramatic heritage (both in terms of literature and performance in printed text form) which is infact one of the many constitutional obligations of the apex Akademies and Schools concerning Indian theatre. We hope the theatre buffs enjoy browsing the present volume as much as we have enjoyed in writing it for the new millennium.

Biswajit Sinha

Ashok K. Choudhury

Acknowledgements

A number of people have provided us immense support in collecting materials for this project over the past several years. We would like to thank Mr. J.P. Bengeri and his colleagues in Sangeet Natak Akademi Library, New Delhi for giving access to their resources.

Our thanks for help with illustrations go to Dr. Tarala Mehta, a well-known actress on stage and films in Bombay.

We are indebted to M/S Raj Publications for understanding the need for this book.

Finally and most importantly our deepest gratitude to Dr. K.P.A. Menon, Chancellor of the Shri Lal Bahadur Shastri Rashtriya Sanskrit Vidyapeeth, New Delhi.

1

Introduction

Bhasa was one of the famous predecessors of Kalidasa whose works were till recently regarded as lost long ago. In Sanskrit and Prakrit literature, we find ample evidences that confirms the existence of this eminent dramatist of ancient period. Kālidāsa (c. 400 A.D.) in the prologue of his drama 'Malavikagnimitra' mentions Bhasa as an unrivalled poet. In the prelude, the actor asks "How does the assembly show to much of honour to the work of a living author Kālidāsa by passing over poetical works of the widely known poets like Bhāsa, Saumilla, Kaviputra and others?" Bāna, in the introdution to his 'Harshcarita' (c. 620 A.D.) states that Bhāsa obtained fame by plays (nātaka) in the beginning of which the sūtradhāra (stage-manager) appeared. Kautilya's Arthasastra, a fourth century B.C, treatise quotes in it, a verse (Book X, Chap. 3, Para 368) exactly like verse 2 of Act IV of Yaugandharayana's vows. Thus, Bhāsa must have been a contemporary of Kautilya. Dandin, praises the scientific perfection of Bhāsa's dramas which are said to be the embodiment of his glory (Avantisundarikāthā). In Avnti Sundari Katha (7th or 8th centuri A.D.), there is the following lines: 'Bhasa is living through his dramas which constitute, as it were, his body, which has assumed so many different forms in his plays'. In the words of A.S.P. Ayyar, there may be an allusion in that passage to the fine scene in Dutavakya, where the body of Vasudeva assumed various forms, and Vasudeva lived in all those different forms, thereby showing that Dutavakya was known to be a play of Bhāsa. A verse of Rājaśekhara, the court poet of the great Gurjara - Pratihāra king of Kānyakubja (c.1000 A.D.) refers to 'Svapnavāsavadatta' as a work of Bhāsa which when thrown into the fire to assess its merit, stood the test successfully (as the fire could not consume it) in a verse in an anthology called "Suktimuktāvati".

In the Gaudavaho (Death of Garuda) by the Prākrit poet Vākpatirāja (c.750 A.D.), Bhāsa receives the title 'Jalanamitta' (Friend of conflagration), probably in allusion to the above event.

Vamara (8th century A.D.) has quoted verses which can be traced to Svapnavasavadatta and Daridracarudatta of Bhāsa, in his 'Kavyalankarasutravritti'. As he was well acquainted with 'Mṛcchakatika', it is clear that Bhasa's Carudatta was a different and was copied to a large extent by Sudraka.

Acharya Bhāmaha (8th century.) discusses the theme of 'Pratijnanatika' of Bhasa.

Mahendrapala (10th century A.D.) praised the dramaturgic excellence of Bhāsa (Bhāsanatakacakram) Abhinavagupta (c.1000 A.D.) of Kashmir in his famous commentary 'Dhavanyāloka', a rhetori work, a quotation attributed to the dramatic poet Bhāsa.

He is being called a 'Mahakavi' (great poet) by him and alludes to the Kṛda (the ball game in Act II) in Svapnavasavadatta and also to a play called Daridracarudatta by Bhāsa. He quotes a verse from a Ramayana play of Bhāsa. The verse is today not available in the Trivandrum versions, may be from one of his many missing plays or probably from Abhiśeka or less probably from Pratima.

Again, Saradatanaya belonging to 11th century, in his descrition of the plot of a Svapnanataka (Dream Play) in his Bhavaprakasa, seems to refer mainly to the Svapnavasavadatta of Bhasa.

In his Sṛngaraprakasa, Bhojadeva of 11th century mentioned to some events from a Svapnanataka, which must refer only to the scene in the Ocean Pavilion in Act-V of Svapnavasavadatta.

Bhāsa has been recalled by Jayadeva as the smile of Sarasvati, a humorist among poets (Bhasohasa). Somadeva quotes two verses under Bhāsa's name. The ancient anthologies have preserved some fifteen verses from Bhāsa's plays, without mentioning the plays from which they are taken.

Natyadarpana of Ramachandra and Gunachandra (12th century A.D.) have specifically mentioned Svapnavasavadatta as Bhasa's work and have referred to the sephalika flowers and the stone bench found in Act IV.

In his own words, Sagaranandin who flourished in 13th century summarised the prelude to Act-1 of Svapnavasavadatta.

A work of the 14th century entitled 'Sakuntavyakhya' quotes from Avimaraka, Balacharita Daridracarudatta, Dutaghatotkaca. Pancharatra and Svapnavasavadatta. The very words from the prelude to Act 1 of Svapnavasavadatta are quoted therein.

Ayyar, Bhat and Pusalkar takes Bhāsa to have lived in the fourth century B.C. in the reign of Chandragupta Maurya and was a senior contemporary of Kautilya. Bhargava, who is doubtful about Bhāsa's authorship of Cārudatta, regards Bhāsa as an old contemporary of Maurya. Rao opines that he was Kautilya's younger contemporary and places under Puṣyamitra Suṇga. At another place, Rao has stated that the playwright must have flourished in two or three centuries after Vālmiki and Vyāsa. On the basis of the historical development of Hindu law with regards to the status of women in the writings of Bhāsa, Kalidasa, Kautilya, Manu, Pataṇjali and Yājṇavalkya, Rao states that Bhāsa belongs to the second century B.C.

Dasgupta, however feels that Bhāsa lived in the third century B.C. and at a time when the Mahābhārata tales had not been worked up in the present form so that he could introduce radical changes in the story without giving a rude shock to the public feeling.

In his introduction to the Bhasa plays K.P.A. Menon has taken a view that the plays dealing with Udayana might have been composed before the Magadhan asendency when the Pradyotas of Avanti and the Pauravas of Kausambi were in full glory and Magadha was a rising power. According to historians Pradyota, ruler of Avanti fought against the king of Kausambi inspite of his being the son-in-law of the former. In the Udayana plays the matrimonial alliance is a saquael to the fight between the two royal families. He has also pointed out that Buddhism had made some headway in the country during the period deal with in the plays. Based upon these historical consideration he has expressed the view, " Bhasa could be dated to 5th century B.C. It could even be a century later since nothing prevents a poet from singing about the glory of the past ". This view has been independently supported by Shrinivas Rath who, on the basis of literary evidence comes to the conclusion that the play Svapnavasavadattam must have been composed towards the closing years of Chandragupta Maurya. According to him, the marriage of Vatsaraja to Padmavati is reminiscent of Chandragupta's marriage with the daughter of Seleukas Nikator.

Krishna Chaitanya assigns Bhāsa to the easy fourth century A.D. and well guesses Bhāsa's period as the fourth century A.D. in his general introduction to 'Six Sanskrit Plays'.

Pusalker writes in the book entitied 'Bhāsa : a study' enlighten us with the new evidence bearing on the date of Bhāsa or his plays from the domain of sculpture broughout by two scholars Krishna Das and Devadhar Krishna Das invites attention to three terracotta plaques from Kauśāmbī, "definitely assignable to the Suṇga period", portraying a scene closely agreeing with the story of the Pratijṇāyaugandharayass of which supports Jayaswal's view placing Bhāsa in the first century B.C. This archaeological evidence indicates that "there is an element of historical truth in the story of the plot" about Vāsavadattā escape as depicted on the plaques. As against this evidence favouring an early date for Bhāsa may be considered the iconographical particulars presented by Devadhar who suggests that two plays of the group, viz. The Dūtavākya and Madhyamavyāyoga, cannot be dated earlier than the seventh century A.D - the date of the Mahābalipuram sculpture depicting Trivikrama and Namuci. The regular appearance of the Ayudha - purusas in sculpture, which begins with the Guptas, is regarded as indicative of the Ayudha - purusas in these two dramas. The arguments, however, are far from convincing and there is no proper evaluation of the literary evidence.

The antiquity of time attributed to Bhāsa is seen from a tradition which refers Bhāsa as a rival of Vyāsa and his poem Visṇuḍharma, as having triumphed over Vyāsa's work of the same name.

T.S.Narayanāsastri, in his introduction to Ratnāvali propounded the opinion that Bhāsa was the later name of Dhāvaka alias Ghatakarpara and he flourished in the days of Śri Harsa of the 6th century B.C. He relied on passages in Rajaśekhara's Kavivimarśa and Hemcandra and Kavyānusāsana to say that Dhāvaka was a washerman by birth and he composed a number of dramas and among which he sold one to King Harsa, it is this sale that is described in Mammata's Kāvyaprakāśa.

T. Ganapati Sastri considers that Bhāsa refers to the Nyāyaśāstra of Medhāṭiṭhi, Pāṇini, an ancient sage prior to Bhārata and Kautilya, Gunadhya, Bhamaha, Sūdraka, and on the basis of these, Gioṛnal places him not later then the 5th century B.C.

V. Venkatachalam has aptly said that Bhāsa's reticence about himself is total. Later dramatists whispered at least their names to their contemporary and future audiences through the conversation of the Sūtradhāra and his assistant in the conventional prolugues to their plays. However, unlike Kalidasa and others, who came in his wake, Bhāsa did not care to record for posteritya even his name in the prologues, which are invariably very brief and conform to a set pattern, typically Bhāsa's. We are, therefore, left with the Hobson's choice of squeezing whatever information is possible about Bhāsa, the man, out of the scanty and uncommunicative external references to him and his works in the writings of later poets an critics.

Few scholars opins that Bhāsa hailed from Kerala and argues that his plays were discovered in Kerala. The Chakyar actors of Kerala have for a long time produced these plays in parts. Above all, agreement in technique with other known Kerala Sanskrit plays and other factors have led to the Kerala thesis.

However, majority of scholars agrees that Bhāsa's home must have been somewhere in the country between the Himalayas and the Vindhyas, through it is difficult to specially mention the exact region or the place.

From his writings, it can be said that he was a Brahmin. If not, at least a strict follower of Brāhmanical religion and practices and ardent devotee of Viṣṇu. In his dramas, he mentions various Brāhmanical rites and customs and with great pride he stresses upon the supreme status of the Brahmins. To justify the above, we can quote from his works where he says "Everywhere and everymoment are the Brahmins worthy of the highest honour on the earth"; "The king should hand over to the Brahmins the entire wealth of his kingdom and leave only his bow for his sons" etc.

MM DR. T. GANAPATI SASTRI (1860-1926)

The dramatists strong faith in lord Viṣṇu is evident in his plays such as Dūtavākya and the Bālacarita. Throughout the length and breadth of these two plays, the feeling of absolute surrender to the devotion of Viṣṇu can be seen for him Kṛṣṇa is the highest god and he is an authority on Kṛṣṇa - legend. This shows that he was a devotee of Vishnu as can be gathered in his constant reference to Him in the prolugue verses and the obvions worshipful tone of his references.

The dramalist had accepted the Hindu view of life. It is significant that Bhasa was not his name, any more than Valmiki or Vyasa being the names of grent sages and that Bhāsa is only a gotra name, like Patanjali, Yaugandharayana etc, the Bhāsa gotra being a branch of the Agastyagotra.

The existance of Bhāsa's works was not known until the early years of the century. Till 1910, Bhāsa was only a great name. In that year, T.Ganapati Sastri (1860-1926) discovered a collection of manuscripts of Bhasa's thirteen plays. These manuscripts were discovered in a Kerala Brahmin home named Maralikkara Matham near Trivandrum in Kerala.

At first, T. Ganapati Sastri, then Curator of the Maharaja's palace library found ten plays and a fragment written in Malyalam on 105 palm leaves. This was followed by two more plays and thirteen plays of Bhasa ended their undetected existance. Almost simultaneously, one of these plays was discovered by R. Narasimhachar, Head of the Archaeology Department, in Mysore.

T. Ganapati Sastri published them in the Trivandrum Sanskrit Series from 1912 to 1917 A.D. and in the preface he identified those plays as the plays of Bhāsa. If we adhere to the subject matter, plays could be grouped as under:-

(I) Udayana or Historical Plays

- Pratijṇāyangandharāyaṇam (The Minister's vows)
- Svapnavāsavadattam (The vision of Vāsavadatta)

(II) Fiction or Original Plays

- Avimāraka
- Daridra Cārudatta (Carudatta in poverty)

(III) Mahabhārata Plays

- Bālacaritam (The Adventures of the boy Krishna)

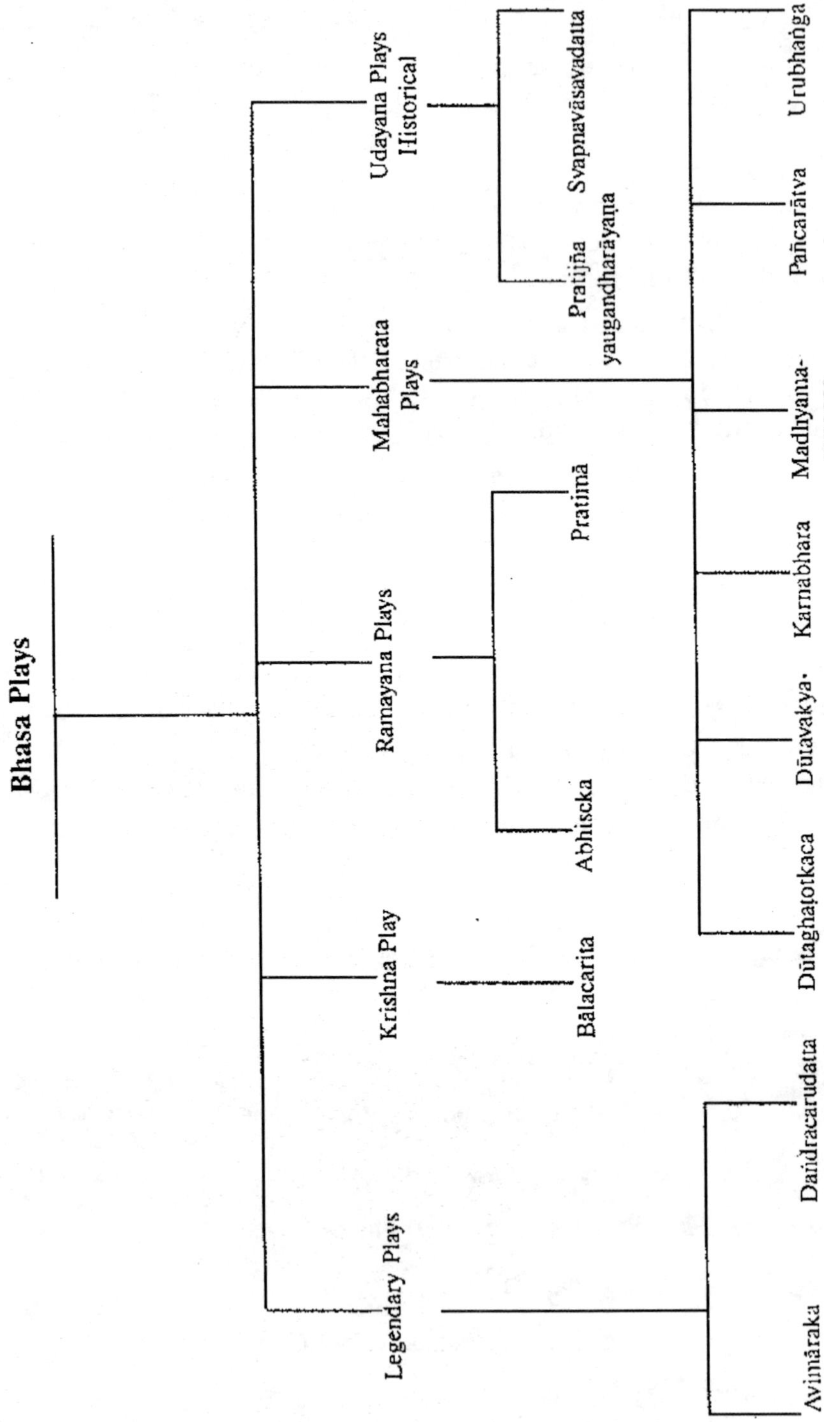
Bhasa Plays
Udayana Plays Historical
Mahabharata Plays
Ramayana Plays
Krishna Play
Legendary Plays
Svapnavāsavadatta
Pratijña yaugandharāyaṇa
Pratimā
Abhiseka
Bālacarita
Urubhaṅga
Pañcarātra
Madhyama-vyayoga
Karnabhara
Dūtavakya
Dūtaghaṭotkaca
Daridracarudatta
Avimāraka

- Dutaghatotkaca (Potsherd as an Envoy)
- Dutavakyam (The Embassy)
- Karṇabharam (Karṇa's task)
- Madhyamavyayoga (The Middle one)
- Paṇcaratram (The Fire nights)
- Urubhangam (The Broken thighs)

(IV) Rāmāyana Plays

- Abhisekanātakam (The Censecration)
- Pratimānatakam (The Statue play)

Popularly known as the Trivandrum plays, these plays are the subject of great controversy.

From the point of view of technique and art, all the thirteen plays shows striking resemblance that indicate or common authorship.

Some of these are :-

(I) All classical dramas begin with the nāndi, that is followed by the stage - direction : "After the nāndi is over the sūtradhara enters" and then the prelude commences with the talk of the sūtradhāra. But Trivandrum plays starts with the words: After the nāndi is over, the sūtradhāra enters, and then he utters the introductory benedictory prayer to Viṣṇu in which the names of the main characters of the play are usually mentioned in a significant manner.

(II) In Sanskrit classical works, something is said in praise of the work that is being presented and at the sametime, it glorifies the dramatist too in the prelude. But this is not the case with plays discovered by T. Ganapati Sastri where the prelude is very short and abruptly takes us to the beginning of the first act.

(III) The play begins with a benedictory stanza and end as well with it. The Bharatavākya or the concluding verse is very much different in other dramas, but in those ascribed to Bhāsa, in most of the cases, and at any rate concluding verse expresses the same meaning : May Rājasimha, the lion-strong king rule over the whole of this earth (or our country).

(IV) In respect of syntax and idiom, these drama show all sorts of uniformity.

(V) In classical dramas, the title and the name of the author are mentioned at the end. But this is not found in these thirteen theatrical pieces.

Though the text of any of these plays does not offer any direct evidence to settle the problem of their authorship but majority of the scholars assign them to Bhāsa. Therefore the credit goes to this ancient playwright for being the auothor of the largest number of extant Sanskrit dramas with variety in his writings, which is not found elsewhere.

But when we go through the citations from the Svapnavāsadatta of Bhasa, as found in works on poetics and dramaturgy, it would be seen that such citations are not found in the manuscript of Svapnavasavadatta as handed down to us by T. Ganapati Sastri. Few situations and verses are absent in it. This leads us to believe that the Trivandrum plays could be the abridgement of the original plays of Bhāsa.

If Svapnavasavadatta is an abridgement of an older text, then it is quite possible that the some is true of the other plays in the group. T.N.Mainkar states that the Chakyars (Cākyār) of Kerala are known to have given performances of plays for which they had prepared their own obridgements of stage editions. It is probable that these thirteen plays are such stage editions.

He has shown his versatility in the choice and use of the types of drama. From several one-act plays to a full-fledged drama in six acts. Bhasa has experimented with plays in two, three or four acts also. From a purely academic point of view, he alone provides examples of so many Sanskrit Roopakas—Nataka, Vyayoga, Anka, Veethi, Samavakara, Prakarana and Natika. If we ramify his entire output according to types, then, which 'Anka' will fall 'Urubhanga'; in 'Nataka category we will have Abhiseka, Avimaraka, Balacarita, Pratima and Svapnavasavadatta; under 'Natika' comes Pratijna - yangandharāyana in four acts; Carudatta is 'Prakasana' type; Pancarātra is 'Samavakāra'; Dutaghototkaca and Madhayumavyayoga are 'Vyāyoga'; 'Dūtavākya and Karnabhāra are 'Vithi'. These are shown in the following table:-

Bhasa Plays

Title	**Types**	**Acts**	**Sentiment**
Avimāraka	Nāṭaka	6	Śṛṅgāra
Balacarita	Nāṭaka	5	Vīra

Cārudatta	Prakarana	4	Śṛṅgāra
Dūtaghaṭoṭkaca	Vyāyoga	1	Vīra
Dūtavākya	Vīthī	1	Vīra
Karṇabhāra	Vīthī	1	Dīptarasa Karunapradhāna
Madhyamavyāyoga	Vyāyoga	1	Vīra
Pañcarātra	Samavakāra	3	Vīra
Pratijñāyaugandharāyaṇa	Nāṭika	4	Dīptarasa
Pratima	Nāṭaka	7	Sarvarasa
Svapnavāsavadatta	Nāṭaka	6	Śṛṅgāra
Ūrubhaṅga	Aṅka	6	Karuṇa

It can be seen that the length of his plays varies from one to six acts with Pratima - Nataka with 7 acts in shown below:

Dūtavākya	1
Dūtughaṭotkaca	1
Karnabhāra	1
Madhyamavyayoga	1
Ūrubhaṇga	1
Paṇcarātra	3
Cārudatta	4
Pratijṇāyaugandha Vāyaṇa	4
Bālacarita	5
Abhiṣeka	6
Avimāraka	6
Svapnavāsavadatta	6
Pratimā	7

The Rāmayana and Mahābhārata plays and the Bālacarita based on Kṛṣna legend bear witness to Bhāsa's deep knowledge of the epic and purānic literature of his days. As discussed earlier, the thematic material in Bhasa comes from both Mahabharata and Ramayana as well as from Akhyanas and legends, it in also both Prakhyat and Utpadya, i.e., well known and imaginary.

To quote Biswanath Bhattacharya, Bhāsa has used all the three type of it viz: the Legendary, the Invented and the Mixed in his plays. Though all the dramas have their origin in the Rāmayana, the Mahābhārata, the Bhāgavata or the Bṛhatkatha yet the poet has not followed the sources blindly. His inventive and creative brain has worked upon them and as a result, we find in his works all the three types of the plot.

Scrictly Legendary are the Pratima, Abhiseka, Dūtavakya, Urubhṇga and Bātacarita. The Invented are Svapnavāsavadattā, Prajṇāyaugandharāyana. Avimāraka and Cārudatta. The Mixed are Paṇcarātra, Madhyamavyāyoga, Dūtaghatotkaca and Karnabhāra.

In his Mahabharata plays, it can be seen that though based on the epic and not invented themes but the originality shown in the handling of legendary themes speaks of his high dramatic acumen. For example, in Paṇcarātra, the peculiar scenes depicted in the play is his own creation. The conclusion of the drama in shown by Bhāsa is again original as such it is in contrary to the Mahābhārata. If Duryoddhara would have given the half of his kingdom to the Pāṇḍavas, the great war of the Kuruksetra would have never occured.

His Madhyamavyāyogas also bears his his creative bent of mind. The meeting of Bhima with Ghatotkacag, (his son through Hidimbā) in which the play portray is entirely imaginative. In Dūtaghatotkaca is also an ivention of the playwright. Because in original epic, there is no mention of such sending of messenger.

The plot of Karnabhāra is entirely created by the dramatist by his fancy, though some of the events have been taken from the great epic.

The two Rāmāyana plays of Bhāsa are Abhisekanatakam and Pratimānātakam. Taken together, they practically covers the whole Rāma story except Bālakānda, Uttarakānda and the first half of Aranyakānda.

Abhisekanātakam of Bhāsa tries to cover a great part of Rāma story called from the Kiskindhā, Sundara and Yuddha kāṇḍa, but this drama gives more details and major emphasis on the presentation of the heroic sentiment. Though the predominant sentiment of the play is heroice, but other sentiments are also depicted in the play to support the main sentiment.

In his 'Pratimanātakam', the hero and the heroine are Rama and Sita, but special importance is given to the character of Bharata and Kaikeyi. Drama mainly shows Bharata in relation to Rāma. Bharata's mental or deal, his heart agonised by internal conflicts that started with his very visit to the Pratimā graha.

V.Venkatachalam points out that " There is an essential point of difference between these two plays. Abhiśekanātaka is practically nothing more than a dramatised version of Vālmiki's epic story with little or no changes in the plot or characteerisation. The incidents and persons are all the same, the characters are cast in the same stereotyped mould, the only difference is in respect of the external form. The few minor changes made here and there are not of much consequence, so much so, that Keith dubbed the play as "a somewhat dreary summary of the corresponding books of the Rāmāyana". As against this, Bhāsa had a definite dramatic purpose while writing the Pratimā. It is a recreation by Bhāsa out of Vālmiki's materials, written with the express purpose of removing the stain out of Vālmiki's Kaikeyī and elevating Vālmiki's, Bharat still further making him a bit taller than Rāma himself. Bhāsa has, accordingy made for reaching changes in the story in tune with his basic aim of presenting Bharata and Kaikeyī in a totally different perspective. As a result, the play is replete with remarkable innovations, which bring out Bhāsa's inventive genius in full relief. It is, therefore, not correct to say that Bhāsa's aim in writing more than one play on the Rāmāyana - theme was just to cover the whole of the epic.

His dramas based in the Ramayana show little ingenuity on the part of the author. Scholars opine that they vary from the original only in unimportant details and also no efforts is being made by him in the delireation of epic characters.

Keith comments that in the Rāma dramas only is there lacking any sign of his ability, the Abhisekanātaka is a somewhat dreary summary of the corresponding books (IV - VI) of the Rāmāyana, nor is the Pratimānātaka substantially superior. The variations are in the main few and unimportant, the two struggles between Sugrīva and Vālin are condensed into one which leaves the treacherous slaying of Vālin without shadow of excuse, and casts a blemish on Rāma's character which later dramatists avoid. The pathetic scene of the epic in which Tārā, his wife, laments Vālin's death is omitted, Vālin forbidding any woman to gaze on him in his fall. The two efforts of Rāvana to deceive Sītā, first by showing her Rāma's head, and later Rāma and Laksmana bound and seemingly dead, are reduced to one, the showing of the heads of both, and Sīta's constancy is made inhuman by denying her the comfort are senseless. To secure a happy ending, Agni is made to vindicate Sītā by the test of fire, and to hand her over to Rāma as Laksmī and his mate. The characters remain stereotyped and dull, Rāvana is nothing more than a miles glorious, if not comic, and Laksmana acts a very poor figure.

The Mahabharata plays show the dramatist in better relief. Critic observes that when he departs from the original, he shows immense skin and intelligence and the characters appears more lively and vivid.

Amongst his six Mahabhārata plays, five are small one-act play namely Dūtaghatotkaca, Dūtavākya, Karnabhāra, Madhyamavyāyoga and Urubhanga. The six play 'Paṇcarātra' is a full length drama in three acts, of the rare Samavakāra type. Keeping aside Dūtavākya, all the remaining three one acts are laid on the battle field. The formers has pre-war theme.

Though based on Mahabharata events, Paṇcarātra and Madhyamavyāyoga are playwrights own creation. The latter has an entirely new structure even in Paṇcarātra, Bhāsa made a number of changes to suit his dramatic purpose.

Biswanath Bhattacharya has aptly pointed out that his one act plays are never fragmentary. It is a very rare power of integration of all the aspects of the drama, which marks all his one act plays. Interestingly in his one acts all the events occur in a single day and the action gets completed with the very exist of all the characters in the end.

Although the shortest among his one-act plays, Karnabharān is an excellent literary work that is perhaps the best for his dramatic skill. The plot is simple and straight, without being weighed down by undramatic descriptions or more poetic flights of imagination. Besides, there is very little action in it. A critic hails the play as in psychological exerecise, laying bare the currents and cross - currents that storm the mind of Karna at a critical moment of his career. His character is enveloped in a halo of tragic grandeur as he still insists upon his march against Arjuna which, as he well realises, is foredomed to failure. Prof. G.C. Jhala writes that the play is constructed with chiselled neatness gracefulness and is a complete literary piece by itself.

The most well received one act play of Bhasa is perhaps the Madhyamavyayoga which revolvels around Bhima's meeting with his son Ghatotkaca. The play is beautifully crafted and successfully bringout the rasas 'Bhayanaka' 'Karuna' or 'Vira'. In the course of events, one can witness the 'Sentimet' 'Hasya' too.

Meenakshi Dalal writes that the interest of the drama 'Dūtavākyam' lies in the skillful portrayal of Duryodhana's character. His arrogance, self - praise, hatred of the Pāṇḍavas and the inferiority complex in relation to Shri Kṛṣna, and his selfishness, etc. are seen clearly as he clashes with Sri Kṛṣna. The elements of the external conflicts are just enough to enable this pychological portrayal.

His power of dramatisation is unrivalled whether this is Dutaghatotkaca,

Dutavakyam or Karnabhara, his technique super diction and characterisation of legendary figures and freshness in the presentation of the known theme or display of emotion shows that he had dramactic power of vision.

In 'Urubhanga' he presents the great Kuru king as the hero of his one act play and excellent *hard les a* tragic theme with 'Duryodhana' as a tragic figure.

Urubhangam stands out for its violation of Bharata's classical form or injunction against the representation of the death of the hero on the stage.

Most of the commentators on Sanskrit drama finds the delineation of Duryodhana's death as the most striking and to some the only remarkable feature of this play. It has rightly been observed by a critict that this play, a solitary composition of its kind, comes very close to Greek tragedy. The central idea of Greek tragedy is that man learns through suffering and it is through suffering that he becomes modest and humble. Man realises the futility of ambition and accepts his own insignificance. But before he learns his lesson he has to pay heavily for it... that is what happens in Urubhangam.

In the words of Madhusudan Pati 'Urubhangam' dramatises, the events of the final day's battle in the great Mahabharata war. Millions of warriors who had assembled to fight the epochal war at Kurukshetra have now perished. Only a handful of the chief contenders, and some strong soldiers, are left alive. The one who was principally responsible for this terrible carnage, the Kuru monarch Duryodhana, now stands alone, bereft of his legions, his famed generals, and his nineety-nine brothers. The play deals with the final encounter with the redoubtable. Pandava prince Bhima whom he is going to meet in single combat... In order to produce, within a small compass, this powerful impression of a large perspective steadily narrowing down to an intensely concentrated, illuminated focus, Bhasa begins by making a brilliant and novel use of 'Sthapana' (The dramatic introducts)

Play begins with the traditional 'Sutradhara' who moves towards fore-stage alongwith a male attendant who establishes the culminating dramatic moment against the backdrop of the past seventeen days epochal war. Through these two characters, Bhasa elegantly and skifully portrays not only the milieu of the horrors of death and desolation surrounding them. But in particular, he tries to establish in the mind of the audience. The two dimensions of the war, ie, the dharma on one side (war as a sacred duty and righteousness) and on the otherside of evil self-aggrandisement.

Urubhangam is a compact psychological play and with superb dramatic design. In real sense, the proper drama begins only after the feelings of revulsion and fascination of waste and achievements etc are firmly established in the audience's mind through secondary dramatic personal and the choric commentators who vividly described the mace-fight between Duryodhana and Bhima. Though Duryodhana dominates his opponent through his superior training and ability and at times, when his victory becomes certain, Bhima resorts to a course of attack prescribed in the rules of mace-fight, and eventually breacks the thigh of an unwary Duryodhana. The long seventeen days war is now come to an end with dynamic Duryodhana absolutely shattered, fallen and lying abjecting sprawled out, on the floor. The play beautifuly sketches the state of agony, misery and helpless of the Duryodhana who atlast long for the peace. Bhasa proves his mastery in handling the major character Duryodhana whose earlier aggressiveness, state of royal splendour, his authority is now replaced by man with moral clarity who realizes the futility of war and is in the midst of grief and embarrassment. The blind Kuru putriarch, Dhrutarastra alongwith his wife Gandhari, two daughter in law, and his only surving grand child Durjaya looks in the battle field and out calls for the fallen son. At the outset disappointed Duruyodhana remains silent, however, he soon realizes that has had, to response. So he unmindful of his broken thighs but, he moves forward to greet his parents. He collapses on the ground and with unbearable physical and mental agony. He utters painfully "Not only has Bhima plucked my hair and shattered my thighs with his mace, but he has robbed me of my ability to pays respect to seniors also".

Dr. Pati states that there is a reversal of the tragic plot when Duryodhana attains supreme satisfaction and ecstasy while he breathes his last. On the one hand his earthly aspiration is fulfilled when son Durjaya is crowned as 'Kuru King' at the instances of Aswatthama, the latter does not abide by the pacifist council of Duryodhana and now ready to fight the Pandavas on the other side. Duryodhana is happy and eager to meet his ancestors in the heaven with sigh of relief, he utters "Hanta, Krtam me hrdayanujan I tam".

Though this play of Bhasa has found recognition as a tragedy but Sanskritists like A.B. Keith takes an exceptional stand and holds the view that the play can not be called a tragedy as it depicts the just punishment of an evil person. Nevertheless, by and large, Urubhangam is recokned as the lone tragedy in the classical Sanskrit repertoire.

Amongst Mahabharat plays, his Pancaratra is a Samavakara type where he has follows Bharata and there is ten to twelve main characters in which are drama from the epic to which he has infused life with his unparalled power of characterization.

A scholar states that as his Kṛṣṇa legend play 'Bālacaritam' has a vast theme to cover, he, therefore, fails completely in the deliveations of subtle emotions and internal conflicts. In the plays the heroic feats of the child Kṛṣ ṇa is presented and thus, the sentiment that gets developed is heroic. The erotic episodes of Kṛṣṇa's life as are totally missing. Merely a narrative, this play remains a short and hurried account of the miraculous feats of Kṛṣṇa withtout giving any chance either for the development of conflict or the sentiments.

The play 'Avimaraka' being a love story, develops the erotic sentiment. It has a very unusual theme in which the hero Avimāraka remains disguised, while in other erotic drama where the identity of a character is kept back, the particular character happens to be the heroine.

To some critic though the various events that occurs in the story are quite interesting, but the playwright falls in unfolding the plot.

The play 'Daridracarudattam' is full of incidents and characters which are identical with those of Mṛcchakatikam except, of course, the political sub-plot and its attendant situations.

V. Venkatachalam observes that the two quasi-historical plays, 'Pratijṇāyan gandharāyaṇa' in four acts and Svapnavāsavadatta in six acts, are both products of Bhāsa's mellow genius... Pratijṇayangandharāyana is a fiery play teeming with political intrigues and is "an essentially manly drama" as excellently characterised by Mearwarth. Battles and skirmishes, captures and killings, kidnappings and hand - cuffs, assults and injuries, stretchers and first-aids, disguises and espionage, hunting expeditions and drinking bouts, strategic moves and counter-moves, challenges and counter-challanges - these constitute the main-stuff, of which the plot - fabric of Pratijnāyangandharāyaṇa is woven. There are only two female roles in the cast and they too have no functional importance. Still this play Pratijṇā - Yangandharāyana is fall with action and dramatic charm. Critics opines that for his simple and meaningful use of prose and verse, the nātikā becomes so charming. His style nowhere suffers from exaggeration, and over burdened with a great number of verses, though in the power of versification Bhāsa is one among the best poets.

Yaugandharayana is shown as a shrewd, dedicated minister for its main protagonist who carries himself into the thick of action, infilters into enemy kingdom with his loyal followers and participate in a heroic adventure to rescue his captive king Pratijnā Yangandharāyanam of Bhasa stands out as a memorable play that ensures mass appeal.

As against Pratijṇayagandharayana, Svapravasavadatta is a play of tender love, in both its phases of union and separation.

The predominant rasa in this play is Vipralambha Śṛṇgāra, ie, love in separation. However glimpses of Śṛṇgāra, Hāsya and Virā rasas could be found here and there to bring out the main sentiment.

In her thesis 'conflict in Sanskrit drama' Minakshi L.Dalal observes that Bhāsa with his simple style, direct and brief, paints the internal conflict of Vāsavadattā with such a realistic touch that Svapnavasavadattam can claim a place among the world's classics. Set in a politically disturbed background the theme of his magnum opus is essentially a study in psychological conflict. What would Svapnavāsavādatta be like without this psychological conflicts? She further states that Svapnavāsavadatta is practically a sequel to the Pratijṇa - Yangandharayan dealing as both do with incidents in the life of Udayana - king of Vatsa country. But there is a vital difference in the approach and treatment of the theme in both. Pratijṇā - Yaugandharāyana is mainly a drama of political intrigue - the erotic episode being sandwiched as a lovely diversifying element in it: the conflict in Pratijṇa - Yangandharāyana is mainly external with threads of internal conflict interwoven. In the Svapnavāsavadattam, the political eclipse of Udayana serves as a peg on which the main psychological drama of Vāsavadattā's emotions has been hung. Svapnavāsavadattam is more delicate, more subtle, more human, and on that account, more interesting than Pratijṇa - Yaugandharāyana.

S.K.De comments that more effectively devised in plot is the Svapna-Vāsavadatta that deals with the same theme of courtly love but rises above its bandity, for the motif of the dream in this play is finely conceived, the characters of the two heroines are more successfully differentiated and the gay old lover of Harsa's dramas is figured as a more serious, if somewhat love - sick and imaginative, lover. The main interest of the play lies in the dramatic skill and delicacy with which the feelings of Vāsavadattā love no sacrifice is too great; while her willing martyrdom is set off by the equally true, but helpless, love of Udayana a victim of divided affections and the demands of statecraft. It is a drama of fine sentiments, the movement is smooth, measured, and dignified, and the treatment, brisk and forceful, is free from the intrusion of melodrama, or of rant and rhetoric, to which such sentimental plays often in cline.

About this masterpiece, Venkatachalam states that "in the play no word is wasted, no technique misapplied, no incident pourposeless, no character superfluous, no device abused, no inbalance in the portrayal of emotion, no jarring excess in poetic embellishment, no incursion of melodrama, no intrusion of the supernatural, no flagging of the tempo, no violation of versimilitude - it is well nigh impossible to point the critical finger at any lampse or short coming, serious enough to upset the total harmony of the play..." In one word, this play stands out for its uniformity of excellence from start to finish.

Svapnavasavadattam (Vasavadatta seen in a dream) is recognised as the most prominent landmark in the pre-Kalidasa period of Sanskrit drama. N.P. Unni writes that Bhasa's style throughout the play is elegant, transparent and flowing. He uses figurative expression with graceful ease, whether it be prose or verse. Infact he is considered by some scholars as a fore runner and a master in the field of dramatic literature. There is a doubt that his Svapnavasavadattam is the brimming with action and rasa. The love in union end separation as depicted in the play has few equals. In the second and third acts Vasavadatta has to undergo in disguise the agony of being close to Padmavati who is to marry Udayana and has also to string her martial garland. Even in this moving situation Bhasa makes Vasavadatta make only simple and cryptic but very effective statements. The crucial fifth act in which Udayan meeting Vasavadatta in Padmavathi's chamber, and considering it only as a dream, is skilfully conceived and developed. Udayana is more appealing in this play than in others like the Ratnavali of Harsha where also he figures as a hero. The two heroines Padmavati and Vasavadatta are cleverly discriminated. The special feature of the play is the dramatic skill and delicacy with which the feelings of Vasavadatta are depicted. It is a drama of fine sentiments; the movement is smooth, measured and dignified, without any tinge of melodrama.

In technique, Bhasa has sometimes openly violated the rules laid down by the Nātyaśāstra.

He belonged to the period during which Alexander invaded India. In a number of his plays, he discribes king Rajasimha as his parton and some historians believe that this Rajasimha was none other than Maurya Emperor Chandragupta. The latter's Greek contacts are known to all. Therefore, it can be said that Bhasa might have the oppartunity to know about Greek theatrical traditions.

Bhasa is not only the first Indian classical writers of drama genre who wrote a tragic play in one act 'Urubhangam' Duryodhana, the hero of the play is a typical example of tragic hero in the Greek sense and his portrayal of tragic hero is in conformity with Aristotle's poetics. But he was also the first and only one who used 'Chorus' in the sense of a group of narrators delivering their dialogues in prose and verse as part of the dramatic plot. Bhasa might have borrowed the device of chorus from the Greek source. In all three plays namely Abhisheka, Urubhangam and Pancharatra, there are three persons who speak in unison and who individually and compries the chorus. Unlike chorus of Greek plays, Bhasa's chorus performs very little functions. They describe some events furnishing information about them and after they depart from the scene such as in Abhisheka, the chorus narrates the fight between Rama and Ravana and in Urubhangam, its reports the fierce battle between Bhima and Duryodhana. However in Pancharatra, it tells us the glory of the five sacrifice performed by King Duryodhana.

Unlike other Sanskrit playwright his work is devoid of too much poetic fancy, but are stagable with consistent well dramatic development and rapid actions.

The most striking feature of his play is do not strictly follow the rules of Natyashastra. This led many to opined that to he was ansterior to Bharata and floured before the great master. If not, then he might have been a dramatist who enjoyed consideration freedom having innovative mind. His style is simple and direct.

So with regard to language, his sanskrit usually agrees with the norm fixed by Pānini, while the Prakrit normally used by Bhāsa is Śaurasoni, with occanonal use of Māgadhī.

So for as the rasas are concered, Bhasa has used Diptarasa in 'Pratijnāyangandharāyana'; 'Dīptirasa - Karunapradhana is his Karnabhāra; 'Urubhangam is fall of Karuṇa', Avimāraka, Cārudatta and Svapnavāsavadatta contains Sṛingāra rasa, the plays 'Abhiseka', Balacharita Dūtaghatotkaca, Dūtavākya, Madhyamavyāyoga and Pañcarātra shows 'Vira' sentiments and finally 'Pratima' is having 'Sarvarasa'.

In the words of M.Krishnamachariar "Bhasa's language posses a peculiar grace, his dramas are well designed and variety of characters in their feature and in versatility of imagery and originatily of conception. Bhasa attained a name".

In 1941, Rajavaidya Kalidasa Sastri broughtout an anonymous play called Yajṇaphalam from Gondal in Kathiawar, claiming it to be a genuine play of Bhasa, and basing its text on two manuscripts in Devanagari, one copied by Swami Suddhananda Tirtha in 1727 V.E. (1670 A.D.) and another by Devaprasad Sharma at Harstinapura in 1859 V.E. (1802 A.D.)

There is a controversy over this 14th play, the 'Yajṇaaphala' or The Fruit of sacrifice. It is said that this is an imitation of Bhasa's plays and have been sought to be palmed off on Bhasa. But there is no doubt, from the internal and external evidence, that the earlier mestioned 14 plays are genuine plays of Bhasa. Prof. Jhala has held that though, like the thirteen plays discovered by Ganapati Sastri, Yajṇaphala begins with the same stage direction, contains the Mudralamkara in the opening verse, makes to mention whatever of its another in the Introduction which is called Sthapana here too, and the Bharatavakya makes the same reference to Rajasimha ruling the earth bounded by the seas that was only to be expected of an imitator and that a close scruting shows great differences in the Sthapana the words, pharases and idioms, and in ideas and ideals, between the Yajṇaphala and the thirteen plays and that startlingly modern idea are found in the Yajṇaphala, ideas which would never have been found in the old poet Bhasa and his times. Thus, Prof. Jhala holds Yajṇphala to be a modern imitation of the thirteen plays.

A.S.P. Ayyar, the Fellow of the Royal Society of Literature of the United Kingdom opined that Yajṇaphala is a clever imitation of Bhasa's plays by some Sanskrit poet of the 11th or 12th century A.D. and not a genuine play of Bhasa.

But in 1942, Dr. Pusalkar wrote an article holding that Yajṇaphala was *prima facie* a play by Bhasa, and a play of his last and mature period, judging from the language, ideas and the dramatic technique and the close similarity to the thirteen Trivandrum plays discovered my Ganapati Sastri. He also rejioced that a Devanagari manuscript from North India had been discovered regarding one of Bhāsa's plays showing that the thirteen Trivandrum plays, with strong family resemblance, were also Bhasa's.

Apart from the thirteen Trivandrum plays, Mr. Kavi ascribes the authorship of Dāmaka and Traivikrama to Bhāsa, Mr. S. Narayana Sastri adds Ghatakarpara to the list, while Krishnamachariar credits Bhāsa with Kiranāvali and Udātta Rāghava and tradition tells us that Bhāsa's literary output comprises of over twenty plays.

Though only thirteen plays of Bhāsa have survived the vicissitude of time, but still his works out number those of Kalidasa, Bhavabhuti, Sudraka, Sriharsha, Rajasekhera or Vishakhadatta and also surpasses all in respect of stage worthiness.

2

Bhasa's Plays

(I) ABHIṢEKAṆATAKAM

Synopsis:

A Rama play in six acts that begins with the Sugriva episode describing his fight with brother Valin, the coronation of Sugriva after the death of Vālin. Other significant events from the epic such as the abduction of Sita, the search for Sita, Hanuman's finding her in Lanka and later comforting her are stringed together. This is followed by his open insults to Rāvana. Vibhisaṇa gives suggestions for the coercion of the ocean to attain a panuge for the army. Rāvana tries in vain to win Sītā's heart and shows her in appearance the heads of Rāma and Laksmana, but she repudiates his all advances and consequently he is forced to fight.

The play ends with the ordeal of Sita and conscoration of Rāma after his return to Ayodhya.

Dramatis Personae (In order of appearance.)

Stage-manager.

Assistant. - in Prologue.

Rāma.

Sugrīva: a monkey prince.

Hanumān.

Lakshmaṇa.

Vālin: elder brother of Sugriva.

Tarā: his wife.

Aṅgada: a monkey prince.

Kakubha: a monkey officer.

Hollow-face (Bila-mukha): a monkey soldier.

Sītā.

Rāvaṇa.

Spike-ear (Saṅkukarṇa), a demon attendant of Rāvaṇa.

(Vijayā), of Rāvaṇa's place: Portress.

Vibhīshaṇa: younger brother of Rāvaṇa,

Monkey Chamberlain.

Monkey General.

Ocean.

Nīla: Indigo, a monkey officer.

Śuka and Sāraṇa: Parrot and Mate two of Rāvaṇa's ministers disguised as monkeys.

Demon Chamberlain.

Demon Porter.

Lighting-tongue, a demon.

Three Fairies.

Agni. the God of Fire.

Other monkeys and demons.

The Plot:-Act One: In the prelude, the stage manager recites the benedictory stanza in glory of Lord Rama. This is followed by Laksmaṇa's address to Sugriva from the off stage. Now the stage manager tells the audience of the compact between Rāma and Sugriva for mutual cooperation.

The main scene opens in the outskirts of the Kishkindha, where Sugriva and Hanuman go with Rāma and Lakshmana to witness the skill and might of Rāma in archery, then only they will seek Rāma's help in overthrowing Valin and thereby restoring the lost kingdom and wife to Sugriva. They watches how Rāma's arrow pierce through seven saal trees, and comes back. Thus, after being convinced of Rāma's power, they lend their worthy ally. When the four reaches to Kishkindha town, Sugriva asks them to wait, while he goes forward and roars aloud and challanges Vālin his elder brother for fight.

The scene now shifts to Vālin, who hears the roar and when he is about to set off, his wife Tara clings to his robe and prays not to go without consulting the ministers and besides, Sugriva who had earlier ran away, must have returned well equipped to become victorious. Vālin disregards her warnings, as he was sure to put Sugriva to death and orders her to go inside. She departs unhappily. Vālin rushes to the spot where Sugriva was awaiting him.

The next scene depicts the fight of Vālin and Sugriva. Furious Vālin attackes Sugriva. The latter also puts up a terrific fight. The duel goes on and after some times Vālin gives a severe blow to Sugriva from his first. The latter fall down and seeing Vālin very nearly killing Sugriva, Hanumana cries out to Rama and remind him of his pledge to help Sugriva. Rāma then throws his arrow which strikes Vālin who drops down unconsious, badly wounded. After recovery, Vālin picks up the arrow and reads Rāma's name on it. He accuses Rāma for treacherously strking him from behind an ambush and by doing so, he has done an unrighteous and unholy deed. Rāma justifies himself by saying that he has simply punished a guilty beast on account of adultery. Vālin argues that even Sugriva has committed some crime with his wife Rāma explains him the distinction between the wrongs committed by these two brothers. According to the Aryan laws, an elder brother should never touch a younger brother's wife. At last, Rāma's arguments soften's him, he submits himself and in the very last moments he admits that he is now free from all sins by meeting his death at the hand of Rāma. Sugriva breaksdown in grief over his brother death. The latter pacifies him and request them to keep away the wailing women-folk. Then Angada enters and falls to the ground, at the sight of his dying father. Vālin consoles him and asks Sugriva and Rāma to forgive his son and then, places him under Sugriva's custody. He gives Sugriva the golden necklace, the family treasure. His death approaches, Hanuman offers him some water and after sipping it, he gets the visions of the Holy Ganges and the other rivers, the Uruvasi and other heavenly nymphs, the arrival of thousand-swanned chariot for his final departure. After his death, Rāma orders Surgriva to offer funeral obsequies to Vālin and then tells Lakshmana to make arrangements for Sugriva's coronation.

Act Two:- The interlude informs us that the spies of Sugriva headed by Angada have been sent out in all directions in search of Sītā, in pursuance of which Hanuman has also left for Lankā, after learning the whereabouts of Sītā from the great bird-king, to deliver Rāma's message. The Act itself opiens with a garden scene in Pramadavana in Lanka where Sītā is surrounded by demonesses. Keeps meditating on Rāma and terribly grieved, but still confident that her husband's arrows would rescuer her. At this moment, enters Hanuman with the ring in his hand after having searched the entire city extensively yet failed to trace her. All of a sudden in the midst of the hideous demoness, he notices a lady who looks like a streak of lightning amidst dark-blue clouds. He wonder whether she is Sīta and as he sees the glare of torches, he hides himself behind the branches of a tree to ascertain whether the lady guarded by the demonsses is Sita. Ravana enters with his smite means. He feels sad at Sītā's pale and gloomy face, concentrated in love for her mortal husband. Hearing Ravana's antemptuous language towards Rāma, Hanuman becomes sure that his assumption is right and mutters that she is troubled like a gazelle at the sight of a lion.

Ravana then tries to win her heart by various means, but Sīta bears with the indignities inflicted by him. When he addresses Rāma as powerless, Hanuman gets enraged, but restrains himself to avoid any conflict which may spoil his mission.

Finally, Rāvana approaches Sīta with his fruitless requests to accept him, but seeing Sīta adament in her devotion to Rāma and at the power of a chaste woman's curse, Ravana feels dejected and at this moment, the beating of the drums inform him that it was time for his bath, so he departs with his smite.

At once, Hanuman comes down from the tree and tells Sīta that he is an envoy sent to her by Rāma, who is grief-stricken from anxiety for her. At first sight, Sītā susspects that he must be some demon in diguise as monkey. So, she prefers to be silent. Hanuman requests her to cast her suspicious aside and believe that he is Hanuman, a messenger sent to search for her by the monkey king, Sugriva, who is in alliance with Rama. But the mere mention of Rāma's name inspires confidence in her. Now Hanuman shows the ring of Rāma and informs her of Rāma's feeling for Sīta, his grief and pain, on separation from her.

All there makes Sīta's hearts swing between joy and sorrow. He further tells her of the slaying of Vālin, the coronation of Sugrıva, Rama's moves and gives her hope that with his new allies, surrounded by hosts of monkeys, Rāma will soon invade Lanka and over power Ravana. Sīta requests Hanuman to inform Rāma of her plight in such a manners that he maynot be over whelmed with sorrow. Then Hanuman starts ravaging the garden to announce his arrival.

Act Three:- The brave deeds of Hanuman is narrated by Śaṇkukarṇa, Rāvana's servant. At first, he brings the news of that a monkey has spoiled the entire Aśoka garden. Infuriated Rāvana orders him to capture the monkey. But Sankukarna returns in a shortwhile to tell him step by step of the havoc wrought by Hanuman. He learns that all the saal trees and the crrper bowers were crushed, the Daruparvata broken, made the guards unconscious simply with his roar.

Sankukarna request him to depute more force to capturc him. Rāvana now orders an army comprising of thousand slaves. But soon he receives the news that all of them have been killed by the monkey who uprooted the trees and striked them with them, Rāvana orders his son Akṣa to encounter the monkey. The reports comes that not only Aksha, but without waiting for his orders, the fire generals had also joined the prince to chase the monkey which fled to the gate-house and there, slained all the fire generals with the golden gateway and then caught the prince by the throat and killed him with a blow of his fist. Ravana prepares to meet the monkey himself, but is told by Sankukarna that prince Indrajit has already rushed to attack the enemy. Atlast comes the gladdening news that Indrajit has been able to over come the monkey and tied him up with a rope. Ravana bids Sankukarna bring Vibhishana and Hanuman. Vibhishana enters talking to himself that Ravana has not had the sense to listen to good counsel and restore the pious lady to her husband. Ravana does not see eye to eye with Vibhishana on this point and orders him to bring Hanuman. Accordingly the latter is being taken before Ravana. Hanuman confronts him bravely and fearlessly.

He exclaims that has not been caught by the devil; as he might have thought. But he allowed himself to be caught in order to see the demon-king Ravana asks his name and the reason why he entered the private quarters. Hanuman tells him about his parentage being the son of the wind-god by Anjana Devi and his name Hanuman, who have been sent there by Rama and goes to deliver his commands. Intolerant Ravana at once orders his killing. On being told by Vibhishana that envoys 'are never to be killed' Ravana agrees to hear the messeage that reads, Ravana should seek the best protection he can get, he should either go to Siva or hide in the nethermost hell. Rāma would send him to the hell, with every limb cleft with his goodly arrows. Rāvana laughts at Rama's warnings and boasts of his strength such as his victory over the gods with the celestial weapons, robbing of Kubera's aerial car. He wonders who a mere mortal like Rāma, pit himself against him. But Hanuman gives him a fitting reply that if he is so powerful, then why did he not fight Rama and take his wife, instend of abducting her after luring him away by magic? Now Vibhishana also becomes bold enough to disagree with Rāvana on the point of Sīta and requests Rāvana to send her back to

Rāma. Rāvana abuses him and in self - praise, fells that a long maned lion is never killed by the deer, a powerful elephant is not struck down by a jackal. After hearing this, Hanuman becomes so annoyed that he calls him by name and enraged Rāvana at first orders his death, but later modifies the order into one for setting monkey's tail on fire and to throw him out of Lanka. Rāvana asks Hanuman to tell Rāma to offer him a great battle. Before Hanuman is being driven out, he warns Rāvana of the ensuing danger, the destruction of the whole city and his eventual death.

After Hanuman's departure, Vibhishana again offers his advice to restore Sītā, as keeping her means a fierce battle and a danger for the demon race. Ravana doubts that Vibhishana might have joined the enemies and thus, put him to exile. Vibhishana tells Rāvana to abandon his wrath and passion, and in order to save the demon race from inevitable destruction, Vibhishana sets out to go to Rāma.

Act Four:- In the interlude, Sugriva's chamber lawn is seen in conversation with the general. He informs about Hanuman's discovering Sītā and asking Sugriva to make preparations to start for Lanka with the Vanarasena. The main scene begins on the shores of the sea, where Rāma enteres with Laksmana, Sugriva, Hanuman and the rest of the army. Just after their arrivals, Vibhishana comes flying from Lanka. From the distance, Hanuman fails to recognize him and alerts his forces to be ready to attack. Vibhishana say to himself that he has sent Rāma no word and being the younger brother of Rāma's arch-enemy, Vibhishana expresses his doubt as to the sort of treatment that would be accorded to him by Rāma. But Rāma is the essence of goodness and that he would definitely make him his ally. Hanuman sees him and at once greets Vibhishana. At the latter's bidding, Hanuman goes to Rāma and informs about Vibhishana's plea to protect the exiled brother of Rāvana Rāma sends Lakshamana to bring him in will all honour. Sugriva, for a moment, does not trust Vibhishana. Hanuman reassures them by telling that Vibhishana was opposring Ravana in Lanka itself and can be trusted fully.

After mutual salutations and greetings Rāma accepts him as the king of Lanka and takes his advice as to how to cross the ocean.

Rama hurls his divine shaft at the ocean, at Vibhishana's councel and threatens to dry up the waters. Varuna, the God of the ocean appears and seeks Rāma's protection. This is followed by Varuna's granting Rāma a passage by divided water. Rāma with his army crosses the ocean and encamps at Suvela mountain near Lanka. Meanwhile comes Neela, the Commander-in-Chief of the Vānarasena, with two monkey's caught spying. Vibhishana ricognizes them as Suka and Sārana, two loyal ministers of Rāvana, who ought to be punished. But Rāma feels otherwise, according to him by punishing them, neither victory will be gained nor Rāvana be destroyed and orders their release. But Lakshmana gives him a suitable suggestion to take the spieces round the whole camp and then only set them free. Rama accepts his advice and sends Suka and Sarana with his message to Ravana that by abducting Sītā, Ravana has brought the battle on his own head and report Ravana of his arrival. After their departure, Rama sets off to reviews his forces before the sun set.

Act Five:- The interlude to Act V tells us through Ravana's chamber lain, the serious reverses of the demen forces, of the death of all the great warriors of rote, such as killings of Prahasta, Kumbhakarna and other leaders except the king and of Indrajit's entry on the battle field. It is also been reported that driven by his passion, he disregards his minister's good counsel and wants to fight on till death. As ordered by Rāvana, the two replicas of the heads of Rāma and Laksmana have been made.

The venue of the main scene is Aśoka Vatikā, where Sītā is shown surrounded by demonsses, and seen bad omen inspite of the fact that her husband has already arrived at the shore. She prays gods for their well beings. At this moment enters who finds on his way that lady Lanka is leaving him. Still he approaches Sītā and makes his last supreme effort to persuade her to accept him. Ravana even tries to tempt her by suave words. Failing he threatens that he would slay Rama and Lakshmana and would win over Sītā.

Vidyujjihva appears at this juncture and gives Ravana the two replicas of the heads and informs that prince Indrajit has killed Rāma and Lakshmana in the battle and he carried them here for king's pleasure. Ravana shows her the talked heads to deceive Sītā and make her accept Rāvana. On seeing them, Sīta fall down and faint. When she recovers her consciousness, she prays Ravana to kill her with the very sword with which he killed her husband. Meanwhile, a messenger arrives with the news that Indrajit has been killed and the news gives terrible shock to Rāvana, who falls down in a swoon and cries out that his son had even conquered Indra and his hosts, but killed slain by a mere man. On recovering he lamens over the demise of his dearest son, at a great warrior and faints again. Recovering consiousness, he sends a messenger to bring news about the enemy camp. The messenger comes into short while to report that Rāma is rushing at Lanka, to set it ablaze. Enraged Rāvana draws his sword to fight with Rāma. He angrily looks at Sītā, who was the cause of all his misfortune. But his attendent presents him from killing a woman. Finally Rāvana mounts his chariot and hasten to the battle field.

The act closes with Sītā's prayers to the god for the victory of Rāma.

Act Six:- *[Interlude of the Act Six forms the Act VI of the Lahore Edition and also of the Trippunithura Sanskrit College manuscript used by Prof. Pisharoti. Main scene of the Act Six forms the Act VII of the above mentioned*

Lahore edition and the Trippunithura manuscript].

In the interlude the great battle between Rāma and Ravana is described meticulously by three Vidyādharas, who witness the battle from a distance. Each in his turn gives details of the duel such as Rama's monkeys rush with tails and ears erect, they hurls rocks and trees and gives fist blows to the demons and battering their heads. While demon army speeding rushes with their swords to counter attack.

Ravana employs his spear to which Rama easily splits into two. The former hurls his arrows against Rama, but remains unhurt when is seen on foot. Ravana taking advantage, mounts a car and rushes towards him. Indra offers his own car, driven by Matali, to Rāma who mounts it and fierce battle goes on. Both the car's wheel round in military movement, in such a manner that it looks as if two suns moving in the sky. The interlude ends in the death of Rāvana, when Rāma finally discharges his Brahmastra and vividly describing his end, the shower of flowers from the heaven and in the blowing of the divine trumpels.

Thus the main scene opens after Ravana's death and now Rāma enters Lanka to meet his beloved. He proclaims his victory and successful mission to rescue Sītā by killing Rāvana. He crowns Vibhishana as the King of Lanka. Lakshmana and Vibhishana inform Rāma of the approaching Sītā. Rama asks Vibhishana to make her wait and insists on the fire - ordeal for her, as Sītā has become a stain on Ikshwaku's house by her long stay with the demons.

Lakshmana informs Rāma that Sītā wants his permission to mount the funeral pyre. When Rāma grants her permission, Lakshmana gets upset at his consent. But as he has to obey his elder brother's order, he deputes Hanuman to make the pyre. When Hanuman departs, Lakshmana reminds Rāma that he is going to lose Sīta forever, as she is entering the fire and his all past efforts have been fruitless. Rāma becomes terribly upset and asks him to prevent her. At this point, Hanuman and Sugriva, watch Sītā entering fire. Hanuman exclaims that Sītā under goes the ordeal successfully and sees Agni lead Sitā out of the fire.

Agni salutes Rāma and guarantees the purity of Sītā, who is but Gooddess Lakshmi in human form. The celestial musicians come and song from behind the curtain in praise of Rāma, who is Lord Vishnu. Rama and Sītā go in for their coronation and Agni shares them the way. This is followed by Rāma's entry after crowned as king by Agni. After short deliberations. Agni informs Rama that his susbjects are arriving to meet him, led by Bharat and Satrughana on Indra's orders. This gladdens Rama. He becomes much delighted when Agni conveys to Rama the greetings of Mahendra and other goods. The play ends with moral epilogue.

(II) AVIMĀRAKA

Synopsis:- Based on an ancient folklore, this drama in six acts depicts the love of a Sauvira prince (Avimāraka turned into a low caste śvapāka due to the curse of a sage) to a princes called Kurangī, daughter of king Kuntibhoja and his maternal uncle. Avimāraka, the hero stakes his life to save the heroine from a furious elephant run amuck. They falls in love. When he was wondering as to how to attain her, the princesses maid helps them to meet secretly in the palace. She carries the message of Kurangi asking him to visit her in her room at night and perform a Gandharva marriage with her. Subsequently, Avimāraka break through the steel - walled security of the royal palace, disguised as a burglar with rope and sword in hand. He climbs the walls of the princesses *hearily guarded* apartment with the aid of rope and meets her at dead of night and accordingly marries her. But the news of their affair reaches the king very soon and Avimaraka run away from the palace. When he is being chased, in despair he tries to commit suicide by falling into a forest fire, but as the god of fire is his father, he is not hurt. He then decides to throw himself down a hill, but is saved by a Vidyādhara, who presents him a magic ring which would make him visible or invisible at will. The ring works as a free passport for him to visit the princess. With the help of this ring, he enters her room, unseen by the guard. When he finds her, Kurangī is about to end her life by hanging herself, but his timely arrival prevents her from doing so. Kuntibhoja on finding him there becomes perplexed and thinks of marrying her to Jayavarman, the Prince of Benares and the brother of Avimaraka. The celestial Narada, the celestial sage appears at this juncture and reveals the story of the curse and princely status of Avimaraka. With King's approval, the couple marries publicly this time.

Dramatis Personae (In order of appearance)

Stage-manager in Prologue.

Actress

Kuntibhoja of Vairantya of Vairantya: KING, father of Kuraṅgī.

Portress, Ketumālī.

Queen, wife of Kuntibhoja.

Jayasena: Attendant in Kuntibhoja's palace.

Kaunjāyana: Minister of Kuntibhoja.

Bhūtika: Minister in charge of the princesses palace.

Santushṭa: JESTER, companion of Avimāraka.

Candrika: Maid, of Avimāraka's household.

AVIMĀRAKA: the Hero, really Vishṇusena, elder son of Sudarśanā, Queen of Benares and the God of Fire, adopted by Sueetanā, her sister, Queen of the Sauvīras.

Jayadā: Nurse of Princess Kuraṅgī.

Little Lotus, maid in attendance of Princess Kuraṅgī.

Maid in Avimāraka's house.

Kurangi: the Heroine, daughter of Kuntibhoja.

Māgadhikā - Maids in attendance on Princess Kuraṅgī.

Vilāsinī

Vidyādhara: Fairy.

Saudāmim: the Fairy's ladylove.

Hariṇikā: Serving woman In Kuraṅgī's household.

Vasumitrā

King of the Sauvīras, husband of Sucetanā and reputed father of Avimāraka.

Nārada: the sae and busybody.

Sudarśanā: Queen of Benares, real mother of Avimāraka. Also of Jayavarman, betrothed to Kuraṅgī, but in the end married to her sister Sumitrā.

The Plot:- In praise of Nārāyana, the benedictory stanza is recited by the stage-manager. He then calls his wife, who wants to visit with him to the public garden for some religious purpose. At this juncture it is informed that the princiess Kurangi was in the garden surrounded by the sentries, he advises his wife to wait till the princess leave the place and they departs. The main scene opens with king Kuntibhoja's entrance along with his retinue. He sends for his queen. They seem to be worried about their daughter, who has attained the marriageable age. The king is eager to see his daughter happily married. At this moment some noise is heard and the queen is anxious about her daughter, who had gone to the garden. Kaunjāyana, the minister, arrived with the news of the princess having been attacked by a mad elephant. The minister went on with his long - winded tale, but king cuts him short and enquires him whether Kurangi is safe. He replies that she is being saved by an unknown youth. He tells that Bhutika arrived on the spot and the princess was rushed out to the palace. On enquiries it is learnt that the noble youth declared himself to be low caste person. The queen remarks that a low born person cannot be so brave and compassionate. The king sends the queen away to meet comfort Kurungi.

Bhūtika who had gone to get details about the rescure of Kuraṇgī enters and tells that the person is concealing his true identity. His striking figure, his flowless speech, his warrior build, and his innate strength and tenderness all prove his noble birth. Bhutika further informs the king that he learnt of the youth's father being quite noble and royal in appreance.

The king orders further investigations to be made in connection with the young man and then goes to resume the question of his daughter's marriage. Kaunjayana replies that the sons of the kings of Sauvira and Benares are the fittest. The king asks for his candid view from Bhūtika and he votes in favour of Sauviraraja as the latter was in addition, the brother of the queen. Kuntibhoja enquires as to why no ambassador has been sent subsequently by the king of Sauviras.

Bhutika replies that the king of the Sauviras has disappeared my teriously with his queen and prince, leaving he kingdom in the hands of the minister. Today none is admitted into the palace. The king wonders whom could be the reason for this and orders further investigations in this matter also and Kaunjayana what he should do with the ambassador from Benares. The minister says that the envoy should be treated with all honours, but keep him waiting. Thus, the decision regarding princess marriage should be postponed as marriage are best arranged with many door ways open. At this moment, the beating of the drum announces the time for the royal bath.

Bhutika asks him to go to the bath, console the princess, congratulate the queen, and apper himself his subjects who have assembled in large numbers to see him after the lucky escape of the princes. While leaving, the king refers to the heavy burden and onerous duties of the king and the First Act closes with that.

Act Two:- It starts with an interlude where in Santhushta, the jester, who is a Brahmana but a close friend of the hero, is seen to be strolling in the street and bewailing the recklessness of Avimaraka who has forgotten his outcaste state and ever since he saved the princess from the tusker, has fallen deeply in love with her. He says to himself that he must avoid the censure of the Brahmans. He will visit some of their houses and then go quietly to meet Avimaraka at his place, while this on a round of visits without rousing their suspicions.

Chandrika, a maid servant the Sauvira household dupes the jester and disappears with his ring which she borrows from him on the pretext of reading the monogram on it. The jester chases her, but all his efforts go in futile and he threatens to report the matter to his friend Avimaraka. The main scene opens with love-sick. Avimaraka sitting in his house and is seen brooding over his newly acquired love. Beloging to a low caste, he realizes the impossibility of his heart's desire being fulfilled, so he tries to control his feelings, but to no effect, as repeadedly his mind turns to his love only. He says to himself that his will is no match for his mind. That being so, he shall think about her and is again engrossed in his love throughts.

The scene is shifted to the princess's nurse and Nalinika, the princess's maid, who come to meet Avimaraka. From them it is learnt that the princess Kurangi also is in a similar plight. The nurse feels that if he invite him to meet princess clandestinely, she bring disgrace on the royal house. If she do not do it, the princess will die. Unable to bear the love lorn condition of Kurangi they have decided to visit this young man's abode.

Nalini is astonished that how could such a man be low-born. Nurse informs her that the over heard the minister felling the queen that he must be of noble birth and must be in disguise. Some super natural power assures them of his noble birth and asks them to cast away all doubts regarding his lineage and bring this matter to a happy end.

This inspires confidence in them and proceed further and set struck by the beautiful carved door and the oblations of flowers and fried rice, when enter the house of Avimaraka they find him alone and engaged in meditating on the princess. They inform him of the pitiable condition of Kurangi who can longer bear the pangs or separation and invite him to the Kanyāpura in disguise at night, to save the life of the princess. This infuses new spirit in him and he accepts the invitation. He learns all the details about the way to Kurangi's rooms. They give him a ring to convince him of their bonafides. He asks them to expect him at midnight and the nurse and Nalini depart.

At the fall of night jester as usual comes back home. He had heard in the market terrace about the visit of the nurse and Nalinika to Avimaraka. He meets the latter and Avimaraka informs him of his plan to secretly meet the princess at her palace that night and seeks his consent. At first, the jester presses him no to go alone on the dangerous mission, but finally allows him to go. The jester further suggests that they should wait in a friend's house in the town till the time comes for their nocturnal adventure.

Avimaraka decides to go in now, for a bath, say his prayer, salute his father, go into his room as if to go to bed and slip out and come with his friend.

It is sun set now and the cover of darkness in the east and the west that glows with red appears to him as if Siva is in his Ardhavariswara form, half god, half goddess. Avimaraka witnesses as altogether new world.

Act Three:- This act opens with Kurangi and her two maids, Vilāsinī and Magadhika. After some deliberations Magadhika ascertains from Vilasini that the bed is ready on the royal terrace for the princess to rest and watch sunset. They all go up, but Kurangi rests on a stone-slab. Magadhika wants to tell a story to the princess. But the latter shows no interest, as she fears that her secret love Avimaraka might be revealed. Vilasini requests Magadhika to narrate the story. She says that the ambassador from Kāśirạja, who had come for asking Kurangi's marriage, has been sent back alone with Bhutika and that the marriage has been postponed as the queen feels that her daughter is still young and she can not bear a separation from her.

Now enters Nalinikā who is returning from Avimaraka's abode. She speaks about her successful venture and assures her that the youth must be born of noble family. This is a happy news for the princess, who then enters the inter apartments with Nalinikā to serve her. The night comes on. Disguised as a burglar, arrives Avimaraka and carries a rope in one hand and a sword in the other. He is seen engaged in a lengthy monologue in which he vividly describes his wandering on dark night, with the many intersting sights such as a couple in love; a lover lingering out side a door-step of another house; then notices a theif running the town guards. The city at night is full of danger yet he is delighted. After the guards disappears, he proceeds towards the royal palace.

He throws his rope on the up, and it catches the coping at the very first throw. Gladly he starts climbing up and as instructed by the maids, he ascends to the top of the palace wall and from there, he descends through the same rope and again, throws up in the elephant's stable. He comes across the water-course, the audience hall and finally reaches Kanyāpura Prasāda, i.e., princess's palace. He opens the mechanical door with the magic key and effects his entry into palace. He throws off his disguise and as he is about to present himself, he hears Nalinikā's remark that the princess has fallen asleep after many a night, when she hard that her lover would come tonight. Nalinika welcomes Avimaraka and asks him whether she should wake up the princess who is half asleep.

But Avimaraka stops her from doing so and keeps gazings at Kurangi. In her semidrowsy state, she mutters and later asks Nalinikā to embrace her. Nalinikā exploits the situation and tells Avimāraka to embrace the princess and she herself manages the body of Kurangī. The latter realizes that she has given a loving embrace to the person standing, while a second one managing her body she atonce opens her eyes when Nalinikā whisper something in her ears. She gets embarrassed and exclaims that her reputation is ruined. Avimaraka pacifies her and at this point, enters the nurse to inform that a couch has been prepared for them in the inner chamber and asks Nalinikā to direct Avimāraka and Kuraṇgī to the sleeping chamber. She leads them both and the princess joyously, makes her wallk seven steps and exclaims that this is their Saptapati, the sacred seven steps, the chief custom in a Hindu marriage.

Act Four:- It is understood from the fourth act that the lovers have happily passed a full uyear in the company of each other, when the king suddenly comes to know about this love affair, he drives away Avimāraka. The Act itself opens with Avimaraka, who have managed to escape from the princess's palace by god's grace. But he is dissapointed and keeps repenting that he has left her in a sad plight. Seized with fear and shame on one hand and the pang of separation on the other, she still took no thought of herself, and was only anxious for her lover's safety.

Avimaraka, thus feels guilty and thoughts of suicide enter his mind. In his long soliloquy, he describes the excessive heat of the sun which was burning the whole earth, as if it is in high fever. He further says that the sun's heat is nothing compared to the heat in his burning heart.

At first, he thinks of ending his worthless life by drowning. But later gives up the idea, as being contrary to the religious precepls. He notices a forest - conflagration nearby and tries to commit suicide by throwing himself into that fire, but finds it as cool as sandal pask that makes him exclaim that this fire embraces him like a father hugging his son with joy. He, then climbs up a hill to throw himself down from its top when he is about to jump down, a Vidyadhara named Meghanada comes, flying in the air along with his wife, Saudamini, to attend a festival at Malay mountain organized by the Vidyadhaṛas in honour of the sage Agastya. At first Meghanāda takes him to be a Vidyadhara, but later comes to know about Avimaraka that he is the son of the king of Sauvira. By his magical skill, he finds out Avimaraka parentage, as the son of Agni. They becomes friend and Avimaraka tells him that he has been separated from his lady - love and is about to throw himself down from the precipice. Vidyadhara offers to help Avimāraka to gain access to the Kanyāpura. A magic ring is given rendering the wearer and anyone touching him invisible.

Vidyadhara demonstrate it by putting it on, first on a finger of his right hand, and then on a finger of his left. Avimaraka tries the ring on himself and get convinces of the efficacy of the magic ring that brings hope. Avimaraka rejoices and expresses his sense of gratitude to Meghanada. The latter, now flies away with Saudamini. After their departure, he rests on a stone seat and then seek out his friend. He finds the jester asleep under a tree. Both are glad at meetings each other and Avimaraka tells his friend of his recent possession.

But before this he puts the ring on a finger of his right hand and becomes invisible. The jester becomes confused and shows out and threatens to curse if Avimaraka hide himself. So Avimaraka puts the ring on a finger of his left hand and reveals himself. He, then applies its magic power to the jester and the latter becomes dumb-struck and even spits on his own hand to see whether it is still there. Without wasting any more time, they decide to proceed towards the prnciess's palace in their invisible forms. After entering Kanyapura, Avimaraka tells the jester that Kurangi must have finished her bath and gone to her rooms. So they enter to the inner apartments.

Act Five:-In the Fifth Act, Kurangi is found to be sunk in gloomy hopelessness. She can not bear her separation from Avimaraka and decides to put an end to her existence by suicide. She and Nalinika go up the terrace to relieve her mental agony. Nalinika asks her to look at the black cloud lit up by lightening. Similarly another maid Harinika comes from the queen to know how her headache is. All these add to her discomfort but she takes the medicine sent by the Queen. She even embraces Nalinika, because she knows that this will be the last time that she is going to clasp Nalinika in her arms. Princess sends her deliberately to fetch Magadhika and make arrangements for her bath. She sends Harinika also away and fasten her upper garments tightly round her neck to kill herself. At this moment as a result of terrible thunder and lightening, she gets scared and cries out for help.

Meanwhile both Avimaraka and jester had come along flying in their invisible conditions. However when she proceeds to hang herself with the rope, Avimaraka puts the ring on his left hand appears on the terrace. He lifts up Kurangi and ask her to put all her fear away. Seeing her lover, she exclaims that how could it be possible. In a moment she feels refreshed they both embrace each other wildly and cries at being reunited. The jester makes mockery for them. Meanwhile, Nalinika returns back and is confused to find the door bolted from within. She already had some inkling of princess's intention to end her life to free herself from the pain.

He shouts for the maid Harinika. Avimaraka asks Vidusaka to open the door and Nalinika is surprised at seeing the men there and enquires about the intrader, ie, the jester and also how Avimaraka has arrived, eluding the crowds along the route. These follow some humourous exchange of dialogues between Nalinika and the jester. Aavimaraka tells Nalinika that the jester will tell her the whole story. So she drags the jester away to the hall. Avimaraka is happy again at being reunited with the princess. They enjoys the beauty of the rain clouds and when the rains actually begins to come down, they extol it. Avimaraka takes her in for love making.

Act Six:-The interlude informs us through the conversation between the nurse and Vasumitra, one of the Queen's maids. They are worried about the confusion prevailing over Kuranigi's marriage. The king Kuntibjoja intended to give the princess in marriage in Viṣṇusena, the son of Suvirarāja, who was the brother-in-law of Kuntibhoja and also the brother of his Queen. But the princess is already being united to a handsome man, but whose origin is not known.

What is more confusing is that the minister Bhūtika has come with Jayavarman, the prince of Benares and his mother Sudarsana to finalize the marriage.

But as Sauviraraja is not heard of for a year and the king of Benares had sent an ambassador on behalf of his son for Kuranigi's hand in marriage. So the king Kuntibhoja has finally gives his consent in favour of Jayavarman and the marriage party has already reached the capital of Kuntibhoja. But Queen is adamant and does not want to marry the princess to Jayavarman till she hears something of Vishunsena.

At this juncture, enters Nalinika with the lastest news that the king has just received a letter from the minister of Sauvira that their master with his family is staying in secret in Vairantya (capital of Kuntibhoja) with his parents for the last one year. On receiving this letter, the King has started investigations through his secret agencies to search the king of the Sauviras.

The main scene begins at Kuntibhoja's palace, where the king Kuntibhoja, king Sauviraraja and Minister Bhūtika are present. Both the king embrace each other, but on seeing Sauviraraja with a gloomy face with voice choked with tears, with his eyers wet, he enquiries him the reason there of. Sauvira replies that he has not heard of his son Avimaraka for a year to divert his mind, the minister enquiries about the reason of his exile. He then unfolds about the curse which the great sage Caṇdabhārgava had pronounced on him. Accordingly he is living like a low-castle Caṇdāla for one year and that very day marked the end the curse. This is followed by the incident as to how prince Viṣṇusena came to be known as Avimāraka, because of his killing of a giant named Dhumaketu, when he was a little boy.

Sauviraraja feels sad about his over expectation of the efficacy of the secret service of king Kuntibhoja. But Bhūtika replies that his efforts to trace the prince have been in vain. Enters Narada, the divine sage on the scene to reveal the whereabouts of Avimaraka to Kuntibhoja and Sauvira who are in deep sorrow owing to Avimaraka's disappearance. He is received with great honour by the two kings. Narada's instructs Bhutika to bring Sudarsana there and then explains the whole affairs to both the parents right from Avimaraka's story in the same house with them to his marriage with Kurangi, the daughter of Kuntibhoja, according to the Gandharva form. But for the satisfaction of Kuntibhoja, Narada asks them to bring the couple and have the ceremony performed once again by the priest, in the presence of sacred fire, ie, in accordance with family tradition. Kuntibhoja prepares to go, but Narada detains him and sends the minister to bring the couple. Kuntibhoja explains to Narada his false position, as he has already given his word for the marriage of his daughter with Sudarsana's son. Narada tactfuly settle the matter right by taking Sudarsana aside and reveals before her the true identity of Avimaraka, as her son by Agni and had exchanged the child with the dead son of her sister Sucetana. She is being further told the story of the curse, his encountes with the mad elephant, Karangi's resene, his entry in the Princes's palace, his escape, his attempt to commit suicide, the magic ring, Avimaraka's secret love-marriage in the palace.

As described by Narada, Saudamini gives her consent to the marriage Jayavarmana to Kurangi's younger sister, Sumitra. Then arrives Avimaraka and Kurangi in their marital dress alongwith Bhūtika. Avimaraka feels ashemed for his secret deed and finds all the elders there. But reassures himself on seeing Narada. They go and pay their respects to the sage, Kuntibhoja, Sauvira and Sudarsana. They all suitably bless them. Avimaraka and Kurangi then go in to pay their respect to Suchetana.

Before leaving, Narada instructs Sauvira to return to his Kingodm and Sumitra be offered in marriage to Jayavarman and assures Kuntibhoja to be ever by his side. The play ends happily with the usual Bharatavakya.

(III) BĀLACARITA

Synopsis:- A Mahabharat play in Five Acts that describe the birth of Kṛṣṇa and successive events in his life such as the slaying of the demoness Pūtanā in Yaśodā's disguise; the killing of the demons Dhenuka and Keśin, his fight with the fierce bull Ariṣṭa, the destruction of the Kāliyanāga of the Yamunāpool; the death of the notorious wrestless Cāṇūra and Muṣṭīka and finally the killing of his main adversary Kamsa and release of the old king Ugrasena from the prison who is re-installed as the king of Mathura.

Dramatis Personae (In order of appearance)

Stage-manager	:	In prologue
Nārada	:	divine sage and the Wonderer of the sky.
Devakī	:	wife of Vasudeva, mother of Krishṇa.
Vasudeva	:	father of Krishṇa
Nandagopa	:	headman of the cattle station, foster-father of Krishṇa
Garuḍa	:	the fabulous bird, the vehicle of Vishṇu (of Krishṇa)
Cakra	:	Dscus, one of Vishṇu's weapons.
Sāraṅga	:	Bow another of Vishnu's weapons.
Kaumodakī	:	Club, another of Vishṇu weapons.
Śaṅkha	:	Conch
Nandaka	:	Sword
Cāṇḍāla women		
Kaṃsa	:	King of Mathurā the wicked usurper, brother or cousin of Devaki.

Curse of the seer Madhuka. 'Arms of Thunderbolt'.

Śrī	:	Fortune, the king's good fortune.

(Other spectres-Ill-luck, Baldhead, Midnight, Deep-sleep, and Yellow eye do not speak)

Yāśodharā	:	Portress.

Bālāki	:	Chamberlain
Nurse		
Kātyāyanī	:	the goddess Dūrgā, arising from the body of the daughter of Nandagopa and Yaśodā.
Kuṇḍodara	:	Pot-belly, the serpent in the goddess's train.
Spear	:	the goddess's weapon.
Speed of Thought		another figure in the goddess's train.
Nīla	:	Dark-blue.
Old Herdsman.		
Dāmaka	:	a herdsman.

Girls gopas of the cattle station.

Belle of the station Ghashasundan.

Wool garland, Vamanāta.

Crescent. Candralekhā

Gazettle Mṛīgākshī.

Damodara	:	Kṛsṅa.
Saṅkarshaṇa	:	Ploughter. Halāyudha or Balarāma. Krishṇa's elder brother, born of Rohiṇī.
Meghanāda	:	a herdsman.

(Other herdsmen-Meghadatta, Bull, Pott, and Herder-do not speak separately.)

Arishṭa-vṛishabha	:	Dreadnought Bull.
Kāliya	:	a Nāga or Serpent.
Dhruvasena	:	Servant of King Kaṃsa's palace.
Cāṇūra	:	a pugilist.
Mushṭika	:	Boxer, a pugilist.
Ugrasena	:	the former king of Mathurā, imprisoned by Kaṃsa.

Portress, sentries, attendents of Katyayani, an old herdsman, cowherds. Gopa damsels, etc.

Plot:- Act One:- After the benedictory verses in glory of Nārāyana, the stage-manager begins to address the audience. In Kamsa's prison in Mathura, there is the fall of a shower of blossoms and one hears the sound of celestial instruments at the birth of Dāmodara (Kṛṣṇa). Nārāda, the wanderer of the sky enters and proclaims that he finds no pleasure in Heaven which is quiet after the last fight between the gods and demons. He, therefore, has descended on the earth to see the Lord Narayana, just born as a child to slay Kamsa. Narada circumambalates Kṛṣṇa who lies by the side of his mother, Devaki and then retursns to his abode at Brahmaloka. The Act proper commenses with Devaki's arrival with her child. She is worried for the life of the new babe, as Kamsa has already killed her six sons.

So this child should be saved from the clutches of Kamsa. Devaki asks her husband to take the child away quickly. He lifts it and proceeds on his way outside the gates of Mathura. The prison doors opens themselves and sentries remains fast asleep.

Amidst pitch darkness, he moves with great difficulty. All of sudden, he notices a powerful light flash and he is able to see his way. But for a moment, he mistakes it to be a light of Kaṃsa who might be following him. So he drawas his sword, but when he looks back, he sees that the light is casted by the lustre of the babe. When he arrives at the Yamuna in flood, he is perplexed for ā while. But soon, the swollen river makes passage for him by the parting of water.

Having crossed the river, he comes to the cowherds quarters where his old friend Nandagopa may arrive there to take care of this child arms whom he finds as the death of Kamsa incarnate. He is waiting under the Nyagrodha tree. Nearby, Nandagopa is seen lamenting with the dead body of his baby girl. Without the knowledge of his wife Yaśodā, he carries away child from her. As he does not want to disturb his tribesmen, in view of the Indrayajṇa festival next day, he wants to throw it away.

Vasudeva calls out Nandagopa in but the latter is at first afraid. That it must be a spirit. But later finds that it is Vasudeva, his old friend. Vasudeva requests him to take the baby, Kṛṣna and save it from the cruel death. After some persuation, Nandagopa agrees to keep the child with him. Through the greatness of the divine child, there rises a column of water and Nandagopa completes his purificatory bath therein, as he was carrying the dead girl. He was more astonished when he lifts babe Damodara who is too heavy for a strong man like him. On Vasudeva's advise he offers prayers to the child to become normal weight. It does so and the five divine weapons such as discuss, bow, club, conch and sword of Visnu and Garuda come to serve the Lord born as the child Nandagopa assures, that the child will be properly cared for and sets out to go back. Now Vasudeva also thinks of returning to Mathura when he hears the cry of child. He is anxious that Nandagopa might have returned back with the babe from the fear of Kamsa. But to his utter disbelief, it proves to be that of the dead child which was alive. He takes it and returns to Devaki and puts the girl by her side.

Act Two:- The act shifts to the palace of Kamśa. He meets with ill-omens and bad dreams. He sees the tumbling down of mansion tops through earth quacks. Even some fearsome outcaste Candala women appear before him and ask him to get married with them. This is followed by the appearance of curse named Vajrabahu, emanated from Mahuka, black as collyrium. five-braned in hand dreadful to look at, with projecting teeth and with eyes yellow in a snake's. He wants to enter Kansa's heart and finish him off. He orders good fortune to leave the palace and enters Kansa's body. Kansa's suddenly wakes up and calls his portress and asks her whether she saw the outcaste maidens entering the palace. She replies that even women of noble families find it difficult to find an entry here. He orders her to call his chamber lein Balaki. The latter arrives and sends him to consult the astrollogers with regard to the ill-omens such as night's storm. earthquake, wined and meteors. Balaki returns with the information that the omens signify the birth of a divine being with some mysterious purpose in view. It is further learnt that Devaki has given birth to daughter and he is astonished to hear that it is a female child. He sumnons Vasudeva to get the correct news. The latter tells him that Devaki has delivered a daughter. The portress enters with Devaki's plea to spare the child, who is only a girl. Vasudeva also joins in this prayer. But cruel Kansa orders the child to be brought before him to be killed. The portress brings the babe and Kansa dashes the girl against the Kansa rock. The child bursts into two, one part falls to the ground, while other part of her rises up into the sky, transformed into Godess Kartyayani. The latter proclaims her mission to kill Kansa. Her attendants Kundodara and others resolve to go to Gokulam to witness the exploits of the boy Kṛsna and exits.

Kansa goes into the palace to perform Santi in order to ward of evil omens, dreams etc.

Act Three :- The interlued to this act tells as that ever since the birth of Damoder Nandgopa's house. The herdsmen happy about that their present condition, about the luxuriante grange, the appearance of fruits and flowers and milk, freedom from disease in the cattle. An old herdsman talks about the killing of the demoness Putana by the babe Damodara who had sucked her breast ferociously, when she tried to murder the ten days child by giving suck to it; killing Śakatasura by a single kick when it was only one month old; the killing of the demons Yamala and Arjuna standing in the form of trees by passing the mortar to which he was tied by Yasoda to present him from stealing milk and mother from the neighbouring homes he eventually smashes the trees to pieces. It is also learnt that a demon called Pralamba gets killed by Sankarshana (Balrama) Damodra's brother, by a timely, fist blow on his head, knocking out his eyes and describes how Dhenuka in gaise of an ass is being seized by its left foot and hurling it on the ground and also killing Kesi who appears in the form of a horse by riding over him, he tolds Kesi firmly and puts Campnor in its mouth, resulting it to break into two parts. Main scene begins wih the performance of the Hallīsaka dance in which both the hardsmen, the cowherds and girls take full part. the dance is accompanied by music and song, the girls are beautifully attired. The old herdsman, however keeps himself contended by witnessing the frolic. He adjures all to worship the kine, the mothers of the world, ever full of nectar, at break of down. Damodara praises the natural beauty of Ghoshasundari, Vanamala, Chandralekha and Mrigakshi, with faces like, full - blown lilies, eyes like lotuses, garments of varied hues, and beautiful tresses adorned with woodland blossoms. They all sings and dances. Suddenly a demon named Ariṣṭarṣabha emerges causing great destruction and panic. Kṛṣna instructs Samkarshana, the cowherds and maidens to go to the hillock nearby. They watches the fight of Damodara with the wretched bull. After a wordy war, the demon realizes the divinity of the boy who stands on one leg and without any weapon confronts the bull. But the demon fails in shaking the boy. He bults at Damodara but falls down senseless. When he rises up, he offers to fight Damodara because he feels that if stained by Visnu, he shall go to heaven. The fight begins and Damodara hurls it down and it falls down dead covered all over with blood.

The herdsman called Dāmaka enters and after greeting him, informs that Samkarshana has gone to the Yamunā on hearing that Kāliya, the lord of sepents has arrived there. Damodara assures that he would break the pride of Kāliya by defeating it and everybody would live in peace.

Act Four:- It shows the scared Gopa damsels requesting Kṛṣna not to enter the pool of the serpent. They approaches Sankarsana to dissuade Damodara. But he even ignores old herdsman's warning that even tigers, elephants and wild boars that have entered the pool, have never come back. Sankarsana assures them that Kaliya is afraid on seeing Damodara and gets into the pool. Damodara steps on the hood of Kaliya, seizes the serpent and stands on its body to play Hallīsaka dance and starts plucking flowers from the trees. The snake emits in poison fumes, but in vain and comes to know the divinity of the boy and begs for protection. Kṛṣṇa orders him to at once leave the Yamunā river saying that it would be free from the fear of Garuda on account of his foot print on its body. Kāliya withdraws his poison and leaves with his retinue from Yamuna.

Damodara now offers flowers he had gathered from the pool to the damsels. Though they delighted to see Damodara, but are affraid to accept the such flowers which they had never seen in their life. But Damodara assured them and makes them accept the flowers. At this juncture, a messenger brought the news from Kansa urging Kṛṣṇa to go with his brother and people to attend the Dhanurmaha Festival (The Consecration of the Bow) at Mathura. Keeping in mind the divine mission to slay Kamsa, both Damodara and Sankarshana accepts the invitation and sets out for Mathura.

Act Five:-In this act, Kamsa unfolds (saying to himself) that Damodara and Sankarshana is being invited today on the pretext of the festival, with the intension of getting them killed by his wrestless. He awaits their arrival and in the meantime periodically calls Dhruvasena and enquires whether they have arrived. Dhruvasena goes out and brings him news of the feats of Damodara and his brothers such as their robbing off the royal washermen of their robes, how Damodara has plucked out the tusks of the great elephant. Dhruvasena returns back to inform that Damodara took the scented unguents from Madanika, the hump-backed girl and annointed his body with them and then made Madanika straight by rubbing her with his hand. From the florist, he snatches the flowers and put them on, and gone to the archery and killed Simhala, the keeper, who tried to prevent him and after breaking the bow kept there, Damodara is now on his way to the audience hall.

Infuriated Kamsa sends for his wrestlers Chanura and Mushtika reminds them of their utmost duty to defeat Damodara. Chanura boasts that he will smash Damodara and Mushtika assures that he will throw Balarama down. Kamsa takes his position to witness the ensuing fight. He orders Dhruvasena to bring the boys into the ring. With their entry, the duels begin. Both pairs start wrestling. Damodara beats Chanura to death and Sankarshana also succeeds in killing Mushtika. Now exclaims Damodara that he will send the demon Kamsa, down to hell. By saying so, he asconds the mansion, seizes Kamsa by the head and strikes him down dead. Just then, Kamsa's army arrives there to attack Damodara and Sankarṣana. But timely appearance of Vasudeva saves the possible fight. He informs the citizen of Mathura that these youths are his sons, by Rohini and Devaki. Both the boys make their salutations to their father and he blesses them and instructs that the dead bodies of Chanura and Mushtika to be removed at once. He orders Ugrasena, Kamsa's father, to be released from prision and, for being consecrated anew as the king of Mathura. To honour the destroyer of Kamsa, the gods rain flowers accompanied by divine music. On the stage, arrives Ugrasena to express his gratitude to Damodara for ending his misery. Finally comes Narada, the representative of the gods. Damodara offers him arghya and padya. Narada identifies Damodara with Vishnu, pays his respect and goes back to his abode.

(IV) DARIDRA CĀRUDATTAM

Synopsis: This play is the last play of Bhasa available only in fragment and based on the story which forms the plot of the later Mṛchhakatika. It has four acts without any benedictory stanzas at the opening and the Bharatavakya at the end. Cārudatta was a young and noble merchant of Ujjain whose generosity has impoverished him. At a festival, a beautiful courtesan called Vasantasena sees him and falls in love at first sight.

She is being chased by a rake, the king's brother-in-law, Samsthāna and Vasantasena escapes into Cārudatta's house where she is given refuge. When she departs, she entrusts her valuable jewels to Cārudatta and is escorted back to her house by the jester and friend of Cārudatta.

The brief episode of the love of a brahmana turned burglar Sajjalaka for Madamika, the courtesan's maid, runs as a paralled theme. In the night the jewels which Vasantasena has deposited, are stolen by Sajjalaka. The jester hand over the jewells in the night to this burglar mistaking him to be Carudatta. Cārudatta is embarrased at learning of the theft of goods kept in his custody and his noble wife offers her pearl necklace for the loss of Vasantasena's ornaments. She gives the necklace to the jester to hand over the same to the *hetaera*.

He takes it to Vasantasena who after learning of the theft, accepts it to have the excuse of visiting the merchant once more.

She allows slave girl to join her burglar lover, Sajjalaka and herself set out to Cārudatta's house to return his necklace in spite of a threatening storm. The play ends here in an unfinished form.

Dramatis Personae (In order of appearance):

Stage - manager in Prologue.

Actress :

Maitreya: friend of Carudatta. Jester.

Cārudatta: the impoverished merchant of Ujjain. Hero.

Sakāra: the king's brother - in - law, a libertine pursuing Vasantasenā, the villain of the play. (Saṃṣthāna).

Parasite, attendant of Sakāra.

Radanikā: maidservant in Cārudatta's house.

Vasantasena. Courtesan, in love with Cārudatta.

Madanikā: Maid, in Vasantasenā's house.

Shampooer, formerly in Cārudatta's service.

Karṇapura: Page in Vasantaseā's household.

Vardhamānavaka: servant in Cārudatta's house.

Sajjalaka: burglar who marries Madanikā.

Brahman lady: wife of Cārudatta.

Vicchittikā: Second maid, in Vasantasenā's house.

Caturikā: Third maid in Vasantasenā's house.

The Plot:-This play is fragmentary forms contain no benedictory verses. It starts with stage - manager's Prakrit speech. He informs us that due to morning walk, he is exhausted and hungry and finds preparations made for a right royal dinner at his house. To his queries, a mistress answers that everything was ready in the market. She tells him of her new vrata called Abhirūpapati and asks him to feed a poor Brāhmana. The stage-manager, therefore, goes out and meets Maitreya, the friend of Carudatta, the hero. They are standing outside Carudatta's house in Ujjain. The stage-manager invites him by stating that apart from a dinner, there would be a gift in gold coins also, but Maitreya declines the invitation and the stage-manager leaves the place to find another Brāhmana.

From Maitreya's soliloquy, we learn that once he used to dire with Carudatta, chewing the cud of sweets and surrounded by countless dishes of various kinds. But today, Carudatta is reduced to poverty and runs elsewhere for Maitreya's food. Today, Maitreya is on his way to deliver him a garland and a thin jasmine scented garment. The noble Carudatta after offering his Shashti prayers enters alongwith the maid with a wood-sorrel in her hands. Then starts dialogues between Carudatta and Maitreya. The former feels that penury is a living death to a high - minded man. He is now a very poor man after having led a prosperous life. He used his wealth all up for the needs of friends. But poverty has crushed his spirit and he would still be generous if recovers his wealth. In this bad days, his all good friends have become indifferent. But the hero finally says that fortunately he is having a wife who follows him in good and bad fortune and a constant friend to share his joys and sorrows.

At this juncture, we are being introduced to the courtesan Vasantasena, going along the deserted street in a hurry (from the other side of the stage). She is being pursued by Śakāra, the brother - in - law of the king and Vita, his attendant, with the intention to kidnap her. In her fright she calls out to her servants but none of them respond. Sakara ridicules her and says that he will catch her by the hair and carry her away just as Duhsasana did Sita. Vita and Śakāra try to terrorize her into submission by showing the sword. Being courtesan, Vita tells her that she is being chased. Vasantasena even offers her jewellery, but Sakara declines by saying that he wants only her love and not her jewels. Meanwhile, Sakara notices that they are close to the side-door of the house of Vasantasena's lover Carudatta, a poverty stricken merchant. He fears that Vasantasena might slip away. She is delighted at hearing this and awaits her chance to give the pursuers the slip and eventually disappears and throw away her garland and ankelts so that she may not be betrayed by the perform of the garland and the jingling of anklets.

In this crucial phase, we see that Carudatta asks Maitreya to go and offer the oblation to the mother goddess in the square. But jester wanted somebody to accompany him. Thus, Radanika, the maid is deputed. Maitreya takes a lamp and opens the side-door, the courtesan cleverly puts out the lamp, as if the wind has put it out. He goes inside the house in search of another lamp. Vasantasena effects her entry into the house and stands in a corner in front of the hero. Radanika is being mistaken for Vasantasena by Sakara and drags her by the hair and harass badly.

Maitreya enters with a lamp and comes to her rescue. He comes to know from Vita that Sakara is in pursuit of a certain lady, mistress of her youth, named Vasantasena and she had deceived them and that they had mistaken Radanika for Vasantasena and through Maitreya Sakara demands that Carudatta should hand over Vasantasena to Sakara or else. The king's brother-in-law would crack his skull and there would ensue a never ending enmity between them. Maitreya tells Madanika that he is going to report to Carudatta that they had made the oblations to the deities. He directs her not to utter a word about the attack on her. She promises to keep mum.

Now the scene focuses on Carudatta who mistakes Vasantasena for the maid and enquires of the oblations have been made to the deities and asks her to carry his garment inside. She hesitates to do so because of the lack of knowledge of the inner apartments of the house. At this moment arrives Radanika and Maitreya. Carudatta hears Sakara's message and Vasantasena comes forwards and seeks the protection and feels guilty for having entered his house uninvited. Carudatta also apologizes for treating her as his servant.

After mutual apologies, Vasantasena states that she was pursued for the sake of her jewels and would leave them with Carudatta, and under his protection, she shall return to her house. On the insistence of Carudatta, the reluctant Maitreya obeys the order and asks Radanika to keep them on the Sasthi and Saptami days and to hand them over to him on Ashtami. As the moon has arisen, Carudatta expresses that there is no need for a lantern. He himself escorts her till the highway and then directs Maitreya to escort her home.

Act Two:- The scene centres on Vasantasena who is in a thoughtful mood. Her maid enquires about the reason and comes to know that Vasantasena has fallen in love with somebody. The maid asks is he some rich merchant's son? The courtesan replies that he is a poor Brahmana named Carudatta. The maid realises that he must be the one who protected her mistress that night. As no poor man would request courtesan's house, so Vasantasena has deposited her ornaments with him.

In great haste, arrives a Shampooer and asks for protection from his creditor. Without paying any heed to maid's objections, Vasantasena asks him the cause of his terror. From long deliberations, it is learnt that he was born at Pataliputra. By birth, he was a trader but as ill-luck would have it, today he is earning his livehood as a Shampooer at Ujjaini. He was working under a young merchant who was handsome, dignified, generous and revered by all. Vasantasena guesses that it must be Carudatta and her assumption appears right. At he instance, he goes on to tell that owing to acute poverty, the kind merchant had to dismiss all his attendants and due to this changed circumstances of his master, he became unemployed and took to gambling. Then he lost ten gold pieces to a man and was being chased by the master of the gambling house.

Hearing his woe, Vasantasena agrees to help him and instructs the maid to pay off and send the creditor off and Madanika comes back soon to tell that she had paid off the creditor. Shampooer requests the courtesan to keep him in her employment. But she declines the offer tactfully and he leaves the place with the intention of renouncing the world.

At this moment, some noise is heard from outside and enters Karnapūraka, a page of Vasantasena. He is excited and rushes in to narrate his heroic deed, which unfortunately the mistress could not witness. He describes how he had saved a monk from the sacred elephant, Bhadrakapota who had nearly killed the monk seeing his ochre robes. The whole crowd cheered him when he drove the elephant away with contiuous blows from his fist. But none wanted to make any gift to him. A young noble man came forward to reward him. He searched in vain for some ornaments, but finding nothing, he cursed his ill fate and gave him his upper garment. Seeing the mantle, Vasantasena suspects it to be that of Carudatta's and asks the page whether he knows his name. But the page could not tell his benefactor's name. Just then, the young man was passing by the road side. From the parapet, Vasantasena exclaims that Carudatta has only his sacred thread for an upper garment and she keeps gazing at her lover.

Act Three:- This act shows both Carudatta and his friend entering Carudatta's house at late night after attending a concert. In their dialogues, the hero speaks in praise of the music and the singer, while Maitreya says that he did not enjoy the cursed lute. Before entering inside, he calls out, after promised 'Vardhamanavaka'. The servent emerges with water and washes Carudatta's feet. Maitreya asks him to wash his feet too, at which he pours the remaining water over his face. Now after a short conversations, they prepare to sleep. The servant leaves the place and Radanikā, the maid entrusts the casket of jewels to Maitreya. Carudatta asks Maitreya to accept it and refuses to send it to the inner apartments so that Carudatta's wife must not see this jewellery. Radanika goes away and Maitreya asks him why had he given away his mantle to the courtesan's page and Carudatta promptly reply that from affection' and then the sleep creeps over them. In a shortwhile, Sajjalaka, a burglar, who is in love with Vasantasena's maid named Madanika, enters the house. He is misled by the huge mansion and hopes to obtain some valuables, as he needs money for securing the freedom of his ladylove. After cutting a hole into the garden-wall he enters the house and then to make a path for the interior of the house, he goes to make another whole. Maitreya says that he cannot sleep properly because of the jewels in his custody and feels as if a thief is boring a hole into the wall. The poor Carudatta ridicules and both drop off to sleep again. Realising that the owner is poor, Sajjalaka thinks of retracing his steps when Maitreya, in his sleep, mutters: "Oh, take this golden casket and rid me of this bother." To his utter surprise, the burglar finds that the man is talking in his sleep. He takes the casket from his hands and Maitreya dreams that it is Carudatta who takes it. Maitreya is now relieved that he would not have to sleep with fright and happy that he would sleep soundly.

Hearing the morning trampels, Sajjalaka packs off with the booty. Now arrives Radanika and finding hole in the wall, she cries out Maitreya wakes up in a hurry. Both of them go to where Carudatta is sleeping. Maitreya feels proud that he handed over the ornaments to the hero at the right moment. Soon, Carudatta guesses the true state of affairs that the golden casket has been stolen. He feels sorry that at the loss and the consequent blot on a poor man. Caudatta's wife calls the maid and asks her whether the burglar has hurt Carudatta or Maitreya. Radanika tells that both are safe and unhurt but learns that Vasantasena's ornaments, kept in the custody of Carudatta, have been stolen. On knowing of the theft, she sacrifies her pearl - necklace. Radanika tells Maitreya that her mistress is giving it to him for handing it over to Carudatta for compensating Vasantasena for the loss of her ornaments. Maitreya takes the necklace and accordingly, gives it to Carudatta. In grief, he accepts it and says "I, who am to maintain her, have to be maintained by her". He dispatches Maitreya to the courtesan with the pearl - necklace.

Act Four: This act focusses on Vasantasena in love, and her maid. The former is holding a paint-box and brushes in her hand and drawing the portrait of Carudatta on the picture - board. When she is being asked, by the Vasantasena, the maid replies that the picture is quite life-like and also remarks that it is just how Carudatta looked when they saw him from the balcony. Another maid enters with ornaments and a message from Vasantasena's mother to put on them and come quickly, as the blue - lotus carriage awaiting at the door. At first, the courtesan assumed that the noble Carudatta might have sent these ornaments, but when she learns that the notorious Samsthana, the king's brother- in-law has sent them, she rejects them and dismisses the maid to inform her mother that she will put on her finery only to meet Carudatta.

At this moment, Sajjalaka, the burglar makes his entry and says to himself about the crime he had commited to buy freedom for his beloved Madanika in lieu of the stolen jewels. He calls her and Madanika enters and finds him nervous and restless. The scene shifts to Vasantasena. She asks her maid to put the painting on her bed, but seeing Madanika gone, she looks around and notices that Madanikā is in conversation with a man and guesses that he must be the one who wants to pay her and let the maid go with him. Though it is unfair to listen to other's conversations but hearing her name from the mouth of Sajjalaka she stays back and overhears them. He places the stolen ornaments which both Madanikā and Vasantasena recognize as beloging to the latter. He confuses just about his violent deed out of love for Madanika. Madanikā abuses him, and calls him an ignoramus. Both are horrified at hearing that it was Carudatta's house which Sajjalaka burgled soon. The ladies relive after learning that Carudatta is unhurt. At the first instance Sajjalaka become sad that his lady love is pining after another man, but later, he comes to know about the real state of affairs. Madanika advises him to return the jewels to Carudatta. But as this is a risky proposal, he seeks her counsel and asks for some other way out. As neither Vasantasena nor Carudatta recognises him, she suggests Sajjalaka to approach Vasantasena and hand over the ornaments in the name of Carudatta. Madanika instructs him to wait in the love god's temple till she informs her mistress and sends word to him. He departs and in the meantime another maid emerges with the news of the arrival of a Brahmana from merchant called Carudatta. He is duly received and Vasantasena pays all respects to the guest. Maitreya is amazed at seeing the royal mansion of the courtesan. He delivers the pearl-necklace to Vasantasena, telling her that Carudatta had lost the ornaments given by her in gambling and in exchange, he has sent the necklace. Vasantasena hesitates for a moment, thinking that if she accepts it, then Carudatta may feel that she is greedy. But if she refuses, that may make him angry and subsequently he would never meet her. Therefore she keeps the necklace.

After the departure of Maitreya, Madanika enters, unaware of his visit. She informs that a messenger from Carudatta has arrived. The messenger is received and he informs that the noble Carudatta has sent back her ornaments as his house is unsafe and his wife too is away. Vasantasena tells her to give the jewels back to Carudatta and request him to keep them for some days more. Sajjalaka declines and Vasantasena says that she knows he has stolen them from his house. This unnerves Sajjalaka and he stands dazed. Madanika is loaded with ornaments from Vasantasena and hearing that the carriage is ready, she places her hand in that of her lover to accept Madanika as his wife. When they leaves, Vasantasena calls another maid and tells her that it was all like a day - dream. The maid replies that as an Amṛtānka nātaka was enacted. Vasantasena then prepares to return the pearl - necklace to Carudatta, but the maid warns her of the treatening storm. Vasantasena gets irritated and angrily calls her a wretch. The maid at once follows her mistress and without any delay, they hastily proceeds towards Carudatta's house.

(V) DUTAGHATOTKACHA

Synopsis: This is an innovative play, but the germinal idea comes from Mahabharata. The playwright employs the story of Abhimanyu's death at the hands of Jayadratha. The Kauravas are jubilant over the victory, but Dhṛtarāṣtra warns them against the ensuing dangers. Ghatotkacha son of Bhima pleads to the Kauravas to be generous to the Pandavas but in vain, and predicts their punishment in the hands of Arjuna. In the original epic, Ghatotkacha had never been acted as an envoy of Śrī Kṛṣṇa.

Dramatis Personae (In the order of their appearance)

Stage-manager, in the Prologue.

Soldier, on the Kuru side.

Dhritarashtra: the blind old king, father of Duryodhana, and the other Kurus.

Gāndhārī: his wife, who bandaged her eyes.

Duhśalā: his daughter, wife of Jayadratha, the king of Sindhu - Sauvir Portress.

Duryodhana: eldest son of Dhritarāshtra, leader of the Kurus.

Duhśāsana: one of Duryodhana's 99 brothers.

Sakuni: the gambling king of Gāndhāra.

Potsherd, Ghatotkacha: son of Bhima and Hidimbā, sent as an envoly by Kṛṣṇa.

The Plot:- The benedictory stanza is interrupted by the sound of a soldier who informs Dhṛtarāshtra that Abhimanyu who spread panic in the Kuru army was atlast killed ruthlessly by a hundred princes rushing at him at the same time.

Dhṛtarashtra, Gandhari and Duśśala comes and hear the announcement. The former protests against the wickedness of Abhimanyu's death and Gandhari bewails the fate of Abhimanyu.

Duśśalā is not aware that her husband Jayadṛatha is the killer of Abhimanyu. She says that the man who inflicted widowhood on Uttarā had ordained widowhood for his own wife and then comes to know from a soldier, to her dismay, that it is Jayadratha who did the deed. She weeps and goes to join Uttarā, prepares to wear widow's weeds like her. From the soldier, Dhṛtaraśtra learns that Arjuna and Kṛśṇa were taken away to a different place by a group of Kaurava soldiers and when Abhimanyu joined in the fray, he got killed. He further learns that Pandavas haven't burnt the corpse, but keeping it for Arjuna to see and take revenge.

Dhṛtaraśtra decides to go to the banks of the Ganges with his wife. At this moment arrives Duryodhana, Dushsasana and Sakuni, jubilant over the death of young Abhimanyu and their victory. Despite Sakuni's resistance, Duryodhana goes to salute Dhritaraśtra and take his blessings. Instead of blessing him, he sarcastically speaks of the gift of widowhood by hundred brothers to their only sister Duśśala. Dhṛtarāstra is horror - struck with the gross iniquity of the child-murder and the ugly shape assumed by this Fratricidal war. He warns them of the impending disaster, and the valorous deeds of Arjuna but Duryodhana is not affected and tries to argue the matter. A terrible noise is heard and the soldier informs Dhṛtarastra about Arjuna's dreadful oath to kill Jayadratha. The following day Duryodhana tells that he would cover Jayadratha with his entire army led by Drona and due to non fulfilment of their vow, the enemy will be forced to enter the flames of fire. Dhṛtarastra answers that even if he enters the earth and hides therein or ascends the aerial regions, Arjuna's arrows guided by Kṛśṇa will follow him everywhere and finally overtake him. The solder exclaims if any other persons had uttered these words to their ruthless king, he would not had been alive for a second after that impending danger.

Ghatotkacha comes as a messenger of Kṛśṇa. He does not pay any heed to Duryodhana's insulting language, but salutes Dhṛtaraṣtra. The latter tells him that his heart is wrung by his brother's fate. He, then begins to deliver the message. At the mere mention of Kṛśṇa's name Dhṛtarāṣtra rises up hastily from his seat. Ghatotkacha clams him to hear the message that in view of the excessive grief to which Arjuna was subjected owing to the death of his single son, the lord asks Dhṛtarastra to prepare himself to bear the impending deaths of all his hundred sons. Duryodhana exclaims that the speech is ridiculous and Duḥśāsana also speaks with disrespect by calling Kṛśṇa, a cow-herd. Ghatotkacha tells Duryodhana of the lightening of the burden of the earth through the destruction of the vile princes. There is also an exchange of fiery words between Sakunī and Ghatotkacha. The former exclaims "could it be done by words alone, the world were won. Were it by words, and nothing but words, the killing of the warriors were done". When Ghatotkaca gives a suitable reply Duhsasana calls him a demon, to which Ghatotkaca retorts that they are *indencent* and more cruel than the demons as they do not burn their brother when asleep, touch their brothers wives hair and do not celebrate the killing of a child.

Duryodhana abuses Ghatotkacha as a mere messenger and tells that he spares his life only on that account. Humiliated Ghatotkacha gets ready for the conflict. In a fighting posture with a clenched fist he throws out an open challenge to them all single - handed.

The bloodshed is averted, when Dhṛtarāstra intervenes and pacify them, fearing another child murder when asked about the reply to be carried back to Kṛśṇa, Duryodhana replies that his arrows would be a fitting answer and that a fight is inevitable. After saying good - bye to Dhṛtarastra, Ghatotkacha takes his leave, not without uttering the final message to Duryodhana and the assembled kings that their final doom is coming to them in the following words "Death will come upon you with the rays of tomorrow's sun, in the guise of the Pandavas". After delivering the message that carried the threat of vengeance by Arjuna, Ghatotkacha departs and the play ends abruptly with no Bharatavākya.

(VI) DŪTAVĀKYA

Synopsis :- This one act play is based on the episode of the Mahabharata dealing with the visit of Kṛśṇa to the Kauravas seeking peace and demands Pandavas due share in the inheritance, which Duryodhana refuses and even tries to imprison the ambassador. Enranged Kṛśṇa takes his Visvarupa and also calls for his magic weapons Sudarshana, Kaumodaki, Pancajanya etc, that baffles Duryodhana. But later, Kṛṣṇa subdues his anger and receives homage from Dhṛtarāstra who falls at the feet of the Lord, on behalf of his sons. The Kṛṣṇa complies with his request, though his mission remains unsuccessful.

Dramatis Personae (In order of appearance):

Stage-manager, in Prologue.

Bādarāyaṇa: Chamberlain.

Duryodhana: eldest son of Dhṛtarāshtra, leader of the Kurus.

Vāsudeva: Krishna, Nārāyana, Vishnu.

Sudarśna: Vishnu's discus, one of his four weapons.

Dhṛtarāshtra: the blind old king, father of Duryodhana and his 99 brothers.

The Plot:- In praise of Upendra, the stage-manager recites the mangala-śloka, but is disturbed by the off-stage announcement by the Chamberlain that king Duryodhana would like to consult the princes in the Council Chamber with regard to the appointment of the supreme Commander-in-Chief of the Kaurava forces. There is hectic preparations for the war. Duryodhana enters and while he proceeds to the assembly hall, his two noble Vaikarna and Varshadev,. Drona, Bhiśma, Sakuni, Karna are all assembled and when they take their proper seats, Duryodhana puts the question as to who is fit to be the Commnder-in-Chief of eleven armies of Kauravas. Sakuni suggests that the veteran Bhīṣma be made the chief and Duryodhana at once seconds the proposal. At this moment enter the Chamberlain who brings a the news that as a messanger from the Pāṇḍavas, Pursottama Nārāyana has arrived.

Duryodhana gets into a rage and warns the assembly not to pay any respect to the cow-herd at the risk of a fine of twelve gold pieces. He plans to insult Kṛṣṇa and deliberately engage himself in looking at a picture scoll depicting the dishonour shown to Draupadi by snatching her hair and clothes, when Yudhisthira gambled her away. But his attempts to insult Kṛṣṇa proves abortive. Kṛśṇa is brought in by the Chamberlain.

When Kṛṣṇa comes, all the assembled councillors stands up to honour him. Even Duryodhana falls from his seat in confusion. At the instruction of Kṛṣṇa the picture-scroll is removed by Badarayana. Kṛṣṇa delivers Yudhisthira's message, pressing the claim of the Pāndavas for the half of the kingdom. Duryodhana refuses to give them their due share in the inheritance. But Kṛṣṇa once again requests Duryodhana to give the Pandavas back what they demand, otherwise, the Kuru race will soon be but a name.

But Duryodhana replies that if they want a kingdom, let them fight and get it.

Thus there goes some wordy war between Kṛśṇa and Duryodhana, followed by abuses from Duryodhana who orders his men to bind him, but they fails. At last Duryodhana himself tries to bind Kṛṣṇa by nooses but his efforts to imprison him prove futile. Kṛṣṇa assumes his universal form and multiplies himself so that the hall becomes filled with Kṛṣṇa all round, Duryodhana becomes baffled and asks each prince to bind one Kṛṣṇa and is surprised to find that, when they try to do this, all of them get bound in their own bonds and fall down. Now Duryodhana takes his bow and arrows to shoot and kill all the Kṛṣṇa's men. Kṛṣṇa assumes cosmic forms and becomes too much enraged, he calls his chief missile, discuss 'Sudarśana' destroy the Kauravas.

Sudarśana appears in human form, pays homage to Kṛṣṇa and sets out to kill Duryodhana.

But Sudarśana softens Kṛṣṇa by saying that "You descended on earth, O God, to ease its burden by riding it of wicked".

Getting into a rage, Kṛṣṇa assumes his universal form, when Duryodhana tries to put the noose on him. Kṛṣṇa becomes bigger and bigger. When the noose is made bigger, Vasudeva becomes smaller and smaller.

Kṛṣṇa's other missiles such as his bow 'Sārnga', mace 'Kaumodakī' conchsell 'Pāṇcajanya', sword 'Nandaka' also appears on the stage, but returns to their respective places, as told by Sudarsana that Kṛṣṇa wrath has subdued and there was no need to manifest their valour.

Now emerges his vehicle Garuda, but leaves the place on being told that Kṛṣṇa is pacified.

Sudarsana also follows Garuda to his abode in Mount Meru. After their departure, Kṛṣṇa also sets out to go, but the old King Dhṛtarastra falls at his feet and apologises on his son's behalf, but his mission remain unsuccessful.

Kṛṣṇa bids farewell to Dhṛtarastra with which the play ends.

(VII) KARNABHĀRA

Synopsis: In the Vanaparvam of the Mahābhārata there is an incident of giving away the armour and ear-rings to Indra who was in disguise of a brahman is taken as the theme of Karnabhāra. Karna gets ready for his fight with Arjuna, tells Salya, king of Mādras, of the trick by which he obtained his armour from the Brāhmana sage, Parasurama. But as he hails from the warrior-class, Paraśurāma curse him that the arms should fail Karna in the hour of his need. This proves to be true, for Indra appears in the guise of a Brāhmana and walks away with Karna's armour and ear-rings. Karna ascends his chariot and asks Salya to drive it to the battle-field.

Dramatis Personae (In order of appearance):

Stage-manager, in the Prologue.

Soldier, on the Kuru side.

Karna: King of the Angas, son of Surya by Prithā (or Kunti before her marriage to Pāndu), and so an elder half-brother of the Pāndavas, but fights on the Kuru side.

Salya: King of the Madras, brother of Mādrī, the second wife of Pāndu, fight on the Kuru side and drives Karna's chariot.

Indra: disguised as a brahman. Speaks Prakrit like a mendicant of an unorthodox order, e.g. Buddhist or Jain.

Angel, disguised as a brahman: a messenger from Indra.

The Plot :- The stage-manager after his benedictory stanza hears some noise caused by the warrior messenger of Duryodhana telling Karna of the imminent fight that is approaching. Karna is, however, ready in his war-dress for the dreadful battle and is proceeding to the battle field with Salya. So the messenger departs. Karna is seen on the battle-field of Kurukshetra in a gloomy mood and preparing himself for his fight with Arjuna. He asks Salya, King of Mādrās, to drive the car to where Arjuna is. But he is held back by the memory of the fact that Pāṇdavas are none, but his younger brothers. As the chariot moves on, he tells Salya of the trick by which he won his armour from the Brāhman sage, Parasurāma.

He narrates the whole episode which runs as follows: Once Karna went to Parasurama, the scion of the Bhrigu race, an excellent sage, the destroyer of the warrior class. He was sitting there with a man of matted locks shining like streaks of lighting, and wielding his famous axe. He went to him humbly saluted, and stood on one side. He blessed Karna and asked him about who he was, the purpose of his visit. He then expressed his desire to learn the art of war and the use of every kind of weapon. He told him that he would teach only Brahmans and not the Ksatriyas, the warrior class. Parashuram started teaching him in the use of weapons. One day, when Karna, as a pupil went with him to fetch some fruits and roots, grass flowers and fuel. While wandering in the forest, Parashuram became exhausted and started taking a nap with his head on Karna's lap. Unfortunately an insect called 'steely-teeth' bored through Karna's thighs. But he did not move and bore the pain with fortitute so that the slumber is not disturbed. The warm blood, oozing out from his thighs, woke him up. Parashurama at once guessed by Karna's endurance that he must be belonging to a warrior class and thus furious Parashurama cursed him that "Useless be thy weapons in thy time of need".

At this juncture Indra comes in disguise as a Brahman and cleverly takes away from Karna his body armour which was born with him and miraculous ear-rings. Thus the curse of Parashurama proves true, he becomes deprived of his divine protection of the eve of his fight with Arjuna.

Salya warns him not to part with them and when Brahman leaves, he tells Karna that he has been cheated by Indra. Though Karna parts with his safety, but not with his generosity. An Angel enters, disguised as a Brahmin and informs Karna that Indra is grateful to him and regrets his taking Karna's armour and ear-rings. That is why he sends a spear, named Vimala, an unfailing weapon to slay one of the Pandavas. But Karna refuses to take a return for his gifts. When the Angel tells him to take it at a Brahmin's bidding. He states that he had never disregarded a Brahmin's bidding and asks the spear. Angel replies that when he bring it to mind and departs.

Karna and Salya start for the battle and proceed in the chariot. The former hears Arjuna's conch and instructs Salya to drive his car to where Arjuna is and with this the play ends.

(VIII) MADHYAM - VYAYOGA

Synopsis :- In this play, Bhasa infuses a Mahabharata theme with a plot-design inspired from a famous story of the Vedic tradition (Sunahśepākhyāna of Aitareya - Brahmana). It depicts how from the hands of Ghatotkacha, Bhima rescues a Brahmana family and demons eventually unites with his wife Hidimbā. There are two madhyama's in the play. When Ghatotkacha attacks on an old brahmana family to fulfill his mothers demand to get a human prey for her meal, the second son of the three sons of this old brahmana was to be offered to Hidimba. But Bhima, also the madhyama, ie, middle of the Pāndavas agrees to sacrifice his life to save the boy. He recognises his son and gets an opportunity to meet his wife Hidimbā. Interestingly Hidimba also tells Bhīma her motive in asking Ghatotkacha to bring a man for her meal, which was to bring back Bhīma himself.

Dramatis Personae (In order of appearance.)

Stage-manager, in Prologue.

Keśavadāsa.: the old brahman.

Wife.

First Son.

Second son, the 'middle one'.

Third Son.

Ghatotkacha ('Postsherd')": son of Bhīma and Hidimbā.

Bhīma or Bhīmasena: the second Pāndava, called her the 'middle one', i.e. considering only the three sons of Kuntī.

Hidimbā: the giantess sister of the slain Hidimba, married to Bhīma and mother Ghatotkacha.

The Plot:- The play opens with the preliminary rites, after which the stage-manager pronounces a benediction on the spectators, and starts addressing them. But he has to stop suddenly because of some noise, which on second hearing proves to be the cry of an old Brahmana called Kesavadasa. This old man with his wife and three sons were passing through the forest (which was then the abode of Ghatotkacha and his mother). They were being pursued by a furious half human, half demonic Ghatotkacha.

Ghatotkacha's mother Hidimba wanted human food and at her bidding, he strolls in the forest in search of a human being and catches sight of the Brahmana family. Ghatotkacha speaks of his peculiarly embarrasing situation - his reverence for the Brahman's but he has to execute his mother's command, one among them will have to sacrifice his life as meal to Hidimba, his mother and would spare the remaining members. Thus begins the discussion among them as to who should sacrifice himself for the sake of the family.

The old man states that his body, decrepit with age, has practically finished its journey of life. So he should offer, to save his sons. But wife cries out "No - no, an ideal wife exists for the sake of her lord only. This body has served it's purpose. I shall offer it as a sacrifice to this demon to save my husband and sons".

On the ground of old age and female sex, Ghatotkaca rules out the offers of the old man and his wife. There is a generous rivalry among the three in self surrendor. Among the three sons, the father wants the eldest, the mother wants the youngest, so the choice falls on the middle one, after much deliberation. He surrenders to Ghatotkacha and accompanies him to fulfil his duty of madhyama son to his family by sacrificing himself. However he asks sometime to slake his thirst in a forest pool in the vicinity. But as disappears for long, impatient Ghatotkacha, in rage, not knowing his real name, shouts for the pray as madhyama, the middle one.

When Ghatotkacha was screaming for the Brahamana boy, Bhīma was engaged in his exercise nearby. He wondered who it might be that disturbed him in his exercise. Nevertheless he had to arrive on the scene to respond to Ghatotkacha's call as he is also the madhyama of the Pandavas. Bhīma stands before him and tells him that he was madhyama by name. Kesavadasa in a whisper to his wife and sons says that he must be the middle Pandava. In a shortwhile, the Brahmana youth, madhyama also appears. The old man requests Bhīma to rescue his son, and Bhīma offers his help. He asks Ghatotkacha to release the Brahmana boy. But Ghatotkacha refuses to set him free and tells even if his own father had commanded, he would not have obliged. He adds that he has seized him by the orders of his mother Hidimba and her lord is the great Pandavas, Bhīma. Bhīma recognises the demon as none other than his own son, but still the playwright brings the son before the father in a duel not found in the original epic. This fight enables Bhīma to have a first hand knowledge of his son's valour.

Bhīma decides to go in the boy's place, but not by force. But Ghatotkacha not recognising his father seeks to compel him. There is a fine blending of comic and the heroic sentiments. There is the melodramatic moves of the son to over power Bhīma with a tree, rock etc. As a last resort, he even tries to bind Bhīma by the magic house given by his mother, but this time also he fails. At the end of the duel, Ghatotkacha accepts Bhīma's offer to go willingly and all go to Hidimbā's residence.

On being called by her son, Hidimba emerges on the stage. Ghatotkacha presents Bhīma to Hidimba as the man brought for her meal . She at once recognises her husband and greets him with unbounded joy. Next the audience witnesses Hidimba's revelation of Bhīma's identily to Ghatotkacha. She reaproaches her son and bids him express regret. She explains that her demand was made only to secure her a visit from Bhīma whom she had missed for many a year. Bhīma asks his son to salute the Brahmana. They expresses their sense of gratitude to Bhīma for saving his son's life and then departs for their destination, escorted to the door by Bhīma, his wife and son. The one act closes with the usual Bharatavākya.

(IX) PAṆCARĀTRA

Synopsis :- Based on the Virātaparvam of Mahābhārata, this Samavakāra type of drama in three acts shows Pāndavas in hiding being forced into battle with the Kurus. Drona has undertaken a sacrifice for Duryodhana and seeks as the free the grant to the Pāndavas of half the Kingdom, Duryodhana agrees to give the same to Pāndavas, but lays down one condition that news of the Pandavas should be received within 'five nights'.

The Pandavas, who are now in the thirteenth year of their exile are in the abode of the king of the Matsya's 'Virāta'. The news of the death of Kīcaka is received and Bhishma rightly informs that the Matsya general must have been slain by Bhīma. Duryodhana at once raids the rich cow-pen of Virata, at the instruction of Bhishma. A battle takes place in which Uttara, the Matsya prince, aided by Arjuna in disguise as a nauch girl 'Bṛhanalā' defeats the Kauravas.

Abhimanyu is taken captive by Bhisma. The real situation is known which the accorded time and Pandavas are given their due share.

Dramatis Personae (In order of appearance):

Stage-manager, in Prologue only.

Three Brahmans, in Prelude of Act I.

Bhīsma: son of Sāmtanu, old warrior who guides the Kurus.

Drona: the old preceptor of the Kuru and of the Pāndava princes.

Duryodhana: eldest of the Kuru princes, sons of Dhritarāshtra.

Karna: King of Anga, elder half-brother of the Pāndavas, being a son of Kunti.

Sakuni: brother of Queen Gāndharī, maternal uncle of the Kuru princes, Prince of Gāndhara.

Servant of the Kurus.

Messenger.

King Bhuriśravas of the Deccan, King Bhīshmaka, King Vasubhadra, and Sahadeva son of Jarāsandha do not speak. (Nor does Abhimanyu in Act I.)

Old Cowherd.

Gomitraka: younger cowherd.

Other Cowherds.

Jayasena: Soldier.

Chamberlain of Virata's palace.

King Virata (of the Mastyas).

Servant of Virata.

Bhagavan, Yudhishthira: (epic Kanka dieer).

Attendant of Virāta.

Charioteer of Virāta.

Brihannala: Arjuna, the great archer.

Bhima or Bhimasena: the powerful Pātna, disguised as a seullion pugilist. (Epic Ballava).

Uttara: Virāta's son.

Charioteer of the Kurus.

The Plot :- In the benedictory stanza, the names of the major characters in the drama are introduced. Then, the stage-manager hears the praise of the grand sacrifice, being performed by Duryodhana.

Act One: With a triangular conversation between three brahmanas, the prelude begins with the description of the sacrifice. These brahmans who are attending the sacrifice, eulogises Duryodhana's nobility and generosity and religious bent of mind. Through brilliant narration of the oblations, fire, the smoke and the holy priests, they glorify the institution of the sacrifice. The Brahamanas announce the entery of Bhīsma and Drona followed by Sakuni, Karna and Duryodhana. The action propers, therefore, shows Duryodhana paying homages and receiving blessings from Bhīsma, Kṛpa, the great Kaurava and his guru Drona and accepting the greatings from his equals such as Karna and others on the successful termination of the sacrifice which the major feat of the Kṣatriyas.

Drona presents Abhimanyu to Duryodhana, but at the same time Sakuni brings Sahadeva, son of Jarāsandha and hence Abhimanyu remains in the background, but Sahadeva receives blessings from Duryodhana.

In the assembly, Duryodhana notices the absence of Virāta, the king of Matsyadesā in the assembly. Sakuni tells that the king must be on his way and a messenger is deputed for the purpose.

As a result of their defeat in the gamble of dice, the Pandavas were living incognite in terms of conditions binding on them.

Duryodhana was desperately looking for them as in that case, they were suppose to go again in exile for another term of twelve years and thereafter live incognite for one year.

Drona, the family preceptor of the Kauravas is well acquainted with the attitude of Duryodhana and others, not to give even bit of land to the Pandavas. Hence he forsee an ensuing desaster resulting from a fratricidal war.

To put an end to their enemity he was looking for an opportune moment and decides to undertake this sacrifice. Now, as the sacrifice is over, Duryodhana offers his gurudakṣina. Seeing tears in Drona's eyes, Bhiśma tells Duryodhana that his all efforts are meaningless, as his preceptor is in grief.

At this, Duryodhana gives a solemn undertaking to offer anything that Drona might be pleased to choose. Drona, now demands as his gurudakṣina the grant to the Pāndavas, half of their realm. Sakuni vehemently protests against any such gift and finds it a deceit practised by Drona on his Sisya.

Bhisma tries to pacify Drona tells Duryodhana that his main intention was to remove all the differences and disputes in the Kuru family and that is why he asked for such a gift. Here the crafty Sakuni plays his usual role of the arch-knave. Duryodhana promises one condition that Pāndavas whereabout should reach him within five days. Drona deems it impossible to fulfil, but later concedes at the suggestion of Bhisma the spies deputed by Duryodhana to find out the news of Pāndavas whereabouts, brings the news of sudden death of Kicaka, the General of Virāta, the king of Matsyadesa by Gandharvas. Duryodhana takes Sakuni and Karna aside and consults them. As per Sakuni's instruction, they also brings the news from Virāta who expresses his inability to attend the ceremony, as he has to mourn the loss of a hundred Kichakas including the chief. Bhīma kills one hundred five Sūtās and the chief called 'Kīchaka' belongs to that class, who attempt to insult Draupadī in Virāta's palace. Bhīsma guesses that Kicaka must have been killed by Bhīma and induces Duryodhana to march against Virāta who has insulted the Kauravas by not attending the sacrifice and they organise a cattle-raid and such expedition would subsequently held them to findout the Pāndavas.

Suśarman, the king of Trigartta country, an enemy of the king Virāta happened to be present there at the assembly is asked first to march against the Kingdom of Virāta and start plundering his wealth.

The following day, Kauravas would be there to carry away the cattle of the King of Matsyadeḍsa. Drona tells Duryodhana that he and Bhīsma are anxious to see his strength and power in battle. He also asks Sakuni to go in the leading chariot. All Kaurava giants, therefore, participates in the march.

Act Two:- This act focuses on the cattle-raid. A vivid picture of pastoral life is shown through an interlude. An old cowherd tells Gumitraka, another cowherd that the cows have been assembled and the king Virata is going to give away cows as gifts, at his birthday festival. Thus the cowherds and cowherdesses of Matsyadeśa are engaged in the merry dances. Their songs raise clouds of dust and provides an opaque canopy, conceals the sun from their view. At the sun set, ther is sundden over running of the colony with the sudden attack of Kauravas who forcibly takes away the cattle. They leave at once to bring it to the notice of the Virata King. Act proper opens with a soldier Jayasena telling the chamberlain about the invasion of the Kuru army. From the chamberlain, the king hears that his cows are stolen. He orders his chariot to the made ready for the fight and calls Bhagavan (Yudhiṣthira in disguise) for consultation. The king also learns from a messenger that all the Kauravas with Drona, Kṛpa, Karna, Salya and Abhimanyu were leading the army for the cattle-raid. Virata asks the charioteer to get his chariot ready at once. But he is further told that his Royal Highness Prince Uttara has gone to repulse the attack. Yudhiṣthira advises him to recall the young prince, as he would not be able to withstand the attack. Virata is nervous about the survival of his inexperienced son in the odds against veteran fighters and sends another chariot and his anxiety doubles hearing that Bṛhanhala has gone as Prince Uttara's charioteer. Yudhiṣthira assures him of the success (as he is conscious of Arjuna's power).

The news is brought of the surrounding of Uttara's chariot by the enemy and later, of the continuous shower of arrows from the chariot, which only Abhimanyu could resist. Hearing of Abhimanyu's valour and fearing that Arjuna may hesitate to fight with his own son, he advises the despatch of another charioteer.

The soldier brings the news about the recovery of the cows and the retreat of the Kauravas. Virata asks for where Uttara is and is being told that he is preparing a report of the heroic deeds of his soldiers. He then enquires about Brihannala. At his instruction, Brihannala called to inform the assembly of the particulars of the fighting at length. At this juncture, a soldier comes with the news of the capture of Abhimanyu by the King's scullion, ie, Bhīma in disguise who went up to Abhimanyu's car boldly and lifted him with his arms.

King Virata is proud of his son's heroism. Bhima enters and remarks to himself that he had to exert himself as much to carry away Abhimanyu as he had to when he rescued all his brothers and mother from the blazing lac house. Arrives Abhimanyu with Brihannala and wonders who it is, who carried him away boldly with so much ease and who this person in lady's garb. Arjuna expresses his willingness to meet Abhimanyu. He takes Bhima aside and asks him to prompt and provoke the boy. Abhimanyu replies that his captor came unarmed and as he was Arjuna's son, he didnot like to strike him and therefore, the captor captured and carried him away. Thus, there followed smart exhanges between this brave boy and his captors. The former remains ignorant about their identity as father and uncle. Then, we find Abhimanyu with his charming arrogance facing Virāta.

Enters prince Uttara and informs the king, his father that the actual credit for this great victory should go to the charioteer who defeated Bhisma and the rest with his arrows and rescued him. Arjuna tries to protest, but later unfolded their identity as the one year term of incognite life of Paṇḍavas is over. Thus this comes as a great surprise for Abhimanyu, when he finds the captors as his own father and uncle. He pleads forgiveness and pays proper respects to all elders and prays for blessings. He is suitably blessed as well Arjuna makes him salute. Virata wishes him to have the magnanimity of Yudhiṣṭhira, the might of Bhima, the skill of Arjuna, the charm of Nakula, the foresight of Sahadeva and the wisdom and glory of Kṛṣṇa.

Now, Virāta, as a mark of gratitude, offers his daughter 'Uttara' (who was in the secure seclusion of the harem during the year with Arjuna) in marriage with Arjuna. Arjuna realizes his anxiety and thus, accept Uttarā for his son as he had treated all the ladies of the palace as his mothers, sisters and daughters.

It is finally settled that Uttara would be married to Abhimanyu. Virāta is overjoyed to hear this and goes to celebrate the marriage that very day.

Yudhiṣṭhira advises to send Uttara to Bhiṣma with tidings of the approaching marriage.

Virata goes inside the palace with Yudhiṣthira, Bhima and Arjuna to celebrate the nupitals.

Act Three :- This act takes us to Hastināpura, after the defeat of Kauravas in the battle. The kidnapper of Abhimanyu is their main agenda of the discussion. Both Bhīma and Drona suspect that it must have been Bhīma.

If this is so, then Duryodhana will have to hand over half of his kingdom to Pandavas. Realizing this Sakuni objects to their suspicions and asks "Are there no other strongmen in the world? Bhiṣma tells that only Bhima and Balarama fight bare-armed, on foot. But Drona and Bhīsma again express their strong suspicions about the person who accompanied prince Uttara as Arjuna who bent his bow with such a loud twang and sent such showers of arrows as could hide even the sun.

At this moment, Bhīsma's charioteer brings in an arrow on his flag that bears the name of Arjuna, who shot it to salute Bhisma and Drona, his teacher. This removes all doubts. But Sakuni still tries in vain to explain that it could be from some other Arjuna. The evidence of the arrow is not sufficient.

Prince Uttara appears on the scene and brings an invitation from Yudhisthira for the marriage of Abhimanyu with his sister. This sets the flimsy objections of Sakuni arid.

Drona appeals Duryodhana to stand by his as word of honour. Five days had not yet ended.

Duryodhana proclaims that half the realm is Yudhiṣṭhira as befor and adds "Man survives only when truth survives".

This makes Drona very happy in the reunion of the mighty houses. An epilogue from Drona stating that "May the lion-like king rule over the whole earth" brings the play to an end.

(X) PRATIJṆAYAUGANDHARAYANAM

Synopsis :- This play of Bhāsa in Six Acts is based on the Udayana legend and is a sequel to the Pratijṇāyaugandharāyaṇa. Udayana losses his kingdom including the capital Kausambi to a foul usurper Aruni who compels him to move to a camp in the border village of Lavanaka.

Meanwhile Udayana's minister heards a prediction from the sooth sayers, Pushpaka and Bhadraka that Padmāvati, a Magadha princes and sister of King Darśaka will marry Udayana. Vatsarāja and with his help he would recover his lost kingdom from the foul usurper, Aruni. To bring about the marriage, the clever Yaugandharayana takes Vāsavadatta into his confidence and she gives her consent to his strategic plan to hoodwink Udayana into believing that Vāsavadatta is dead.

Now, Yaugandharayana succeeds in purusuading Pādmāvatī to take charge of Vāsavadatta in disguise. He doned the garb of a Brahmana mendicant state that she is her sister Avantika and will stay with Padmavati while he goes on a pilgrinage. Udayana and Padmāvati are wedded. Once when asleep, Vasavadatta comes to his side and when she touches him he wakes up and tries to get hold of her, but she runs away.

Dejected Udayana was once diverting himself with a painting of Vāsavadatta in her wedding attire, Padmavati tells the king that there was a young girl in her harem quite like the image in the picture, brought to her by a sage. Vāsavadatta is being produced before the king and the secret is divulged. He retrieves his lost dominions and also reunities with Vasavadatta, his first queen.

Dramatis Personae: **(In order of appearance):**

Stage-manager: Only in the Prologue to introduce the play. The name of the Sūtra-dhāra 'holder of the strings' is derived from some from of puppet play.

Actress

In Kauśāmbī:-

Yaugandharāyana: the principal minister of Udayana the Vatsa king.

Sālaka: the intended messenger not required.

Vijayā-Portress: stock name of a female doorkeeper.

Nirmuṇḍaka: Shaveling', servent in the minster's household.

Hamsaka: 'Gosling' a soldier of Udayana's escort, returned.

Brahman.

In Ujjain:

Chamberlain of the Avantī Court. (Bādarāyaṇa.)

King of Ujjain, Pradyota or Mahāsena.

Queen of Ujjain (Aṇgāravatī).

Jester (Vasantaka) of Kauśāmbi, disguised as a beggar.

Madman-Yaugandharāyana in disguise.

Buddhist Monk-Rumaṇvān the other Vatsa minister.

Two soldiers (or servents).

Page (a Vatsa spy) who feigns intoxication.

Two servants.

Bharatarohaka: Minister of Ujjain.

The Plot: **Act One** — In the prelude, the stage-manager introduces through the benedictory verse the characters of the play and then calls out to his mistress to sing a song. She tells him that she is worried about her kin, as he had a bad dream and wants the stage-manager to sent a messenger to bring news about her relatives. The stage-manager agrees, but from the off stage, he hears the conversations of Yaugandharāyana, the prime minister of the Vatsa king and his loyal messenger, Salaka.

The former is about to send Sālaka to warn Vatsaraja of the ensuing danger, before the king leaves for Nāgavana. On hearing them, both the stage-manager and his mistress departs.

The play begins with a scene in Vatsaraja's palace at Kausambi.

It would be apt to mention here that Udayana Vatsaraja was the descendent of the great Pāṇḍavas and was ruling at Kauśambī. An ardent lover of fine arts and hunting wild elephant. In his neighbouring state Avanti, King Pradyota popularly known as Mahasena (owing to his huge army) was reigning. He had a beautiful daughter called Vāsavadattā, whom he intended to offer in marriage to Vatsaraja. But the latter had not condescended to send any envoy for the purpose. Thus, in order to trap Vatsaraja, Mahasena planned an evil design to trap Udayana and take him capture.

From the words of Vatsaraja's faithful minister Yaugandharayana, the central figure of the play, it is learnt that the king has gone to capture elephants; his favourite past time, in the Nagavana. Through his spies, the minister comes to know that Mahasena has kept a large blue artificial elephant in the forests adjoing the borders of his kingdom to attract Vatsaraja and eventually attacking him by a body of soldiers hidden within that elephant.

Yaugandharayana orders Salaka to go at once and alert the king of the danger, as the king is sure to run the risk of going alone to entice such an elephant of remarkable size. He tells Salaka that he has go a long way to which Salaka replies that he can ever cover a much longer distance and requests the minister to give him a letter for the king. The minister asks Vijaya, the female attendant to hurry with the letter and the auspicious from the queen-mother. Vijaya leaves and comes back shortly to inform that the cord (an amulet to protect Udayana Vatsaraja from harm by demons, enemies wild beasts, etc) is going round of all the married ladies in the palace, for being blessed by them in turn. This makes the minister inpatient and tells that whether blessed by all ladies or only one, he needs the cord immediately. So Vijaya goes back to get the cord. Meanwhile, news is brought about the return of Hamsaka, Vatsaraja's body guard and Yaugandharayana sends away Sālaka to wait outside and eagerly awaits the arrival of Hamsaka. On questioning, he learns of the eventual capture of king Udayana by Pradyota Mahasena, Hamsaka gives him a detailed account of the fight. How the king went near it, hostile warriors rushed out of the Trojan elephant and attacked the king; he fought single-handed with the army for three or four hours and became unconsious owing to sunstroke when the king recovered his consciousness, he found himself fied down with shrubs and suddenly on alien soldier dragged the king brutally by his hair and attempted to behead him, but stumbled and fell down helpless. Then the chief of the enemy forces, Salankayana, who also was hurt by Udayana with his spear and because unconscious in the previous fight, recovered from his swoon rushed to the spot and ordered his warriors not to commit anymore violence and then cut off his bonds, saluted the king and took him to Ujjaini.

When the minister now laments over his master's captivity, Vijaya enters with the auspicious cord. Yaugandharayana asks her to throw it away since it has come too late. She asks him what she is suppose to tells the Queen-mother. The minister is so grief-stricken that he is unable to spell the doleful news at first instance. But later directs her to reveal the news of the capture to the Queen-mother.

After Vijaya's departure, the minister asks Hamsaka why he did follow the king Ujjaini. Hamsaka replies that Śālankayana had sent him to inform Yaugandharāyana of the whole incident and that Vatsarāja himself asked Hamsaka to go and see him. Yaugandharayana, vows to save his master from the terrible fate, by meeting him in the forest or in bondage, and defeating Mahasena or sacrificing his own life. At this junture, some noise is heard and the whole harem is in mourning at the news. Vijaya comes with the message from the Queen-mother stating that Yaugandharayana was at first a friend of Vatsaraja and then his minister. But he is like a son to the Queen. She asks one son to bring her another son. Yaugandharayana feels deeply honoured at the confidence in him shown by the Queen-mother and the Vatsarāja. So he pronounces his vow that he is not Yaugandharāyana, if he doesnot release his master seized by his enemies, like the Moon seized by Rahu. Vijaya goes inside and then emerges Nirmundaka with a madman's apparel and informs him of a strange happening at the Śānti festival where the Brahmana's were being feasted for the sake of King's welfare. A Brahmana appeared there as a madman laughing and proclaiming aloud that the royal family will recover from adversity and prosper. In great astonishment, he enquires whether all this was true. One of the Brahmanas added that the madman was none other than the blessed Dwaipayana, the great sage Vyasa, who came and vanished leaving his cloth. Yaugandharayana dens these clothes and finds himself transformed beyond recognition. He immediately sets about to effect the release of the King in that guise, without rousing any suspicions. Then Vijaya comes with another message from the Queen-mother who wants to see him. He asks the Brahman to wait in the chapel for him and asks Hamsaka to rest and departs with Vijaya.

Act Two :- This act begins in Mahasena's palace at Ujjaini. In the interlude, through the solilogue of Badarayana, Mahasena's chamberlain, we are told that various kings from all parts of the country have sent their envoys to his court, asking for the hand of Vasavadatta, his daughter in marriage. Of late, Jaivanti, the preceptor of the Raja of Benaras has come and Badarayana directs Abhivaka to look for the comfort of the honourable guests and respęctful treatment palace. He then wonders about Mahasena's indecision to settle the marriage and lives everything up to fate. The main scene opens with the entry of Mahāsena with his retinue. He says to himself that though numerous king have submitted to him, but he will not be satisfied till Vatsaraja's subjugation. He now enquires whether the honourable Jaivanti has been properly lodged and receives a positive answer. On asking the cause of his indecision regarding his daughter's marriage, he replies to Badarayana that he has not arrived at a definite choice of a bridegroom as he wishes to have all the best qualities in the prospective son-in-law such as of his noble birth, compassionate nature, to be of a mighty king to control and protect the bride, to be attractive to the women folk etc. When the queen enters with her retinue, he enquires about Vasavadatta and is told that she is in the concert hall taking her music lessons from Uttara. She now, requests the king to engage a music teacher for Vasavadatta. The king says that Vasavadatta's husband would teach the Narada Veena. The queen expresses her worries regarding Vasavadatta's marriage, since she has attained the marriageable age and at the same time, fears that as a consequence she would be separated from her daughter. The king requests her to make her chocie and at first tells about the alliance proposed by the honourable Jaivanti and then enumerates the royal suitors from Magadha, Kasi, Vanga, Surashatra, Mithila and Surasena. Their conversations get interrupted at the emergence of Badarayana who rushes in and breaks the news that the king of the Vatsus has been captured by Salankayana. On hearing the news and then being convinced of the truth after a series of queries, he orders Badarayana to go and tell Bharatarohaka, his prime minister to receive victorious Salankayana with the honours and also see that none of he citizens be debarred from seeing the captive Vatsaraja.

The queen comments that she has never seen Mahasena so pleased and also tells casually that it is only Vatsaraja alone who didn't send any envoy to ask for her daughter hand in marriage. So this king enumerates all the noble qualities that Vatsaraja possesses. Such has his birth in the Bharata live of Kings, with its long roll of royal sages, and its tradition of vedic learning, his unparralled mastery over music, his youthful beauty etc. The interrupts her by exclaiming that these are the very qualities one would desire in a son-in-law. The chamberlain enters to deliver Ghoshavati, the famous lute of Vatsaraja, an emblem of victory. He also informs that Salankayana has been given warm reception. Then the king ponders as to whom to give the lute and finally decides to make a present of that to Vasavadatta. The king then enquires about Vatasaraja and is told by Badarayana that Vatsaraja is badly wounded. Mahasena orders immediate medical attendance, honourable treatment in right royal manner. The chamberlain leaves and returns in a shortwhile to inform that the Vatsaraja have been dressed on the way, when the king learns that Vatsaraja is being kept near the Peacock perches. He at once orders his removal to a more suitable mosaic room, so that he may be shielded from the scorchy heat. The queen then leaves for inner apartment telling the king that there is no need for hurrying up the marriage of Vasavadatta, who is still quite a child. Later, Mahasena also departs expressly his serious concern over the sorry plight of Vatsaraja who received so many wounds.

Act Three:- The Third Act shows that Yaugandharayana, Rumanvat, the Commander-in-Chief of king Udayana, and his jester and friend, Vasantaka have come to Ujjaini in disguise to effect the escape of Udayana alongwith his lute in accordance with the plans of Yaugandharayana. At first enters Vasantaka disguised as a begger, worrying over the loss of his sugar-balls indicating his non-meeting with Yaugandharayana. He speaks in code language that appears humour and nonsensical, but suggestive from his solilogue, or is indicated that Udayana has fallen in love withthe princess and the consequent failure of their mission. With bottered sweets in hand, arrives Yaugandharana, Vasantaka tells him of the need to modify minister's original plan in his usual funny language. This is followed by his secret signal to Rumanvat, who comes as a Buddhist monk and they move into the secret chamber of the fire-shrine, where their talks begins in ordinary language. Vasantaka informs that the king has recovered from his wounds and taken his bath. Yaugandharayana states that every item in the plot was ready and they will have to depart from this place to carryout the plan tomorrow.

The elephant Nalagira will be infuriated in the good old trick, with charms and herbs there will be dazzling fire, a house near the stables will be set on fire to terrify the elephant and appropriate mileu will be created by loud noise of conches and drums kept in the nearby temple. Vatsaraja was captured by an elephant trick, and will be set free by this elephant trick. When the elephant will go mad, Mahasena would sought Udayana's help to pacify it and then Vatsaraja will mount the elephant and ride away to Kausambi before the pursuers overtakes him.

But Vasantaka tells them that Vatsaraja will not agree to follow the plan suggested by Yaugandharayana. Because the latter has fallen in love with Vasavadatta at first sight, the day the palanquin in which the princesses was travelling had halted near the prison gate, on its way to the temple of the Yakshini. Now the prison has become for him paradise itself. The jester further reveals that there is a message from the king to Yaugandharayana stating that Vatsaraja is not satisfied with Yaugandharayana's plan and he is planning a fitting return to his planning humiliation by abducting Mahasena's daughter. This makes Yaugandharayana little distressed, but after some deliberations it is agreed upon that they would take the king out of the inner apartments of the palace. Yaugandharayana takes his vow to rescue his master and enabling him to carry away Vasavadatta just as Arjuna carried away Subhadra.

Now the citizen of Ujjaini have started moving about the street, they leave the fire-shrine by different doors and Yaugandharayana assumes his role as mad man and shouts out nonsensical and things makes funny gestures.

Act Four :- In the interlude, enters a soldier of Mahasena atached to Vasavadatta palace, coming in search of Gatrasevaka (page) the make out of princesses elephant, Bhadravati, so that the man can take the elephant to Vasavadatta who wants to go out bathing. He goes to a alehouse and finds Gatrasevaka there. Here commences a humorous sence between this intoxicated page, who in reality is a spy of Vatsaraja.

The Gatrasevaka describes how he has powred Bhadravati. Meanwhile the soldier hears some noise and to his disbelief, Gatrasevaka informs that it is Bhadravati, who has broken out of the alehouse and running away. The page casts away his disguise, and tells that Vatsaraja has eloped with Vāsavadattā. He inspires the Vatsa worriers by war songs and describes the valour of Yaugandharayana. The solider witnesses how he plunges himself into the battle with Mahasena's huge army and keeps slaying elephants, drivers and numerous heroes on foot and on horse. But at the end of the fight, Vijayasundara, an elephant breaks Yaugandharayana's sword by striking it with the tip of its task. He is caught hold by two soldiers and taken prisoner of war but he feels proud for his valiant deeds and proclaims that he has rescued his master and there by kept his words. He is being carried hand-cuffed. Yaugandharayana requests the soildlers allow the people of Ujjain to see him. Because they had earlier seen him in mad man's, guise. At this moment, a soilder brings the news of Vatsaraja's arrest to which Yaugandharayana gives no credence. Another soilder enters and tells the other two soilderls that Yaugandharayana is to be kept in the arsenal and to be heavily guarded by Mahasena's men. Yaugandharayana makes mockery of the order and states that they are newly guarding an empty casket after the jewels have been stolen. At the instruction of Bharatarohaka, Mahasena's minister, a soilder comes and untie the nooses that bound Yaugandharayana. When his chains are removed, comes Bharatarohaka taunts Yaugandharayana that it is only his machinations that enabled Vatsaraja to escape. In reply, Yaugandharayana refers to the trick played on Yaugandharayana with the false elephant by Mahasena. Then Bharatarohaka reminded him of the improper act of Vatsaraja who eloped with his disciple. Yaugandharayana answers that his master has already married her in Gandharva form. This way attack and counter attack goes on till Badarayana emerges with a gold chalice from Mahāsena as a gift to be presented to Yaugandharayana. At Bharatarohaka's bidding, Badarayana gives it to Yaugandharayana who exclaims: The houses I set fire to one still burning. This honour shown to one who deserves death is unendurable. At this moment, some noise is heard. Bharatarohaka asked the chamberlain to go and find out the causes of this sudden lamentations. The latter goes and returns in a shortwhile to inform that, the noise is due to the joy expressed by the whole harem when the king Mahasena asked his Queen to rejoice on Vasavadatta's choice. In grief and shame at the*elepement*. the Queen wanted to commits sucide by jumping from the top storey of the palace. The king further assures her that her daughter's marriage has been performed in the Gandharva form and inspite of that, their marriage will be celebrated in absentia by means of portraits.

Yaugandharayana is now convinced of the bonafides of the present and accepts the chalice. The play ends with the Bharatavakya praying for the prosperity of the cows, overcome the foreign attack and the reigning of the earth by Rājasimha.

(XI) PRATIMĀṆATAKAM

Synopsis :- The entire story of the Ramayana is retold in this Seven Acts but the playwright builds a superstructure of his own. The play derives its name from the 'Pratimā - gṛha' or the statue-house in which an image of Daśaratha is installed with his three ancestors. Bharata learns the demise of his father indirectly from the statue and comes to know the role played by his mother in this sad event. The abduction of Sītā by Ravaṇa under the guise of an expert on Srāddha and the absence of Laksmana at the time. Thus Rama's exit to collect the necessary material for the Srāddha or his coronation in the penance forest are some of the playwrights own innovations.

Bhasa presents Kaikeyi on a higher level and seeks to exonerate her from the charges of selfishness and heartlessness that have been levelled against her through centuries.

However, much of the significants events follows Valmik's version like slaying of Jatāyu who seeks to protect Sītā, Rāmā's alliance with Sugriva against Valin etc. Bharata deploys the army of Kosala to aid Rāma, whom he meets on the way returning victorious. He recovers Sītā after killing Rāvana.

He is crowned amidst deafening cries of the masses. "Victory to our King! Victory of the best of men", "Victory to the destroyer of Ravana".

Dramatis Personae (In order of appearance):

Stage-manager in the Prologue

Actress

Vijayā: Portress.

Bālāki: Chamberlain of Ayodhyā court.

Avadatika: one of Sītā maids of honour.

Sītā: wife of Rāma, daughter of Janaka, king of Mithilā. (Hence 'Maithilī, Lady of Mithilā.)

Maid, another of Sītā retinue.

Nandanikā: Second Maid of Sītā's retinue.

Rama: the heir apparent, son of King Dasaratha and Queen Kausalyā.

Lakshmana : brother of Rāma, son of King Daśratha and Queen Sumitrā.

Maid from the tiring room.

King Daśaratha of Ayodhyā.

Kausalyā: chief Queen of Daśaratha, mother of Rāma.

Sumitrā: second Queen, mother of Lakshmana.

Sumantra: Minister of Daśaratha.

Sudhakāra: keeper of the Statue Gallery.

Attendant of Ayodhyā court.

Bharata: Son of King Daśaratha and Queen Kaikcyi.

Soldier of Ayodhyā.

Kaikeyi: Queen, mother of Bharata.

Charioteer of Bharata.

Female ascetie.

Rāvana: the demon King of Lankā.

Two old asceties.

Nandilaka: servant in the hermitage.

Satrughana: twin brother of Lakshmana.

Plot:- In the epilogue, the stage-manager recites the benedictory verse in which the main characters of this Rama play are introduced. He then calls his mistress and asks her to sing a song of the autumn. The mistress sings and the stage-manager gives his comments on the season and at this juncture, some noise is heard, which the stage manager recognizes to be of those of the female door - keeper of Dasaratha's palace. So they depart from there and the main scene begins. Vijaya, the female door - keeper calls the chamberlain named Arya. Balaki tells him that the king Dasaratha desires him to hurry up with the preparations for the coronation of Rāma. The chamberlain answers that everything was already arranged - the umbrella and the fan, the joy drum, the consecration waters, and the sacred chair, were ready; the citizens and ministers were all assembled. His Holiness Vasishtha stood ready at the altar.

Vijaya sends Sambhavaka, an attendant, to the high priest to get ready and Sarasika, a maid - servant to tell the actresses in the court threatre to be ready with a dramatic presentation suitable to the occasion. Now she goes herself to inform. His Majesty that everything had been arranged for the ceremony. After her departure, enters Avadatika, a maid, carrying a bark garment, which she had taken away from the lady Reva, the mistress of the green-room to punish her. When the lady had finished her work on the stage Avadatika 'begged her for one sprig of the Asoka trees'. But Arya Reva defused her request and so she did this mischief. Sīta appears with her retinue and learns of Avadātikā's act. When Avadatika is about to go to return the bark garment, she is being called back. Sita takes the garment and puts it on for mere fun. She asks the maid to bring a mirror. The latter enters with it, but seeing her face, Sītā makes out as if she wanted to say something.

The maid tells her ladyship of some coronation about which Balaki, the chamberlain was talking about. Another maid comes with the news of Rāmā's coronation. Sītā is delighted at the good news and takes off her ornaments and distributes them to the maids. The sound of drum is heard. But suddenly it ceases and the second maid remarks that the coronation might have been postponed. Sītā tells that many unexpected things happen in courts. The maid tells that perhaps, after crowning the prince, the king would retire to a forest. Rama appears on the stage and wonders that why his friends, whom he left at the entrance are astonished at his calmness in leaving the throne at his father's words. Rāma does not seen very anxious and breathed a sigh of relief that he is still just Rāma and not the king. Avadatika alerts Sīta that the prince has arrived, but she has not yet removed the bark garment. Rāma meets Sītā and after short deliberations he tells Sītā how his coronation was cancelled. The king Dasaratha had ordered him to accept the kingdom, taking an oath on his own life. Then Lakshmana and Satrughna held the sacred vessels and the king held the umbrell. While he was going through all these rituals, Manthara arrived there and whispered something in king's ear and he was not king. Sīta is glad to learn that Rāma is still exclusively her own lord, without being, in addition, the lord of all the subjects. Then Rāma asks Sītā why she had removed her ornaments and put on the bark garments. He is told by Avadatika that she wore them out of mere curiosity. He then expresses his desire to have one for himself, but Sītā prevents him as it was unlucky, especially, in view of the recently cancelled coronation. They hear a wailing sound and the chamberlain brings the news that Kaikeyi has stopped Rāma's coronation for the sake of getting her son Bharata to be crowned the king.

Rāma tries to justify Kaikeyi's conduct and tells the chamberlain not to speak a word against his mother. When he enquires about his father, he learns that he has fainted because of the grief at Kaikeyi's distressing demand. At this point, enters Lakshmana, with bow and arrows in his hand. He is seen much agaited at king's decisions and intent on ridding the world of young women like Kaikeyi. Rāma expresses his astonishment at Lakshmana's angry outburst. Lakshmana tells him that it is not that Rāma has just been robbed of the realm, but it was the forest exile for fourteen years which has been enjoined upon Rāma that has unnerved him. Rama now understands why his father fainted. He asks Sīta to give him that bark garments, and decides to go to the forest and Sītā, as the ideal wife, is determined to accompany her husband.

Rama asks Lakshmana to dissuade Sita. But Lakshmana supports her. Then enters a maid with an unworn bark garment, which Rāma put on Lakshmana prays to Rāma to allow him to share the bark garments and forest life with him, and to serve him there. Rāma tries to prevent him but at Sītā's request; he gives half the garments and allows him to accompany him. The trio with the bark robes on, sets out for the forest led by Lakshmana, Rama asks Sītā to take off her veil so that the subjects assembled may freely have a look at her. Meanwhile the chamberlain appears with the news that the grief-stricken king is coming to prevent them from going into exile. Lakshamana tells Rāma that those who are to dwell in forests, clad in bark robes, need not see anybody. Rāma agrees to it and they all leave the palace.

Act Two:- The interlude in the form of a conversation between the female door keeper and Balaki, a chamberlain tells us of Rāma, Sīta and Lakshmana's departure and the sorry plight of king Dasaratha who laments his fate, as he is not able to bear the separation from his sons and is lying in the ocean chamber. Balaki continues that since the day when Rama left, Ayodhya appears to be deserted. The king is attended by Kausalya and Sumitra, rises and falls down and is continuously waiting and gazing at the way Rama went.

The main scene opens with the king in deep sorrow, attended by the two Queens, who witness his over weening love for Rāma ạnd his helplessness. Dasaratha is neither able to control his grief nor can he suffer it. He is even out of his senses and cannot even recognize the Kausalya who weeps and asks Dasaratha not to forment himself and gives assurance that he is bound to see all the three when the period of exile is over. At this juncture, enters the chamberlain with the news of Sumantra's arrival. The king stands up with the hope that Rāma might have returned. But chamberlain informs that the minister has arrived only with the empty chariot. In terrible grief, Dasaratha exclaims that as if death has sent his chariot to fetch Dasaratha.

Sumantra comes and greets the king. The latter anxiously enquires about the trio. But he is disappointed to learn that they all went away into the forest without a word. This adds so much to Dasaratha's grief that he falls into a deep swoon. When he recovers partly, he leaves a message full of irony and sarcasm for Kaikeyi. Then he sees the shades of his ancestors, asks for some water, sips it and with the names of Rāma, Vaidehi and Lakshmana on his lips, he swoons and expires. The chamberlain puts a cloth over him and all mourns his death.

Act Three: The interlude informs us of the arrangements made in the 'Pratima Gṛha' (statue-house) in view of the intended visit of the queen-mothers through the conversations between Sudhakara, a professional palace cleaner and an orderly from court. The scene provides some comic relief where in Sudhākara is seen enjoying a little nap after tidying up the palace, as directd by Sambhavaka, the emissary from the court. The orderly comes to see whether the tidying up is over, goes and strikes the cleaner over and over again. The cleaner weeps and asks about his fault. The orderly reminds him of the Queen mothers visit today to see the statue of king Dasaratha who left for his heavenly abode with broken heart, because Rama could not be crowned the king and had to go into exile. The cleaner says that has cleaned up the entire house by white washing the walls, decorating the door-ways with garlands and wreaths, cleaning the dovecotes, strewned fresh sand on the floor. On knowing these, the orderly allows him to take rest and goes to inform the minister that everything is ready for the queen-mothers to come.

The main scene opens with Bharata coming in a chariot. As he was away at the time of Dasaratha's death, he knew nothing of the tragic happenings in Ayodhya. He tells the charioteer that his long stay with his uncle has made him a total stranger to Ayodhya. He keeps enquiring about his fathers, as he was only informed of his ill health. On Bharata's questionings, the charioteer gives evasive replies such as when being asked, what disease afflicted the king, he answered 'a great affliction of the heart'. When Bharata asked whether he take his food as usual and, sleep well. The charioteer replied "No, he takes nothing and lies on the earth'. Thus the charioteer spoke of the dead king, which Bharata understood in a different sense.

At getting on satisfactory replies, Bharata becomes purturbed and instructs the charioteer to drive the car faster. The speed of the chariot diverts the attention of the prince, he gives beautiful desicriptions of the surrounding, the trees, the flooded rivers, the steady wheels etc. The charioteer informs that they have reached the outskirts of Ayodhya. Bharata becomes nostalgia and says to himself that he would fall at his father's feet, he will be soaked by the tears of his mothers, servents would speak in his praise, he will be mocked at by Lakshmana for his unconventional dress and speech.

The charioteer feels sorry for his master who is all ignorant of the triple bane, his father's death, his mothers greed, and the exile of his elder brother. At this point a soldier-messenger comes and Bharata asks him whether Satrughna is coming to see him. The soldier says that he is coming but requests him to wait outside and enter Ayodhya only after the advent of the star Rohini, and that half an hour of Krithigai has still to elapse, as directed by the preceptor. Bharata obey's his preceptor's word and suddenly he comes across the statue-house which he notices in the avenue of the trees. He mistakes it for a temple and resolves to take rest there and serve the double purpose of worship and repose. He gets down from the chariot and dismisses the charioteer for a while. Seeing the special preparations in the temple such as the walls being marked with imprints of hards dipped in sandal, the doors beautifuylly decorated with garlands, fresh sand on the ground, he wonders whether this is for Krithigai festival or is to what deity come this place belong to. He finds no outward sign of banner or weapons. Thus he incidentally visits the 'Pratimā Gṛha'.

He sees four statues and curiosly inspects the images which are life-like and not those of deities, but look like men. He expresses the artistic skills of the sculptors and goes to bow his head and utter a hymn of praise. At this juncture, Devakulika, the priests enters, after having his meals, finds a person resembling those worshipping the statues. He prevents Bharata and informs that they are not deities, but the statues of the kings of Iksvāku family. He pays his respect to them in turn when he knows them as the bygone Iksvāku kings, namely Dilipa, Raghu, Aja. Now when the image of Dasaratha catches his eyes and shocked Bharata gets puzzled, but cannot ask a direct question but at first requests him to repeat what he had said. Then he enquires whether they do put up statues of living kings also. He is told that only the statues of dead ones are installed.

The truth downs upon Bharata's mind, and he hastily starts to go. The priest is surprised that he doesnot ask any question about the fourth statue, that of Dasaratha over who gave up his life and Kingdom for the sake of the dowry contract. This news gives a terrible blow to Bharata and not being able to bear the impact of the tragic news he again and again, faints. He gets the details of his fathers death, the exile of Rāma with Sīta and Lakshmana and Kaikeyi's evil desire to instal Bharata on the throne. On one side he loves Rāma and will never think of becoming a king; on the other, his mother has committed the wicked act on his accounts only. As a result, Bharata feels guilty and his heart is wounded.

At this precise moment, a voice is heard that announces the entry of the queens led by Sumantra. Sumantra appears, but seeing Bharata lying on the floor, asks the queens not to enter. But the priest informs that he is Bharata and makes his exist. Bharata recovers, but not knowing of his departure, keeps muttering. But after a shortwhile, he recognizes Sumantra. The latter tells him to pay respects to Kausalyā and Sumitra. He salutes them and is suitably blessed by the queen mothers. Then Sumantra points to Kaikeyi. On hearing his mother's name, Bharata rises up angrily and tells that she doesnot deserve to stand between his two mothers. Kausalya asks him to salute Kaikeyi, but he dishonours her and more so, he openly denounces her and proclaims that he would establish a new law in the world that a mother be no mother for perfidy to her husband. Kaikeyi tries to justify herself on the ground of the fulfilment of the ground of the dowry contract, but he asks the reason of Rāma's punishment and asks whether that was too agreed to at the time of her marriage. Kaikeyi patiently submits to her son's insults for a greater reason, which she doesnot want to reveal at this moment. But Bharata is not satisfied and subjects his mother to wholesale condemnation, her crave for the title of King's mother, her lust for power, making Rāma dwell in the forests and sending Sīta dressed in bark etc. Sumantra then announces the arrivals of Vasistha, Vamadeva and others for Bharata's coronation. Bharata is not only grieved, but ashmed of Kaikeyi's behaviour, so he asks them to crown her ladyship and tells that without Rāma Ayodhya is not Ayodhya, Ayodhya is where Rāma lives. His heart aches to meet Rāma and beseech his forgiveness, so he sets out to meet him.

Act Four:- The interlude to this Act shows Vijaya and Nandinika, two maids of the harem, talking about the happening in the Pratima Gṛha. We are told that Bharata's refusal to accept the crown and his departure for the penance grove has endeared him to all the citizen of Ayodhyā and eventually put his mother more humiliation.

The main scene opens with Bharata and Sumantra in a chariot, approaching Chitrakuta, the then abode of Rāma. Bharata is seen in supreme haste to meet his brother whom he regards as his greatest deity. On reaching the hermitage, they get down from the chariot. Bharata asks Sumantra to announce him as the 'Son of greedy Kaikeyi'. But Sumantra objects to it. Then he proposes another mode of announcing himself to Rāma, by calling " Bharata, the disgrace of the Ikshavaku race". But Sumantra says that he would simply declare that "Bharata has come". He asks Sumantra to get away to give repose to the horses and Bharata cries out that an ordinary, cruel ungrateful, barbarous and violent - but devoted person has arrived to see Rāma. The trio listens to him wonderful voice and feels some affnity to the speaker from it, so Rāma sends Lakshmana to findout who the stranger is. Lakshmana goes and sees Bharata and is astonished to find stark resemblance between the stranger and that of Rāma. Sumantra hails Lakshmana and Bharata at once salutes his brother and Sumantra then introduces Bharata to Lakshmana, who welcomes him and goes in to tell Rama that Bharata wants to see Rāma. Rama is surprised to know that Lakshmana wants his order for this and directs him to bring in Bharta immediately, but later sends Sītā to receive him by showing honour like a mother. Sīta for a moment mistakes Bharata for her husband, as both of them bears remarkable resemblance. Sumantra tells Bharata that it is Sīta. He pays his respect and Sītā notices similarty in voice too. She blesses him and takes him to Rāma. Sumantra waits outside, while Bharata enters the hermitage led by Sītā. Bharata salutes Rama and the latter blesses him and asks him to embrace.

Meanwhile Sumantra arrives, who reminds Rāma of Dasaratha and his heart is torn. Sumantra expresses that his long lfe is a curse, as it lingers even after experiencing king's death, Rāma's punishment, Bharata's distress and the helpless state of the royal house. Both Sumantra and Rāma weep and he asks Lakshmana to bring water. But Bharata atonce snatches the pitcher from Lakshmana and goes fetches water. Rāma sips it and remarks that Lakshmana's right to serve him is gone. Sita replies that Bharta should also attend on him. Rāma admits the right of both, but desires that Lakshmana would serve him in the forest, while Bharata in Ayodhya. Bharata is broken hearted and distressed at Rāma's words and says that he would carry on Rāma's task even by staying in the forest, as the kingdom will be safe in the name of Rāma. But Rāma reminds him of his father's words and adds that he ought to keep his vow and would curse Bharata, if he neglects the kingdom. Subsequently Bharata agrees to perform his kingly duties on condition that Rama should resume the kingdom, entrusted to him, at the end of the fourteen years. Rāma accepts it and Bharata makes the rest three, ie, Lakshmana, Sītā and Sumantra witness to this compact. Bharata again asks him to give his two sandals, stating that he will be their vassal till Rama returns from exile. After receiving the sandals, Bharata desires to crown them by sprinkling coronation water. Rāma's approve gives him immense pleasure as he will be hence forth called as the virtuous son of the deceased king and lead life in a dignified way. At this moment Rāma tells him that a kingdom should not be neglected even for a moment, so he must take leave without any delay. Bharata is ready to setout. Rama bids Sumantra to protect Bharata. The latter mounts the chariot in Rāma's presence. The trio accompany Bharata as far as the gate of the hermitage.

Act Five:- The interlude takes to the hermitage in Janasthana, where Sīta has assumed her new duties in the forest, by sweeping the hermitage, worshipping the deities with flowers and watering the shrubs and trees. Then enters Rāma in search of Sītā and is pained at seeing Sīta who feels no fatigue in carrying at water - pot, while the same Sīta used to be worn by carrying mirror in her hand. The forest makes delicate ladies as hard as creepers. Rāma is already in very sad since Bharata's departure and at the thought of the deserted city of Ayodhya. Sīta finds her lord in pensive mood and asks him to reason. Rama asks her to sit and discuss with him. Then he tells Sīta about the approaching Sraddha ceremony of his father the next that worries him. He is perturbed and unhappy as he is not able to offer oblations to his father with proper rites. Sīta assures him that Bharata will perform the rites in royal style, while Rāma may perform it with fruits and water available in the forest. Rama answers that when his father would see the fruits placed on the sacrificial grass with their own hands, it will remind him of their life in exile. Rama wants to ensure the happiness of his father, but his oblaions would bring tears in Dasaratha's eyes.

The main scene of this Act begins with Rāvana's appearance in the hermitage dressed as an ascetic and takes advantage of the situation. He declares his intention to abduct Sītā after deceiving Rāma, to avenge the murder of Khara. He, thus, pretends to be a guest. He knocks at the entrace to Rama's hermitage. Rama comes out and after saluting the guest, offers him a seat and directs Sītā to bring water to wash the feet of the holy man. At the command of her lord, she brings water to pour it on Rāvana's feet. But the latter is afraid that his disguise may be known at her approach. When Rāvana stops her from doing so, Rāma offers himself to serve the guest. Ravana tells that he is honoured by Rāma's words and asks him to be seated. Then Ravana introduces himself as a Brahman, who belongs to Kasyapa gotra. He declares his mastery over various branches of learning such as Vedas and Vedangas, the Dharma Sastra of Manu, the Yogasastra of Mahasewara, the Neelisastra of Brihaspati, the Tarkasastra of Medhatithi and the scripture on funeral rites written by Prachetas. On hearing this, Rāma evinces special predilection for the rituals of Srāddha and states that he is anxious to know what can satisfy the shades of the ancestors at this ceremony. Ravana replies that anything given with love and faith (sraddha) constitute a Srāddha. Rama enquires about the meritorious offerings Ravana now employs his trick and starts mentioning objects such as Darbha grass, sesam amongst the herbs, Kalāya among the vegetables, the crane among the birds, and among the beasts, the cow or the rhinoceros or, indicating something else in addition also. Rama desires his willingness to know that alternative beast. Ravana tempts him with the golden deer and informs that, it lives in the Himalayas and great seers like Vaikhahasa, Valakhilya and Naimisiya brought it by the power of thought and sacrifice it at the Srāddhas to their ancestors. Rāma atonce asks Sītā to get ready for the Himalayas. Ravana discourages him by telling that it was an impossible feat for human beings and the deer will not be visible to him. Rāma proudly declares that it would not be difficult task for him. At this moment, a flash of lightning is seen and the golden - planked antelope makes it appearance to Ravana. Rama instructs Sītā to send Lakshmana to catch it. Sīta informs that Lakshmana has already been sent to meet Kulapati, the chief of the hermitage returning from a pilgrimage.

After advising Sītā to attend on the ascetic, Rama goes out to catch the deer himself. Rāvana praises Rama's strength, valour and the speed, but is happy that the deer has spurfed beyond the range of his arrows and disappeared in the thickest part of the forest. Sītā feels uneasy in the presence of the guest and tells Rāvanaa that she is going into the hut. As she is about to leave, Ravana assumes his true form, as a demon and says her to stay back. Sita is terrified and exclaims who this could be. Ravana reveals his identity and of his intention to carry her off. Sīta cries out for help and in reply to her prayers for help from Rāma or Lakshmana. Ravana says that there is no point in lamenting and asks her to look upon him as her lord. Sīta says to him "Be thou accursed". This mere words burn Rāvana and he seizes Sīta and carries her off and at the same time, proclaims the challange to Rama. Sīta cries out for her lord. At this precise moment, Jatāyu, the vurture friend of Dasaratha comes to oppose Ravana on the way with his terrible beak. Ravana threatens to cut his wings and bleed him to death and thus, draws his sword.

Act Six:- In the interlude, two old men in the penance grove are seen observing the aerial fight between Rāvana and Jatayu, resulting int he death of the latter. The two hermits then go to report the matter to Rāma.

The venue of the main scene in Ayodhya, where the chamberlain instructs Vijaya, the female door-keeper, to inform Bharata of the arrival of Sumantra from Janasthāna after visitng Rāma. The door-keeper goes away and the chamberlain finds Bharata coming along, clad in a bark robe and with all his locks matted, eagerly awaiting the news from Sumantra. Then appears Bharata and Pratihari. Bharata orders the chamberlain to bring Sumantra at once, and both the servants make their exit. Sumantra enters through the golden gate and again grieving at his old age that has witnessed a string of calamities right from king's death, his son's exile to Sīta's abduction. He greets Bharata who asks him about Rama, Sīta and Lakshmana in exile. Sumantra tries to circumvent and tells that they have left Janasthana and tries to keep back the tragic news from Bharata. He speaks of Rāma's friendship with Sugriva, the monkey king, who was driven out of his kingdom by his elder brother, Vali, and dwelling on the mountain robbed of his wife.

Sugriva expresses his gratefulness to Rama for relieving him of similar trouble. Bharata asks Sumantra the meaning of the similar trouble and the latter refuses to tell the truth and tells that Sugriva meant that both had lost their realms. Eventually Sumantra has to yield when Bharata adjures him by the feet of Dasaratha to speak out the truth. Sumantra breaks the news of Sīta's kidnapping by Ravana. On hearing this Bharata goes into a swoon. After recovering, he sees broken hearted at the sad plight of his elder brother, who was first robbed of his father, then deprived of the kingship, followed by, his banishment to the forest and now finally separated from his wife. Bharta, now, feels that it is because of Kaikeyi that such a calamity has befallen to Rāma. He then goes to Kaikeyi, after sending word to her through the door - keeper that he wants to meet Kaikeyi with Sumantra who has just come back from Rama. Kaikeyi order the door-keeper to usher Bharata in. Bharata and Sumantra enter. Kaikeyi tells that she is being told by Vijaya that Sumantra has come back from Janasthana. Bharata replies that there is a pleasant news for her. Asked whether Kausalya and Sumitra be called to hear it, with extreme bitterness, he taunts her that they are not to hear it.

He abuses Kaikeyi for her cruel and unjust actions and finally breaks the news of Sīta's kidnapping with his harsh words that the house of great warriors had the good fortune of securing Kaikeyi as a daughter -in-law, it has had the further good fortune of having another daughter-in-law being abducted. So far, circumstances demanded sacrifice and silence on the part of Kaikeyi and now the time has come that she should reveal her secret. She asks Bharata whether he knows anything of Dasratha's curse. But the latter was unaware of the curse on his father. Thus, at Kaikeyi's benest Sumantra tells the whole episode how Dasaratha killed by mistake the only son of a blind sage who cursed him that Dasaratha that he too would perish, with grief for his son. Kaikeyi then states that in order for the curse to operate, she had to effect the separation of the son.

Then, Bharata asks why she didnot ask for the exile of her own son. Kaikeyi replies that it is because he was dready separated from his father and was away his uncle's house.

Now Bharata puts another query that why she asked for such a long period of exile. Kaikeyi explains that she meant to say "fourteen days" but there was a slip, and she said "fourteen years". Bharata now puts another question to Sumantra whether the story given out by her is known to the preceptors. Sumantra replies that Vasistha, Vamadeva and other knew the whole incidents and assented to it. At this point, Bharata repents for his past behaviour towards his mother and prays her to forgive him.

Kaikeyi, who had so longer silently suffered, readily forgive him. Now Bharata rises up and proclaims that he would organise his entire army to help Rama against Ravana. Some noise is heard from the inner apartment and Vijaya enters to inform that on hearing the news of Sītā's abduction the senior queen has fainted aways. Kaikeyi at once departs with his son to comfort the noble lady.

Act Seven:- This Act shifts to Janasthana, where a hermit is seen in conversation with Nandilaka, a servent in the hermitage. The former brings the order of the Kulapati to make everything ready to the best of their resources for receiving the victorious Rama, who is returning to the hermitage along with Sītā (whom he has rescued after killing Ravana) and Vibhishana (whom Rama has installed on the throne of Lanka). The latter is surrounded by the chiefs of demons, meonkeys, bears. This worries Nandilaka who states that everything is ready, but as Vibhishana and his followers are demons who eat men as food. He asks what to do for their meal. The hermit assures that the demons fully under the control of noble Vibhishana. There ends the interlude.

The mains scene itself commences with Rama's arrival in the hermitage. He speaks to himself about the fulfillment of his mission by slaying Ravana in the great war and there by regained Sita, the soul of purity, the abode of all virtues. He keeps waiting for Sītā who has gone inside to meet wives of the sages and other old friends. Sītā enters with a female ascetie, the latter tells Sīta to go up to Rama from whom she had long been separated. Then, the couple reminicised their past life in Janasthana, the trees that Sīta planted the herd of deer that startled on seeing Bharata, the great tortoise that witnessed their austerities. However, the memory of the golden deer for the Srāddha ceremony frightens Sītā, who trembles from head to foot with fear. Rāma reassures her and at this point, they hears the blare of conches and the din of kettle - drums. Lakshmana comes to announce the arrival of Bharata with the queen mothers and a huge army. Bharata's joy knows no bound and exclaims that he is happy to see them free from calamities. Rama, Lakshmana and Sīta pay their homage to the queen - mothers and are suitably blessed. He embraces his brothers and salutes Sīta and is blessed by them.

He now requests Rāma to shoulder the burden of the kingdom and then Kaikeyi also tells that she has long been cherished this desire. At this juncture, arrives Shatrughna who salutes the trio and declared the desire of Vasistha and Vamadeva and the citizen of Ayodhya to see Rāma crowned with the consecrated water which they have collected from many a river and stream. To Kaikeyi's bidding, Rama agrees to go in for his coronation and makes his exit. From the off stage, many triumphal proclamation like "victory to our king", "victory of the best of men", "victory to the killer of Ravana" etc are heard. Kaikeyi and Sumitra rejoices at the celebration and refer to the priests, ministers and servants. After the coronation, Rāma enters and looking up at the sky, he asks his father to cast aside his grief and rejoice in the heaven as his wishes were fulfilled and Rāma has sworn to protect his subjects in accordance with the law. Bharata, Shatrughna are all in praise for Rāma and then Lakshmana offers his felicitations. Meanwhile, the chamberlain announces that Vibhishana, Sugriva, Hanuman, Nila, Mainda, Jambavan seek permission to offer their congratulation. To this Rāma says that he has attained victory by their assistance. Then they all congratulate Rāma and finally Kaikeyi desires to see the coronation ceremony again performed in Ayodhya. Rāma says that she would see it soon there. Everyone leaves for Ayodhya that very day by the 'Puspaka' ariel car and thus the drama ends happily with the epilogue that states many our king be united to glory, and rule the earth in the same way as Rāma was united to Sītā and his brothers.

(XII) SVAPNAVASAVADATTA

Synopsis :- In 'Svapnavasavadatta" he has proved himself to be one of the great masters of the erotic sentiment. The story is about the stratagem used by a clever minister called 'Yaugandharayana' to sustain his monarch's kingdom. A marriage with a neighbouring princes 'Padmavati' is essential to gain this objective. But the king Udayana is already married to Vasavadatta to whom he is inordinately devoted. The minister contrives during a temporary absence of the Queen to make out that both he and the Queen are lost in the burning of a village. But in reality he prevails upon her to become a lady - in -waiting to the princess Padmavati to whom Udayana is to be married. Udayana, never fully resigned to the death of Vasavadatta finally agrees to meet Padmavati. In her palace by a chance, Vasavadatta meets Udayana and the king believes that it is her vision that he sees All his old passion sweeps him and he is in the torment of having to honour Padmavati whom he has married, while yet loving Vasavadatta whom he believes dead. This predicament it resolved when Vasavadatta reveals herself not as a vision but a reality and all three- the King, the Queen and the new Consort - reconcile themselves to the new reletionship.

Dramatis Personae (In order of appearance):

Stage-manager

Sūtradhara in Prologue only.

Two guards in the retinue of Princess Padmavati.

Yaugandharāyana: Chief Minister of Udayana, king of the Vatsas.

Vāsavadatta: Princess of Ujjain, daughter of King Pradyota-Mahasena, and the first Queen of Udayana, supposed to have been burnt alive and brought to Magadha in disguise as the Lady of Avanti.

Chamberlain

Maid from Magadha with Princess Padmāvatī.

Padmāvati: Princess of Magadha, sister of King Darsaka. In the last three acts the second queen of Udayana.

Lady hermit.

Student of theology.

Nurse of the princess of Magadha.

Second maid, of the princess of Magadha.

Jester (Vasantaka) of King Udayana.

Udayana: King of the Vatsas.

Padminikā

Madhukarika

Maids in attendance on the princess of Magadha.

Chamberlain of the Vasta king at Kausambi.

Vijayā: Portress at Kausambi palace.

Raibhya: Chamberlain from the Avanti court at Ujjain.

Vasundharā: nurse of Vāsavadattā from Ujjain.

The Plot: Act One: — In prelude, the stage-manager recietes the benedictory stanza that introduces major dramatis personae. Then he is about to begin his speech when some noise is heard from the off stage. The two soldiers of the king of Magadha, escorting Padmavati who is on her way to the penance grove, are asking the public to make way. The stage manager exits and the main scene begins with the arrival of Yaugandharayana and Vasavadatta, the former disguised as a mendicant and the latter's as his sister called 'Avantika'. Yaugandharayana is surprised that even in this holy hermitage, the people are pushed away. Vasavadatta is humiliated as being told that she too can be ordered to make way. She tells Yaugandharayana that the fatigue of the journey do not cause her as much pain as his insult. Yaugandharayana consoles her by saying that the wheel of fortune turns with time and she will have her good days once her husband is victorious again. The chamberlain, however, orders one of the guards Sambhashaka, not to drive the people away. Yaugandharayana approaches this noble man and asks why people are being turned away. He comes to know that Padmavati, the princess of Magadha, is to visit the hermitage to see the queen - mother who has made a hermitage her home and thus, Padmavati, the sister of king Darsaka is to stay there for a night. Yaugandharayana says to himself that is the princess about whom the astrologers and others had predicted that she will marry Udayana, a prophecy on which Yaugandharayana has based all his plans. And on hearing that she is princess, Vasavadatta develops a sisterly affection for her. Padmavati enters with her retinue and a maid. The Queen-mother, now a hermit, welcomes the princess who salutes her. She asks Padmavati's maid whether any king has applied for the princess hand. The maid replies that Pradyoda has sent an envoy for the hand of the princess for his son. Through her chamberlain, Padmavati proclaims her desire.

The proposal of Udayana fðr her hand gladdens Vasavadatta at the prospect of Padmavati becoming her sister - in - law. Now Padmavati announces her alligness to help others, taking advantage of which Yaugandharayana, who presents himself as a suppliant (arthi) and expresses his wish to place his sister (Vasavadatta) under her custody till the former's husband returns. But the chamberlain objects to this unreasonable request. But Padmavati tells that she has already proclaimed that she shall grant any request and therefore it would be now improper to refuse him. The chamberlain, the maid and the queen-mother all praise Padmavati's feelings. Yaugandharayana hands over Vasavadatta to Padmavati and later says to himself that everything is happening according to his plan and that his task is almost half-finished and he would be successful in his venture, according to the prophecy of the astrologers. A brahmacharin, who is a student of theology comes along towards the hermitage at this point, but is taken back on seeing ladies there. But chamberlain assures him that a hermitage is common to one and all and offers the student some water which he gratefully accepts. From the student, all there learn of the fire accident at Lavanaka in which both minister Yaugandharayana and the queen Vasavadatta have perished and of the immense grief of the king Udayana after his return from hunting, and of the ministers preventing him from ending his life in the fire and he is now being taken away forcibly by the ministers from Lavanaka as his life was in danger owing to his sufferings and lamentations, and neglects of the body. This draws the sympathy of everyone in the hermitage towards Udayana. But Vasavadatta becomes sad on hearing that the king is very much distressed and unhappy. Now Padmavati's maid wonders whether Udayana will marry again and Padmavati begins to cherish the desire to become his wife. The brahmacharin takes his leave and goes away. To fulfil his errand Yaugandharayana also takes his leave from the princess. The chamberlain then tells Padmavati that it is time to return.

Princess takes leave of the queen mother, who suitably blesses her. Now Vasavadatta also salutes the lady-hermit, who tells her that she would soon meet her husband. The chamberlain and Padmavati then setout for their halting place.

Act Two:- The interlude of this act shows a maid in search of Padmavati and she ascertain from Kunjarika, also a maid that the princess is enjoying the game of ball with her maids and Vasavadatta. The latter is well established in the new house hold. The maid watches the princess at the game near the jasmine bower. The main scene commences with Padmavati playing with a ball, and followed by her retinue and Vasavadatta. The princess exhausted, Vasavadatta picks up the ball and refers to her red hands as being due to raga (red colour or love). Vasavadatta keeps gazing at her beautiful face and later by various questions, tries to read Padmavati's mind and learns from the maid that Padmavati does not desire any alliance with Mahasena's son, but the princess is enamoured of king Udayana's virtues, his understanding and tender hearted nature. The maid asks what Padmavati would do if Udayana happends to be ugly looking. But at this point, Vasavadatta unwittingly refers to the handsome features of Udayana, but gets over her indiscretion by promptly explaining her knowledge as due to the impression of the residents of Ujjain. Now a nurse enters to inform that Padmavati has been betrothed to Udayana who has come to the palace hale and healthy. Vasavadatta who hears the news of the king having accepted Padmavati as his wife, words of resentment and misery escape from her in an unguarded moment, but, she controls herself immediately, since she willingly chose her position to help her husband regain his kingdom. She feels grateful, when she learns from the nurse that Udayana, still remembers Vasavadatta, needed much persuation before he finally agrees to marry Padmavati.

Act Three:- The interlude to this Act shows Vasavadatta's retirement and loneliness, in the midst of nuptial gaiety. To ease her grieved heart, she sits on a stone bench under the Priyangu creeper, at the pleasure-garden of Padmavati and immersed in thought. She is pained that her husband has become another woman's and mutters that blessed is Padmavati that the queen had sent for her as the **Kautukamangalavidhi**, the ceremony of tying the nupitial thread was to be celebrated that very auspicious day. This shocks Padmavati, but she bravely bears the suffering by says to herself that "The more they hasten, the more is her heart covered as it were with darkness". They all go into the palace.

The female bird Chakravaka, separated form her mate, does not live. But how wretched she is to be alive in the hope of being reunited to his lord one day. At this jucture a maid comes with a basket of flowers and leaves, looking for her. She tells that the queen has requested her to weave the auspicious wedding gardland of Padmavati. Padmavati is going to be her co-wife and what else can a helpless woman like her do, save to blame gods who have become unkind to her. The maid urges her to make the garland quickly, as the bridegroom is already having his bath in the mosaic room. Vasavadatta asks the maid whether she has seen the bridegroom. The maid relates her impressions of the Udayana that he is cupid incarnate without his bow and arrows. Then Vasavadatta sorrowfully begins her work. She asks the maid about a leaf and learning that it is Avidhavākarana (widowhood - preventer), decides to use them profusely. Again she comes across another leaf called Supatnīmardana (rival - exterminator), Vasavadatta excludes this leaf and tells the maid that it was unnecessary, since Padmavati's co-wife is no more. Another maid comes to ask to hasten the wreathing, as the bridegroom is being conducted to the ladies' court by married women. Vasavadatta handsover the finished garland and the maids go away with it. Broken hearted Vasavadatta gets no relief in the garden, she retires to get some sleep in a lonely place.

Act Four:- The interlude to this act inform us through the soliloque of Vasantaka, the jester-friend of Udayana of the successful termination of the marriage ceremony of Udayana and Padmavati and presently he is leading a joyous life at the Magadha palace, after his master having been submerged in a whirlpool of misforture in the past. The jester feels sad that no celestial nymphs to entertain him and his stomach trouble due to excessive eating and consequent sleeplessness. A maid comes to know whether the royal bridgegroom has finished his bath, as flowers and ointment were to be brought for him after his bath. He replies that His Majesty has bathed and she may bring anything except food-stuffs, as his bowels were playing him false. Then he goes to join His Majesty. The main scene begins with Padmāvati entrance to the Pramoda-garden with Vāsavadatta and a maid to see whether the Sephālika clusters have blossomed. They find the plants and creepers in full boom. While Padmavati and Vasavadatt sit on a stone bench, the maid gathers some of the sephalika flowers and takes them to Padmavati who admires their brilliant colour, but asks her not to pick up any more flowers, so that when Udayana comes there, he may see them and be pleased. Now they engage in some pleasant conversations and soon their topic shifts to Udayana and on questioning, Padmavati tells Vasavadatta that she was much devoted to Udayana and when he is not by her side, she feels ever so lonely. In the course of conversation, Padmavati expresses her doubt whether Vasavadatta had to much regard for her Lord, and Vasavadatta immediately replies that she loved Udayana even more.

Padmavati wonders how Avantika (Vasavadatta is disguise) know it. Vasavadatta tactfully refers to her elopement for the sake of Udayana, who had forsaken her own people. The maid requests Padmavati that she should approach her husband to teach her how to play on the lute. Padmavati replies sadly that she had made this request, and the king heaved a deep sigh and turned his face away. She further adds that out of courtesy for her, the king restrained his tears, and thus, her inference from this peculiar behaviour was that his memory of Vasavadatta was still fresh, to which Vasavadatta feels gratified.

The king and the jester arrives at the pleasure-garden, the former recalls his past relations with Vasavadatta. In order to divert his melancholy, the jester refers to Padmavati and to the flock of cranes flying in the sky. The king appreciates the sight, and Padmavati, her retinue and Vasavadatta also watches the cranes. Vasavadatta elects to enter a bower to avoid the sight of strangers. While the ladies retires under that bower, the jester approaches the stone-bench occupied by Padmavati and infers from the plucking and gathering of flowers that Padmavati must have left a shortwhile ago. They decide to take rest on the stone-bench, but due to excessive heat, they propose to enter the bower. At this precise moment, the maid shakes the creeper which lets loose a swarm of bees, that prevents their entry. So they retrace their steps and sit outside that very bower. Unaware of the presence of these ladies, in the course of conversation, Vasavadatta asks which one of his two queens Udayana loved more. The king tries to avoid this meaningless query, but the jester forces him to reply, stating that the king should not be worried, as of the queens, one was dead, and other was away. Seated inside the bower, this conversation is overheard by both Padmavati and Vasavadatta. The king is forced to admit that he is having a very high esteem for Padmavati on account of her beauty, sweetness of temper, but Vasavadatta holds the key of his heart. On hearing this, Vāsavadatta feels amply rewarded for all her suffering. The maid remarks that the king has shown his lack of courtesy. Padmavati reports that her husband is sympathetic and kind as he still remembers the merit of Vasavadatta. Meanwhile Udayana asks Vasantaka to give out his impressions of the two queens. The latter cleverly remarks that his opinion is worthless and he holds both the queens in very high esteem. When the king pesters him, he still keeps praising both, indicating his slight preference for Padmāvati who used to serve him with delicious dishes. The king mistakingly utters that he shall tell queen Vasavadatta all this, but realizing that she is no more, the king cannot control his emotions and he sheds tears. The jester- friend immediately leaves to bring water for washing the face of his master. Vasavadatta and the maids make their exit, unseen by the king whose face is hidden in a veil of tears. At the suggestion of the maid, Padmavati goes to meet the king, but on the way meets Vidusaka. On asking he tells her that the pollers of Kāsa flowers had fallen into his master's eyes and hence they were streaming with tears. Padmavati takes the water from his lord's chivalrous servant. The king feels embarrassed when Padmavati arrives there and enquires him about his condition. The king at once consults aside with Vasantaka who whispers the same into his tears and thus king in order not to pain his new queen, hides the truth. He asks Padmavati to be seated, and gives out the same reason for his tears. To save the king from further embarrassment, proclaims that the king should retire as it is the time to meet his brother-in-law Darsaka, who is giving a reception that afternoon to all his friends in Udayana's honour. At the benest of his frined Vasantaka, he agrees and rises up.

Act Five:- In the interlude, we find two maids of the Magadha palace called Padminika and Madhukarika in conversation. In the course of their conversation it is learnt that Padmavati is suffering from headache. Thus, Padminika asks Madhukarika to report the matter to Avantika and tell her to go to the Samudragriha (The Ocean Pavilion, where Padmavati's bed has been spread) and attend the princess and relieve her pain by telling her some amusing stories. Padminika herself goes out to call Vasantaka and asks him to inform Udayana about her ill health. She meets Vasantaka and tells him to convey the news to the king, and then goes to get some medicine for Padmavati. Vasantaka also departs to meet his master.

The main scene opens with broken hearted Udayana, constantly doting on Vasavadatta and lamenting her apparent loss. The jester comes and tells him about the severe headche of Padmavati and Udayana at once starts the Samudragriha to comfort her. In the way, the jester mistakes a garland for a cobra. They go to the room and find the bed vacant. Vasantaka remarks that the queen must have come there and gone away. The king after seeing the bed in perfect condition becomes sure that Padmavati had not occupied the bed.

The king agrees to the jester's suggestion that they should await her arrival on the same bed and thus reposes there for sometime listening to the stories of his jester friend. But its beginning reminds the king of the Ujjain city and Vasavadatta, the daughter of Avanti's king. When Vasantaka starts narrating another story, Udayana fulls asleep and his friend leaves him to bring some blanket, as it was very cold at that hour. At this precise moment Vasavadatta makes her entrance and in the dim light, seeing somebody on the bed mistakes the person to be Padmavati and sits on the bed and embraces its occupant. The king, however, cries out in his sleep and calls Vasavadatta by her name. Vasavadatta at once rises from the bed and finds that it is her noble lord and not Padmavati. Realizes that if she is caught, an efforts of Yaugandharayana would go fruitless. The king again speaks in sleep and she regains her confidence that he is only dreaming her presence. She stays there for sometimes and unknowingly gives response to his calls. In his sleep, the king asks her few questions and she replies to him. Not to upset Yaugandharayana's plan, Vasavadatta decides to go away now and eventually tries to replace the arm of Udayana that is hanging down from the bed. She does so and goes away to avoid the possibility of being recognized. The touch of her hand slightly revives him and he gets up to hold on to her while she flees the room hastily. Udayana rushes after her and knocks his head against the door. In the meantime arrives Vasantaka, to whom Udayana narrates his experience of the dream in which he felt that the lady of Avanti is still alive. But Vasantaka dismisses it all as being a mere dream, since he mentioned the bathing pools of Ujjaini and that set him thinking about Vasavadatta. But the king begins to feel that his minister Rumanvan and others have deceived him. The king tells him meticulously to convince that Vasavadatta is alive. He shows his arm which was clasped by her in sleep and points to the the hair of his body that stands on end still by her touch. Vasantaka asks him to go back to the ladies court. Now the chamberlain brings the news of the battle to criush Aruni that shakes the king from his stupor.

Act Six:- The action of this act takes place after the termination of the war with Aruni and the restoration of the Vatsa kingdom. In the interlude, we find that in Vatsaraja's Suyamuna palace in Kausambi, comes Badarayana, Mahasena's chamberlain alongwith Vasundhara, Vasavadatta's nurse with a message for Udayana from Mahasena and queen Angaravati. The chamberlain calles Vijaya, the female door-keeper of Udayana to carry the message that congratulate Udayana on his recent victory, Vijaya replies that this would not be the proper time, as Udayana is again in sorrow, being reminded of Vasavadatta by the recovery of his famous lute, Ghosavati by someone in the Suyamuna palace from a thicket of reeds on the Narmada bank. The king falls in a swoon after seeing it and has just regained his consciousness. The chamberlain convinces the door-keeper that their mission too has something to do with it. Vijaya thus agrees to inform the king about their arrival and then, declares that His Majesty is coming down from the Suyamuna palace.

The main scene itself focuses on the king who is holding the lute in hand and mourning Vasavadatta's loss. He relates the sweet memories of the past to his jester friend and tells that his grief has been reawakened by this lute. He instructs Vasantaka to take it to some skilful artisan and have it restrung and bring back the same to him at his earliest. Vasantaka goes out with the lute. The messengers from Ujjayni are announced by the door-keeper and the king calls Padmāvatī. The couple is now anxiously awaits their arrival to infact know what message from the mighty Mahāsena could be and feels ashmed as he fled with his daughter, without telling him and then allowed her to perish by fire. Udayana honours the envoys from his father-in-law and the messenger offers him the felicitations of Mahasena on his great victory. Udayana inquires of Vasundhara about Angaravati. The nurse replies that the queen is well and has inquired if all was well there, which again grieves Udayana very much, reminding him painfully of Mahasena's daughter, his pupil and the beloved queen. The nurse then reads the message from Angaravati that in breif states that when Udayana had eloped with Vasavadatta, without waiting for the traditional nupital celebration. Then, the royal couple had the portraits of Udayana and their daughter done and used it in celebrating their marriage ceremony.

The queen has requested him to forget his grief by looking at Vasavadatta's picture on seeing which Padmavati recognises her friend Avantika as Vasavadatta. At this juncture, the portress arrives to announce that the ascetic from Ujjayini has arrived there to reclaim his sister. The king asks Avantika to be brought at once. Padmavati goes and brings her. Yaugandharayana is also brought in, by Vijaya, who pronounces victory to the king. The voice of Yaugandharayana, in guise of Brahman, appears to the king as familiar. but not exactly identifiable. He asks Yaugandharayana whether he has come for his deposit, and receives a reply in the affirmative. When Padmavati returns back with Avantika, the king ask her to give back Avantika to the Brahman in the presence of Badarayana, and Vasundhara as witnesses. Padmavati hands over Avantika to Yaugandharayana and meanwhile, the nurse of Vasavadatta recognises her and king orders that Mahasena's daughter be taken into the ladies court. Yaugandharayana objects to his unkingly act and asks him not to take her by force, being a noble scion of the Bharata race. The king orders that her veil be removed and subsequently Vasavadatta removes it and then the whole plot is gradually unfolded by the minister who begs pardon of his kings for his acts of omission and commission. Padmavati falls at the feet of Vasavadatta and tells that she has unconsciously been guilty of gross impropriety pays her homage. Yaugandharayana explains his main object in the whole design was to save the realm and adds that even Rumanvat and all knew of the plan.

Now the king decides to go with Padmavati to convey Mahasena and queen Angaravati that Vasavadatta is safe and the drama ends with happy note.

(XIII) URUBHANGA

Synopsis: Based on the Mahabharata, this tragic play in One Act depicts the duel between Duryodhana and Bhima. There is the elevation of Duryodhana character who has been made to behave better by Bhasa than as shown in the original epic. Bhima defies the rule of battle and to fulfil his own, smashes Duryodhana's thighs in the godā-yuddha (fight with maces) and hence the title is most appropriate.

Dramatis Personae (In order of appearance):

Stage-manager in the Prologue.

Assistant of the Manager

Therc Soldicrs of Duryodhana's army, who describe the battlefield and then the duel with maces.

Baladeva or Balarāma: the wielder of the Plough (Halāyudha), elder brother of Kṛṣṇa.

Duryodhana: eldest of the hundred sons of the blind king Dhṛtarāshṭra, leader of the Kurus.

Dhṛtarāshṭra: the old blind king.

Gāndharī: his wife, who wore a bandage on her eyes.

Mālavī: one of Duryodhana's Queens.

Pauravī: another of Duryodhana's Queens.

Durjaya: Duryodhana's young son.

Aśvatthāmā: son of the old preceptor Droṇa.

The Plot: At the close of Mahabharata war, the fight betwcen Bhimā and Duryodhana begins. The prelude features three warriors who witness their gadā-yuddha (mace-fight) and give a graphic description of the battle field on the eighteen day of the great Mahabharata war. The whole battle field is full of corpses of kings, soldiers, horses and elephants slain in battle and of jackals and vultures assembled to eat the flesh of dead bodies.

From the off-stage, some noise is heard and later on it is found that a terrible mace-fight is going on between the two giants in the presence of

Vyāsa, Vidura, Balarāma and Kṛśna. The fighters are equally matched. Though Duryodhana has greater skill in the club-fighting but Bhīma has an edge over him, with his susperior strength, as opined by the second warrior. At the fight progresses suddenly Bhīma gets a blow on his head and falls down. The anxiety of the Pāṇḍava supporters grow, while Balarāma becomes glad at the victory, of his disciple.

Duryodhana makes mockery of Bhīma by telling him not to be afraid, as he is not going to kill him, though his life was at Duryodhana's hand. Kṛśṇa now makes a secret sign to Bhīma by striking on his own thighs and gazes at the sky indicating that the thighs are the weak spots of Duryodhana. This infuses a new spirit in Bhīma. With a loud thundering noise, he rises up to confront Duryodhana. Both exchange dreadful blows and after fighting for sometime, Bhīma hurls his mace with both hands on the thighs of Duryodhana, as directed by Kṛśṇa and thus, disobeys the standing norms of mace-fight.

Duryodhana's thighs are broken and bleeds profusely. He falls to the ground. Vyāsa set out to fly to the heavens, after this unfair mace-fight. Balarāma gets infuriated for this unfair means. On Vyasa's instruction, Bhīma is led elsewhere by the Pāṇḍavas helped by Kṛśṇa.

In Act proper Duryodhana is first shows with Balarāma, who indignantly out bursts at Bhīma's foul play and affirms that Duryodhana had been cheated and he is going to kill Bhima. This provides greatest consolation to the fallen Duryodhan. Balarāma asks Duryodhana to hold on a little longer. With great effort, Duryodhana crawls in and tries to pacify Balarāma but the latter becomes more enraged and talks of killing all the Pāṇḍavas. He realizes that it was not Bhima, but the great Lord Kṛṣṇa who has deceived him and says that it was no use fighting in this circumstances. Now there is touching scene of Duryodhana's meeting with his parents, wives and son.

Enters Dhrtarāṣṭra, Gāṇdhārī, the queens of Duryodhana, called Malavi and Pauravi and his son Durjaya. They all bewailing his sad lot and searching for him on the battle field. The queens are crying on aloud, walking on foot and bare-headed, without their usual veils with hair in disarray. All this pierce Duryodhana poignantly than his physical injuries.

To fulfil this father's desire to salute him Duryodhana tries to get up to fall at the feet of his father but falls down again. He utters "..When Bhima hurled his mace at me, he didnot rob me of my thighs alone, he robbed me also of the power to go and prostrate at my father's feet."

His son comes to him in his childish way to sit on his lap but the father prevents him from doing so. His inability to offer his lap as a resting place for his beloved son is the unkindest cut all to Duryodhana. He breaks down in grief.

Gandhari too comes to the spot and softly weeps. He seeks to comfort his parents. He requests Dhṛtarāṣṭra to console his mother by telling her that her son died in the war without showing his back. He is dying in the same dignity in which he was born.

He expresses his love for his mother by his desire to be her son in all his future lives, if he has earned any merit. He consoles the warrior queens by stating that their husband is meeting with the hero's death having performed in all earnest all his kingly duties. They should not weep, but only think of his glory with pride.

In his parting advice to his son, he preaches reconciliation and his enmity with the Pāṇḍavas gives place to a sort of repentance and purification of the soul. He asks him to honour Draupadi and Kunti like his own mother and to join with the Pandavas in giving him the last oblation. At this moment, arrives Aśvatthāman who makes a big sound with his bow. He is infuriated at the news of the condition of Duryodhana. Duryodhana, however, replies that his condition is due to his discontent. But Aśvatthāman is firm in his decision to kill all the Pāṇḍavas and Kṛṣṇā.

Duryodhana tries to dissuade him by stating that after the lose of his brothers, Karṇa and others, it is of no use to revive enmity. Unconvinced Aśvatthaman tells him that it appears as if his dignity has been killed along with his thighs. But Duryodhana replies that dignity in the life of the king and it was for dignity alone that he fought. He further says that the sins committed by the Pāṇḍavas are nothing as compared to his ill treatment towards Paṇḍāvas such as the dragging of Draupadi, the slaying of Abhimanyu or the making of the Pandavas wonder in the forest.

Despite Duryodhana's every councels to peace, Aśvatthāmā swears vengeance, with Balarāma as a witness, to fight with the Pāṇḍavas and crown Durjaya as the emperor. At this, Duryodhana feels satisfied.

Visions of his revered ancestors, his brothers, Abhimanyu and Apsarās etc float before Duryodhana and he passes away. They cover the corpse with a cloth. Grief stricken Dhṛtarastṛa decides to go to the forests for penance. Will upraised weapon, Aśvatthāman departs to kill the Pāṇḍavas in their sleep.

Drona ends with the general praise by all for the protection of the earth by "Our King" after destroying his enemies.

(XIV) YAJṆAPHALA

Synopsis: This Seven Acts drama is based on the Balakanda of the Ramayana and is similar to Abhisheka and Pratima of Bhasa. The play deals with the early life of Rāma up to his marriage with Sītā. It glorifies vedic sacrifices and penances. Four sons are born to Dasaratha owing to his Yajṇa. Viswamitra becomes a Brahmarishi owing to his Yajṇa in the form of peace of all living beings in the hermitage consequent on. Rāma's killing Subāhu and Marīca's flight in fright and finally Rāma marries Sīta owing to Janaka's Yajṇa.

Hence the title "Yajṇaphala" is most appropriate.

Dramatis Personae (In order of appearance):

Vidūsaka

Dasaratha

Sumantra

Kausalya

Kaikeyi

Sumitra

A Spy

Ravana

Viswamitra

Vasistha

Rama

Laksmana

Bharata

Satrughana

Manthara

Sita

Janaka

Parasurama

(Dasaratha's retinue, spy, servents, Palace bards, an aged cowherd woman, Warriors deputed by Janaka Sita's maids, Satananda and other distinguished guest at the court of Janaka).

The Plot: Act One:- The First Act shows that a festival is in progress to celebrate the birthday of the four sons of Dasaratha. At first Vīdūṣaka supplies some humour, after which enters Dasaratha who has obtained sons owing to a Yajṇa. Sumantra distributes lavish gifts among the subjects on his happy occasion. An order is passed to release all prisoners from the jails. But, Dasaratha finds no one in bonds, except himself in bonds of love towards his sons. He is seen worried over the education of his princes, despite his victories, performances of Yajṇa's and protection of the subjects and the Brāhmanas. He also feels uneasy about his promise to Kaikeyi, at the time of her marriage, to make her son king. Dasaratha holds conference with Sumantra. At this point, messages come from the three queens desirous of meeting the king at once. The king replies that he would accord the same treatment to all and receive them all simultaneously. As evening approaches, the king rises to retire.

Act Two:- At the command of Dasaratha, Grīṣmodyāna (The palace garden) has been cleared of all persons by the chamberlain. The maids, coming to gather flowers are kept out as the conference is to take place. Dasaratha enters with his retinue, who wants to make Rama crown Prince, but is perplessed owing to his promise to Kaikeyī. He desires that Sumantra should convince the queens, servants and subjects and especially Bharata.

At the sight of the queens, Sumantra departs. After long deliberations regarding inheritance - according to seniority of age or greatness of merit and King's wise decision for the equal division of the kingdom etc. Eventually the queens give their consent to install Rāma as crown Prince. But when Kaikeyi is reminded of the promise to make her son king, she states that Rāma alone deserve to be crowned because of his extra ordinary virtues and ability to rule the kingdom. When the queen goes away, the king calls Sumantra and inform him of the ultimate decision. Sumantra tells Dasaratha of Vasiṣṭha's message to arrange for the education of Rāma. Vidusaka supplies some more humour. A spy breaks the news of Rāvana's arrival at Ayodhya in disguise. Dasaratha leaves the place thinking about how to prevent Rāvana.

Act Three:- From the interlude it is learnt that Kubera, under orders from Indra, sends two Gandharvas to protect Rāma. Enters Rāvana invisible by his magic power and has come to do some mischief to Rama about whose prowess he has heard. He finds Viswamitra entering who is in search for a student Athibala and finds that Rama would make an even better pupil to teach the famous Jhrumbhakastra. His intention is to take Rāma for the protection of his sacrifice and is also invisible. Each thinks that he is invisible to the other. Arrives Vasiṣṭha along with the four princess. Being holiday, Vasiṣṭha goes away and the princess discharges their arrows to test their knowledge of archery. Rāvana and Vīśvāmitra watch the skills of Bharata, Lakṣmaṇa and Satrughana. When Rāma fixes his bow at a target, both of them catches Rāma's arrows. He is being obstructed twice that forces him to declare that he would use Agneya Astra. Rāvana get terrified at its vrey mention and leaves at once. Rāma is pursued by his brothers not to use it as their palace maids were in the vicinity. Comes Manthara and other maids to collect flowers and seeing arrow-marks on trees and the marks of the chariot of Rāvana, they run away in fright, but are reassured by the Princes. The latter are informed of the arrival of Rāvana and Viswamitra by Vasiṣṭha who advises them to pay homage to Vīśvāmitra when they see him the next day. They are also told that Visvamitra will request Dasaratha to send Rāma with him to thwart the demons. When they all leave, Sumantra enters and advises the palace servants to be on the guard as Rāvana has made for Ayodhyā in disguise.

Act Four:- This act shows four palace bards engaged in a scuffle about their skill as musician and also hold some humorous discussion about Viśvāmitra, his qualities as Kshatriya and as a Brahmana. Now arrives Viśvamitra in the palace. Daśaratha, Sumantra and all others pays respects to Vīśvāmitra. The latter enquires about the learning, skill and accomplishments of the princes. He tests their knowledge and is impressed with Rāma's modest and intelligent answers. But, Viśvamitra feels that the princes do not know the Jṛmbhakāstra and the Brahmāstra and thus, need a deeper practical training in archery. With a view to Rāma and to protect his sacrifice from the demons, Viśvamitra asks that Rāma be sent with him. Daśaratha agrees, on Vasiṣṭha's supporting the request to send Rāma and Laksmana with Viśvāmitra.

Act Five :- The interlude to this act shows a discussion among Viśvamitra's disciples as to why his sacrifices were obstructed. We are learnt that Visvamitra being a non-Brahman a promoted as a Brahmana has resulted in strong resenment among Brahmana. The latter have provoked the demons, headed by Rāvana to obstruct his sacrifices. Visvamitra had guessed this and brought Rama along to fight the demons, after instructing them in those rare astrtas. Finally when Rāma is taught, he sets out to defeat the demons, Maricha, Subahu and others. Besides, the successful termination of Vīśvāmitra's sacrifice is also known through the interlude and how the people move about freely in the hermitage. Now arrives Viśvamitra along with Rāma and Lakṣmaṇa.

Rāma gives credit to Vīśvāmitra for his own feat, while Viśvāmitra praises his valour and courage. He also hints about the approaching battle with Ravana to protect Dharma. They discuss the natural beauty of the hermitage and at the same time, condemns urban life. In order to acquaint them with pastoral life, Viśvamitra takes them out for a stroll. Rāma talks to an aged cowherd woman, whose simplicity impresses the young princes. Then, Viśvamitra wishes to take them to Mithila to attend Janaka's sacrifice and promises some extraordinary benefit as fruit of sacrifice, meaning Rāma's marriage with Sīta.

Act Six :- The warriors deputed by Janaka to serve Viśvamitra, tells us through the interlude that at first sight. Rāma has fallen love with Sītā. Rāma enters meditating over Sītā, but in vain, he tries to cast away thoughts of love. Sītā arrives with her maids. Rāma overhears their conversation and learns that Sītā is deeply in love with some one and from her maid, he comes to know that he was the object of Sītā's love. But Janaka's vow to give Sīta in marriage to the person who bends Siva's bow. But Sītā fears that Rāma's delicate body would be incapable of performing the feat. Rāma appears before her to console her and reassures the maidens that he would surely bend the bow. Suddenly Janaka arrives there and Rāma runs away. Sītā pays her respect to Janaka and the latter informs Sītā about her approaching marriage believing Viśvamitra's word that Rāma will bend it and he fixes up a day for that and then departs.

Act Seven :- This act shows that at the court of Janaka, the marriages of Rāma and Sita and Janaka's nieces to the other princes in the presence of distinguished assembly comprising of Daśaratha, Vīśvamitra, Vasiṣṭha, Satananda etc. When Janaka asks for the sanction of the assembly to which all readily gives their consent. At this juncture, enters Paraśurāma after hearing the thundering noise of bow breaking and expresses his anger over it, but Janaka, Vasiṣṭha, Viśvamitra and others pacify him. But when he sees the divinity (Maha Vīṣṇu) in Rāma, he gives him his bow and also gives the fruits of his penance to those assembled there and to earn immortal bliss, goes away to the forest.

3

Bhasa Mahotsavam

To commemorate the 75th anniversary of the discovery of the Bhasa's plays, National Academy of Letters (Sahitya Akadami) organised in collaboration with Sopanam Institute, Trivandrum, a six day festival on Bhasa, one of the ancient masters of Sanskrit drama. The festival was inauguarated at Trivandrum on 14th April 1987 by Sri P. Ramachandran, the then Governor of Kerala. A Seminar was organised on the occasion and the inaugural session was presided over by Dr. Birendra Kumar Bhattacharya (the then Vice-President of Sahitya Akademi) and addressed by Dr. P.S. Habeeb Muhammad, Vice-Chancellor, Kerala University make a new peryrphi.

The First Session on 15 April 1987 was presided over by Prof. Vidya Niwas Misra and a paper on '*Bhasa's Text, Stage Directions and Performance*' was presented by Dr. Farley Richmond.

The Second Session on 16th April 1987 was presided over by Dr. K.Krishnamoorthy and Dr. K.D. Tripathi presented his paper on '*Bhasa and Bharata*'.

The Third Session on 17th April 1987 was presided by Dr. K.K. Kunjunni Raja and Sri D. Appukuttan Nair presented a paper on '*Bhasa and Kutiyattam*'.

At the Fourth Session on 18th April 1987, Dr. P.K. Narayana Pillai presided over and Dr. S.S. Janaki presented her paper on *Bhasa and Later Sanskrit Playwright*.

In the Concluding Session, on 20th April 1987, Dr. K. Sivaram Karanth presided over while Prof. Nemi Chandra Jain presented the paper on '*Contemporary Production of Bhasa's Plays*

Each session was marked by scholarly discussions, and the presentation of Bhasa's plays in different styles in each evening.

Bhasa plays in performance:- Nemi Chandra Jain in his article entitled 'Contemporary productions of Bhasa plays wrote: It is no exaggeration to say that Bhasa in his various plays has something or the other to offer to every theatre practitioner and enthusiast - playwright, director, actor, and the spectator. His plays have a great diversity and flexibility of structure, with inventive devices to advance or intensify the dramatic action. His treatment of many episodes and situations has that directness and the individual touch of the singer - narrator, and it would seem that the story - telling or ballad-singing tradition was very live and powerful in his time. Here are some very important features for the modern playwright to draw upon.

Bhasa plays are the most outstanding examples of what K.N. Panikkar calls the 'minimal script', which offers fantastic unfettered opportunities for the creative imagination of the director, as he and many others have more than demonstrated in their work. To the actor, the Bhasa plays present not only a great challange, but also the limitless possiblities for the creative exploration of his own talent and potential. This has become evident again and again in many modern productions, but more than that in the work of the great Chakyar masters, some of whom are regaling us with their creations of great beauty and insight on a number of occasaions.

Eminent theatre personality B.V. Karanth once said that he like Bhasa's plays very much.

In Bhasa's plays, particularly 'Svapnavasavadatta' he found the nearest approach to the ideal play with appropriate character delineation and economy of speech.

It will be appropriate to mention the finding of Dr. G.K. Bhat regarding Bhāsa's talents as a director of plays and bases his conclusions on his refreshingly original interpretation of the punning epithets employed by Bāna in his verse, describing Bhāsa's plays and equating them with temples.

According to Dr. Bhat, Bhasa was personally concerned with the staging of his plays 'either as director, who trained the actors for various roles or as an actor himself, who performed several roles in his own plays'. This is Dr. Bhat's novel interpretation of the expression *bahubhumika* in the verse.

This eminent playwright of the pre - Christian period wrote plays that present a diversity of forms and techniques as well as plots, characters and sentiment. This is the reason why Bhasa plays have captured the imagination of many contemporary directors who have discovered in them unlimited possibilities for innovative theatrical treatment in varying styles and idioms.

4

Kutiyattam and Bhasa Plays

One of the oldest traditional dance dramas of Kerala, Kudiyattam is a slow, stylised art-form which emerged from the precincts of temples. The word derives from the root 'Kudi' meaning group and 'attam' meaning dance. The object of this form as always is to generate Rasa. Traditionally, the staging of this form of theatre is confined to a few specific families. Even today the actors hail only from the 'Chakyar family' and the actresses from the 'Nangiars'. Also, the female vocalist is always chosen from the Nangiar family. The male members of the Nangiar family called 'Nambiars' are the percussionists. These families were in earlier times patronised by the king and acting was not just a hobby but a profession for them. As a result, the quality of their art is exceptional.

A ritual performance takes place in the temple complex. A special auditorium called "Kuttambalam" is provided for this purpose. The structure is made of wood and stone. Special care is taken for acoustics and an oil lamp is required to serve the lighting purposes. The oil lamp (Nila Vilaku) has three wicks symbolising The Holy Trinity of Brahma, Vishnu and Siva.

The shastras for a Kudiyattam performance are from the 'Attaprakarana' for abhinanaya and 'Krama Deepika' for costumer and production of the plays.

Kūṭṭanpalams of Kerala

Kūttanpalams are theatres in Kerala temples for the performance of Kūttu, and no other art form. They are usually located in front of the Deity outside the inner circumambulatory building called Cuttanpalam and on the right hand side. The performances staged here are usually Prabandha Kūttu, Naṅṅyār Kūttu and Kūtiyāttom all of which come within the broad category of Kūttu, This does not mean that the different types of Kūttu could not be performed outside the Kūttanpalam. In fact, in many of the temples with a great heritage of Kūttu, the performances are held in the Valianpalam (the entrance hall in front of the Deity) or in the Agrasāla (the dining hall). Outdoor performances such as Parakkum Kūttu used to be held in the open space called Kūttu Paranpu (This type of performance has ceased to exist).

A Kudiyattam play begins with the 'Poorvaranga'. where the artists introduce their characters. This is followed by the 'Nirvahana' which is a brief history of main characters. Then the actual play begins.

The slokas are recited in Sanskrit and the actors narrate them with the help of facial expressions, eye movements and hand gestures. The stress is on Satvika Abhinanaya (spiritual expression).

Sutradhara acts as a compere and besides the main characters, there is a 'Vidusaka' who brings a touch of humour to the otherwise serious play.

Kudiyattam uses twenty four basic 'Hasta Mudras' (Hand Gestures) and an equal number of ragas to depict various moods.

The make-up for Kudiyattam is a specialised art in itself and resembles that of Kathakali in some respects. The skirts used here, however, are not as heavy as those worn is Kathakali.

Different colours are used for different types of characters. Green is used for nobility, red for evil characters and black for primitive power.

Characters are also broadly divided into groups depending upon their nature, like Kathi (materialistic), Thadi (evil) and Pacchi (noble).

Therefore, the tempo is provided by a Mizhavu, which is a large copper vessel with its mouth covered with leather. Other percussion instruments like the Edaka and Timila are also used. The Nangiar who provides vocal accompaniment uses Cymbals to provide rhythm.

Kudiyattam is the only surviving tradition of the early Sanskrit theatre in India. Though 'Koothu' the major element in Kudiyattam has a recorded evidence in 'Silappadikaram' dating to 2nd century A.D., classical Sanskrit literature on drama owes to 4th and 5th century A.D. The works of Bhasa. Sudraka, and Kalidasa were the early ones enacted in Kudiyattam. Kudiyattam as it is seen today dates back to 10th century A.D. Kulasekhara Varma who ruled Kerala at that time has made significant contribution to it by writing epics like Subhadra Dhananjayam and Thapati Samvaranam. His versatile minister 'Tholam', introduced the role of Vidhushaka and also started using the newly developing language of Malayalam for Vidhushaka.

Guru M. Kochukuttan Chakyar as Vidushaka

Kudiyāttam is generally acted only during night is one of the most ancient and popular of Kerala's entertainments. It has pan-Indian importance for in this we have the Sanskrit dramas staged. Here the particular act of the particular drama is enacted. Chākyars act the chosen act of the chosen drama, because to produce a whole play require the better part of several months. In Kerala, a Kūdiyattam performance may take atleast five days or it may extend upto eleven days. Thus, in the partial fashion, the Chākyārs stage few dramas and Bhasa's plays finds a special importance in their repertoire.

These are:-

(i). Balacharita

(ii). Third Act of the Pratigṇa - Yaugandharayana or Ministers vow (called *'Mantrankan'*)

(iii). Svapnavāsvadattā (The vision of Vāsavadatta)

(iv). Abhisekanātakam (The Consecration of Rama)

Previously Bhasa's Cārudatam were among about a dozen other works from which acts were enacted but which were eventually dropped from the repertoire.

About 2,000 years old, Kudiyattam was the exclusive preserve of the upper castes of Kerala, even in the post-land reform phase. It was confined to the Kuttambalans (performance area built to the specifications of Natya Sastra and others texts) of temples, and its performers included only Chakyars and Nambiars. Nangiars, who are offshoots of Namboothiris in the caste hierarchy. Until about 30 to 35 years ago, Kudiyattam remained within temples. It was Mani Madhava Chakyar who decided to take Kudiyattam outside the temple, braving excommunication within his community. There are mainly three schools of Kudiyattam today, at the Ammannur Gurukulam in Irinjalakkuda (Thrissur district), Margi in Tiruvananthapuram, and the Kerala Kalamandalam in Cheruthuruthy. The latter is under governmental control. Margi was a club in its infant state, that the late D. Appukuttan Nair started in 1971, adding a Kathakali school in 1974 and another of Kudiyattam in 1981.

The textual base of Kudiyattam is from the treatises of Bhasa, and Kalidasa. The interesting differences between the two texts, as for a Kudiyattam is concerned, that is the more elastic the Attaprakaram (which describeds the movements, etc), the better suited it is to Kudiyattam. Bhāsa's texts lend themselves to acting far more than Kalidasa's for the laltter has in his Attaprakaram, laid down each and every movement and its time specifications for the actor, which limits the scope for improvisation.

Kudiyattam has five major elements that distinguish it. These are:-

It is limited to Chakyars and Nambiars, to temples, to Sanskrit verses, to set conventions and to its ritual orientation. In its adherence to classicism and in terms of antiquity, Kudiyattam is older to Kathakali, which is only about 400 years old. Kathakali depends on Attakathas (performance texts) in Malayalam, while Kudiyattam looks towards Sanskrit texts alone. Ranjini Rajagopal, a critic has rightly observed that while the text and performance of Kathakali do not give room for much elaboration, Kutiyattam is elastic, rendering itself flexible to expand or condense. Kathakali concentrates on completing an episode overnight, but Kudiyattam can play with a single aspect for days on end. An endless reservoir of aesthetic fantasy, of imagination in its wide-winged flight, of improvisation that distances itself from the real in distinguishing between pure art and the absence of it. Kavalam Narayana Panikker, the late Chakyar points out that there is less and less of lokadharmi (realistic represence) in Kudiyattam, but more of natyadharmi (abhinaya-based) and kavyadharmi (poetry/text based), that is, textual and the non-textual for the sake of contexualisation, unlike in Kathakali which has more of lokadharmi. But lokadharmi has its place too in Kudiyatam, in the form of Vidushaka, whose role is to criticise society. This art form was created with the idea of chastising, cleansing society. They could criticise even he king and the would hear it.

Role of Mizhavu in Kudiyattam Performance: A most interesting and intriguing feature of Kudiyattam is its musical accompaniment. Mizhavu, the 'soul' accompaniment of Kudiyattam, is considered a divine instrument, which, though steped in tala (rhythm), substitutes for music as well. Undoubtedly the only instrument that carefully follows vocal and emotional nuances of intonation, it is to the music of Mizhavu that the Chakyar performs. Mizhavu or the Mṛdanga as it is also called, has come from sage Bharata's classification of musical instruments - ghanam, avanaddham, tatam and susiram. The Mṛdanga comes under the group avanaddham.

Guru P.K. Narayanan Nambiar playing the Mizhavu

In Kudiyattam, the Mizhavu player is not just an accompanist, but a fellow-traveller of the Chakyar in performance. For his beats are bound to the gestural aesthetic and emotion of the Chakyar, to his bhava and pace, flowing in and out of intense rhythmic patterns that reflect the performer's mood so acutely as to let the listner follow the bhava of the performers blindly. There is certainly no other (rhythm) instrument that does much, and grinds itself within the soul of the performance.

5

Bhasa Plays in Performance

(i) Abhiṣekanāṭakam in Performances

The Annual Kūdiyāṭṭam performance at the Vaṭakumnāthan Temple Theatre of Trichur commences from Vijayadaśami day, an auspicious occasion in the Hindu calender of events.

From the town of Inriṇjalagada arrives Mādhavan Cākyar and his party of performes to Trichur to perform an act of a play. It would be worthwhile to mention that from October 14 to 20, 1975 they chose to stage the Third Act of conscoration the Rāma (Abhiṣekanāṭakam), a Six Acts drama of Bhāsa. Only two acts of the play are in the repertory of Cakyar families entitled: (i) Bālivadhāṇkam (First Act); (ii) Tarnayudharnkam (Third Act).

On 22 July 1985, Kerala Kala Mandalam staged 'Balivadhankam' from Abhiśekanataka of Bhasa at Sri Chitra Hindu Religious Central Library Auditorium, Trivandrum on the occasion of 'Kootiyattam Kalotsavam' organised by the Trivandrum Cultural Society. On 13th November 1988, from the Abhishekanatakam of Bhasa, the Balivadhanka act was presented in Kutiyattam style at the Bhasa Mahotsavam at Trivandrum. In temple, the play takes over five nights. It was, however, shortened to a little over five hours in the stage performance. Drama critic commented on the production in the following lines "... As it is, the unhurried pace, the enormous attention to detail, the breath taking grandeur of the costumes and the masks, the fascinating moments and mudras, the resonance of the drums with their changing beats were captivating enough and to me the at least, a successful act of interpretation of a dramatic piece in a different art form.

'Balivadham' in Kudiyattam form was produced by The Ammannur Chachu Chakyar Smaraka Gurukulam with the help of the Sangeet Natak Akademi, New Delhi in the Eight Kutiyattam Festival. The venue was Natana Kairali, Ammannur Chakyar Madhom, Irinjalakuda, Trichur District, Kerala. The Act was presented from 7 to 11 January 1995 under the direction of Guru Ammannur Madhava Chakyar.

The Dramatis Personae were:-

First Day (7-1-95)

Sri Rama's Purappad	....	Sreejith Nambiar
Second Day (8-1-95)		
Sri Rama's Nirvahana	...	Sooraj Nambiar
Third Day (9-1-95)		
Sugriva's Purappad	...	Ranjeeth.
Fourth Day (10-1-95)		
Sugriva's Nirvahana	...	Ammannur Rajaneesh
Balivadham (Kutiyattam) (11-1-95)		
Bali	...	Guru Ammannur Madhava Chakyar
Sugriva	...	Ammannur Parameswaram (Kuttan Chakyar)
Sri Rama	...	G. Venu
Lakshmana	...	Sooraj Nambiar
Tara	...	Usha Nangiar
Hanuman	...	Ranjeeth
Angada	...	Ammannur Rajaneesh

The Accompanists were :-

Mizhavu	...	V.K. Hariharan, Kalamandalam Rajeev, C.K. Krishnan Nambiar, Kalamandalam Narayanan, Ramesh.
Idakka	...	Kalanilayam Unnikrishnan
Talam	...	Subhadra Nangiar, Nirmala Paniker etc.
Make-up	...	Kalanilayam Parameswaran.

Ammannur Madhava Chakyar as Bali in 'Bali Vadham'
(Abhisekanatakam: Act - One)

Variously described as the oldest and most undiluted form of Sanskrit theatre, hence perhaps of the world, its use of formal elements of dance and theatre as described by Natyasastra, of techniques like the device of the flashback, moving easily from time present to time past and future and the extraordinary complex language of its abhinaya technique, from netra and hasta to anga and vacika, make Kudiyattam the scholar's delight and the culture preservationists cherished aim, feels critic Shanta Serbjeet Singh. The six day festival on the form from 24-29 March 1995, organised by Sangeet Natak Akademi at its open-air grounds was all this and more a celebratory mahotsava in the true sense. The day after day sizeable audience sat through the performances was equally heartening. The seniormost performer of Kudiyattam today, Ammannur Madhava Chakyar, 79, gave a breath taking performance on the penultimate day of the festival in his role as Bali in Balivadham. Emotions of vira (valour) and Srinagara (romantic / erotic imagery) sat elegantly on him, the 79- year old transformed within moments into the gushing, cupid-struck romantic youth, the gravity and depth of his seasoned gestures, the fluency and ease of his aged body, the clarity of his utterance, through to the end (where Bali is killed by Sugriva), where of course a *tirasseela* was held and cushions substituted for Ammannur's form, for a personal enactment would have been too close to reality, where imagined reality has to florish. Padmashree Ammannur Madhava Chakyar's enactment of the death of Bali in Balivadham in the March 1995 Kudiyattam Festival was strictly on the lives improvised by his Guru, Bhagavattav Kunjunni Thamparan of Kudungallore Palance, who taught him the ingenious technique of breath control for the effective delineation of rasas (emotions). The portrayal of the sequences of Bali's death is inimitable and continues to be his master piece even today.

Balivadham from Abhisekanatakam (Act One) of Bhasa was produced by The Ammannur Chachu Chakyar Smaraka Gurukulam, Irinjalakuda on 28 March 1995 at Rabindra Bhawan Lawn, Ferozeshah Road, New Delhi, on the occasion of this National Festival of Kutiyattam.

A Chakyar actor and his musical accompanist performing in March 1995 Kutiyattam Festival, organised by the Sangeet Natak Akademi, New Delhi.

Presented below is an account of the Plot, Text of Performance, Cast, Accompanists and the Troupe:-

Balivadham: *Abhisekanataka (Act One) of Bhasa:*

Plot:- 'Balivadham' deals with the incidents leading to the killing of Bali, the king of the monkeys. It describes the alliance between Rama and Sugriva (Bali's brother), Sugriva's challenge to Bali for a fight, Bali's acceptance of the challenge despite Tara's plea. While the two brothers are engaged in fight, Rama shoots Bali down with an arrow, hiding behind a tree. The death-scene of Bali, in which he traverses through several conflicting emotions of outrage (at Rama), reconciliation (with his fate, as also with his brother), sorrow, compassion and finally, clam, is the high point of this act.

Text of performance:- After the ritual drumming called Mizhavu Ochappenduttuka, the Nambiar comes and stands in front on the oil-lamp of the stage with great devotion and recites the verse of the prayer with which the play begins.

Meaning of verse:- "May Lord Sri Rama protect you - Rama who entered into a treaty with Sugriva; who lifted and hurled the dead body of the demon Dundubhi; who in no time cut down Sapta Salas (seven palmyra palms) with one arrow to instil confidence in Sugriva; who killed Bali while he was fighting with his brother in order to confirm his friendship with Sugriva and who is a diadem on the crest of Surya (Sun) dynasty."

When the curtain is removed we see Sugriva sitting in a mood of deep sorrow and dejection. Sugriva expresses through hand gestures and facial expression his agonics and his hardships in living alone in a solitary wood.

Sugriva, for fear of his elder brother Bali, has taken refuge in the Malyavan mountain. Hounded out of his palace, Sugriva bemoans his sad lot, living alone in the forest facing the rigours of nature. He sees, around him in the forest, a reflection of his own metnal state. "My good God, will my miseries never end ? Exposed to the sun, drenched by the rains, shivering in the cold and open to the winds, I live in the forest. Would I ever see a normal comfortable life? Is there anything I can do in the matter? Alas! no."

Thus sorrowing he decides to take a peep at what is in store for him in the future. He plucks a small leaf from the bush and tosses it. Scrutinizing the fallen leaf and the oracular message it portends, he pronounces the result, "No friend, but there is, foe!" Some distance away he notices the young one of a deer grazing. Suddenly hearing the twang of a bowstring, the frightened deer runs to take cover. But observing a lion sleeping in the bush he had approached, he stands stunned shivering with fear. Observing this scene he explains, "Oh! God, my destiny is no different than that of this deer; and grieving thus, he repeats the leaf-test and reading the signs reaches the finding, "There is friend and there is foe!" Now looking around he sees a serpent which observing an eagle floating above in the sky, looks out for a hole to hide in. Presently it spots one and promptly takes shelter in it. Not quite satisfied with this omen, Sugriva tries the leaf-tossing test which said, "No foe, but friend, there is." About this time a peacock begins its dance but a sudden forest fire starts; the frightened peacock fly to a high rock and continues its dance when the rains flush out the fire. The sight of this scene pleases Sugriva.

It is at this juncture that Hanuman appears; Sugriva welcomes him and they become friends. When Hanuman and Sugriva are together, they notice two men approaching some distance. Suspecting danger, Sugriva sends Hanuman to find out who they are. Hanuman escorts Rama and Lakshmana to Sugriva and introduces them to him. Rama and Sugriva enter into an agreement of mutual help and Rama agrees to kill Bali. [This is a solo enactment by Sugriva]

[Exit Sugriva]

[Then enter Rama, Lakshmana, Sugriva and Hanuman]

[Sugriva accompanied by Hanuman, Rama and Lakshmana, start for 'Kishkindha', Bali's kingdom. On the way Rama fells the Sapta Sales (seven palmyra palms) with a single arrow]

Rama: Sugriva, look this way, this way. Sugriva, in this fight you will soon find Bali knocked down by me, lying on the ground with his body all cut and tom with my arrows. I am going to fell him in a moment. Standing by me you will presently see him lying dead on the ground.

Sugriva: My lord, I know that with your grace and blessings I can conquer even the kingdom of the gods. How much easy then, it will be to conquer a kingdom, of the monkeys! I am sure of this because: Oh, valiant lord, the arrow that you have discharged from your bow has pierced and passed through the trunks of seven big Sala trees of this forest, each as tall and formidable as a peak of the Himalayas. The arrow after passing successively through these trees has continued its course with unabated speed and force and pierced the earth, reached Patala (the nether world) and has returned to kill Bali after having wahsed itself in the ocean, so I have no doubt at all that Bali will be killed.

Hanuman: Oh lord, the comforting and reassuring words coming from your mouth have dispelled all our fears and sorrows. Now let us proceed towards the mountain (the abode of Bali) as black as clouds to secure victory for Sugriva.

Lakshmana: Look sir, this place which is full of trees must certainly be Kishkindha.

Sugriva: What Lakshmana has said is quite true. Yes lord, we who are protected by your strong arms, have reached Kishkindha which is protected by Bali's strong arms. Sir, please wait here. I shall go and challenge Bali to a duel in a thundering voice which will shake all the three worlds.

Rama: Let it be so, Go now.

Sugriva: I humbly obey your order.

[All exeunt]

[Sugriva re-enters]

Sugriva: Your Majesty, Sugriva who did not wrong you in any way, was disclaimed by you and expelled from your kingdom. Now he has come back, intent upon doing reverence to you at your feet, but in battle!

[Exit Sugriva]

[The entrance of Bali. As a prelude to the entrance, he hammers at the door of the *nepathya* with his fists, and roars out angrily. He then calls out from the *nepathya* in a loud voice with a slight stammer]:

"What? What? It is Sugriva, is it?"

[Bali appears from behind a curtain]

Bali: What? Is it Sugriva, is it? [He gets up and walks across the stage, preparing to leave. Looks towards the left and sees that his wife, Tara has caught hold of his garment.] My beautiful Tara, please release your hold on my dress. I shall fight with Sugriva; you shall see Sugriva lying exhausted on the ground with his body hideously mangled by my blows and covered all over with blood.

Tara: Be gracious to me, your majesty. There must be sufficient reason for Sugriva's arrival. Therefore, better seek the counsel of your ministers before going out to accept his challenge.

Bali: Listen my beautiful Tara, I will surely defeat Sugriva even if he is supported by the mighty Indra himself; or even if he is backed by Lord Shiva himself armed with his sharp-edged axe; or let the lotus-eyed Mahavishnu himself support him against me; or let Mahavishnu take the form of Narasimha and come to protect Sugriva from me. But I assure you none of them will come and take arms against me.

[Here the actor going off the text of the play enacts the story of Prahlada.]

Long ago, Hiranyakasipu, King of the Asuras, had a son named Prahlad who was a great devotee of Vishnu. Chagrined by his inordinate devotion to Vishnu, Hiranyakasipu called his son to his side and angrily asked him: "My son, whom are you adoring and worshipping?" Prahlada replied: "Father, I am devoted to none other than Mahavishnu who is the lord and protector of the three worlds." Hiranyakasipu angrily retorted: "Am I not the protector of the three worlds? Who is this Vishnu of yours? Prahlada calmly and firmly replied: "It is Vishnu who is the lord and protector of all the world." Then Hiranyakasipu asked him: "Where is this Vishnu? Where does he reside?" Prahlada replied: Vishnu is everywhere in all the worlds; he is omnipresent."

Hiranyakasipu : Is he present everywhere?

Prahlada : Yes, he is presented everywhere and in all things.

Hiranyakasipu : Is he presented in this pillar?

Prahlada : Certainly, he is in that pillar.

[Hiranyakasipu, in a fit of anger, struck at that pillar with his sword and split the pillar. Vishnu, in the form of Narasimha, emerged out of the broken pillar and killed the king.]

Bali continues: Tara, even that Narasimha will not take arms against me in the fight with Sugriva. You need not be sad or frightened at all.

Tara : Be gracious to me, your majesty. Please give this person a blessing, your majesty.

Bali : Tara, hear about my valour. In the days of yore, when all the gods and the demons together were churning the sea of milk for obtaining 'Amrita' (the elixir of life), I went there and asked all the gods and the demons to stand aside. Then I grabbed the head of the terrible serpent Vasuki with his wide open eyes, with one hand and his tail with the other hand, alone and unaided, churned the sea, while the gods and the demons stood looking on with amazement.

[Here again the actor enacts the story of Amrit Manthan.]

Listen, Tara, long ago, when the *devas* were all stricken with old age, the Devas and Asuras through out a plan for preventing and remedying old age. They entered into a friendly agreement to churn the ocean of milk in order to obtain Amrita. Their plan was to use the Manthara mountain the churning-rod and the snake, Vasuki as the rope. While churning both the Devas and Asuras became exhausted. At that time I churned the ocean singlehanded, holding one end of Vasuki with one hand. Seeing me do this work, both the Devas and Asuras stood astounded. Therefore, I, who did this astounding work, is not afraid of anybody.

Tara : Be gracious to me, your majesty.

Bali : No more! You simply do as I say! Go inside the house!

Tara : This luckless person is going. [Exit]

Bali : Ah! Tara has gone. Now I will go and finish off Sugriva. [Hurrying forward] Sugriva, stop, stop! Sugriva, even if you have Indra or the almighty Lord Vishnu as your ally, once you come within my field of vision, you will not go away alive.

Sugriva : As your majesty commands.

[They battle with each other]

Sri Rama : Look, look, Bali is rushing towards Sugriva, biting his lips and showing his enormous teeth, his eyes fierce and red with anger, shaking his clenched fists threatening like the fires of deluge to burn everything to ashes.

Lakshmana : Oh, brother, look at Sugriva. Throwing away all civilized rules of behaviour, he has given himself up to the impulses of his beastly or monkey-nature and is fighting with Bali. His eyes shine red like fully-blossomed lotuses; his long round shaping arms, resplendent with gold bracelets, are raised high a threatening gesture.

[Sugriva is struck down of Bali]

Hanuman : [With alarm and anxiety] Alas! Look at Sugriva's fallen and helpless condition. Bali is certainly much more strong and powerful; my master (Sugriva) is weak. Please remember this and the pledge that you have made to protect him.

Sri Rama : Hanuman, don't be alarmed or worried. Look, I have already taken action [discharges an arrow at Bali]. Alas! hit by my arrow Bali has already fallen.

Lakshmana : See, Bali with his strong arms lies with his body split by the arrow and covered all over he is getting ready to go to Yamaloka (the kingdom of the god of death).

Bali : [Reading the letters of the name of the sender on the arrow, to Rama] Rama, is it proper that you who is valorous, who stands steadfast your duties as a prince, and who is intent upon leading the people along the path of righteousness, should deceive me in battle in this manner, without the least suspicion that you are committing an unrighteous act? Oh! What a pity! You who is good by nature and has a good reputation among people, has now earned a bad name by deceptively killing me in this manner. Oh Rama, you have the mated hair of a hermit and have, as garment, the bark of a tree. But your thoughts seem to be at variance with your mode of dress. You concealed yourself and killed me while I was battling against my brother. Isn't this an unrighteous act?

Sri Rama : So you consider that concealing oneself in order to kill is an unrighteous act?

Bali : Undoubtedly it is.

Sri Rama : That is not ture. Look! In hunting, one conceals oneself in order to kill animals. Now this is not considered to be an unrighteous act. Since you are an animal and you deserved to be killed, I concealed myself in order to kill you.

Bali : So you consider that I deserve to be killed?

Sri Rama : Without a shadow of doubt.

Bali : For what reason?

Sri Rama : Because you have accepted a forbidden woman.

Bali : Accepted a forbidden woman, eh? For us this is not an unrighteous act.

Sri Rama : Sir, is it proper that you who is capable of distinguishing between the righteous and the unrighteous, and who is the king of the monkeys, should consider yourself to be a mere animal and accept your brother's wife?

Bali : In this matter of accepting one's brother's wife, I and my brother Sugriva are equally guilty. But you have punished me alone. You have not punished Sugriva.

Sri Rama : I punished you because you deserved to be punished. One does not punish the innocent.

Bali : Sugriva accepted my wife; and I am his elder brother to accept a younger brother's wife.

Sri Rama : These is no law which permits an elder brother to accept a younger brother's wife.

Bali : In that case I have nothing to say by way of reply. Since it is you who has punished me, I am now indeed purged of all my sins.

Sri Rama: So be it!

Sugriva : Alas! Oh! king of the monkeys, with a gait resembling that of an elephant, seeing your two arms which resemble the trunk of an elephant with their shoulder rings fallen off due to the force of the enemy's weapon, lying stretched over the bare earth, my mind seems to lose its balance.

Bali : Sugriva, do not grieve. This is simply the way of the world.

[From inside] Alas! Alas! His majesty!

Bali : Sugriva, don't let the women come here. They need not see me in this condition.

Sugriva : As your majesty commands! Hanuman, go and carry out the order.

Hanuman : As the prince commands! [Exit]

[Re-enters Hanuman bringing Angada, Bali's son, with him]

Hanuman : Angada, this way, this way!

Angada : Having heard that his majesty, the king of the monkeys, is approaching his end, I am on my way to see him, with a heart laid down with grief. Hanuman, where is his majesty?

Hanuman : Here is his majesty, his chest rent by the arrow, lying on the earth like the Krauncha mountain pierced by the lance of Lord Subramanya.

Angada : [approaching] Alas! Alas! His majesty! In former times the mighty king of the monkeys always used to lie down in comfort. I now see you rolling on the earth, with your limbs weakened, Sir, do you now wish to leave this body, pierced by the arrows, and enter the paradise of heroes?

[Prostrates himself at the feet of Bali]

Bali : Angada, don't grieve unncessarily. Oh Sugriva, forgetting all the wrongs committed by me towards you and leaving aside anger, you, who has now become the king of the monkeys, should tread the path of righteousness and accept the protection of this boy, the heir of our race.

Sugriva : As your majesty commands.

Bali : Oh Rama, you should consider any wrongs these persons may commit as arising due to the fickleness common to all monkeys, and forgive them.

Sri Rama : By all means.

Bali: Sugriva, accept this golden necklace, the hereditary wealth of our race.

Sugriva : I am indeed honoured.

Bali : Hanuman, get me some water.

Hanuman : As your majestry commands!

[Makes his exit and then re-enters]

Hanuman : Here is water.

Bali : [sipping the water] It seems that my soul is leaving this body. Here are the great rivers, headed by Ganga! Here are the celestial damsels headed by Urvasi! And here is the air-chariot, borne by one thousand swans. sent by the Lord of Death to convey the souls of heroes! So be it! I am coming!

[Bali on the point of death makes convulsive movements of his face and limbs and climacteric breathing of Vayus such as Kshudraka, Tamaka. Cohinna, Mahan and Urdhva. These laboured breaths become more intense showing that death is close. Bali dies.]

[All say together: "Ha! Ha! the great king".]

Sri Rama : Alas! Bali is dead and he has attained heaven. Sugriva, perform his funeral rites.

Sugriva : As the Lord orders, so it will be done.

Sri Rama : Lakshmana, perform the coronation ceremony of Sugriva.

Lakshmana : As brother orders, so it will be done.

Cast :

Bali	:	Ammannur Madhava Chakyar
Sugriva	:	Ammannur Parameswaran Chakyar
Sri Rama	:	G. Venu
Lakshmana	:	Sooraj Nambiar
Tara	:	Usha Nangiar
Hanuman	:	Kalamandalam Radhakrishnan
Angada	:	Ranjeeth

Accompanists :

Mizhavu	:	C.K. Krishnan Nambiar, V.K. Hariharan,P.P. Rajeev, K.P. Narayanan Nambiar
Edakka	:	O.N. Gopinathan Nambiar, Kalanilayam Unnikrishnan
Kurum Kuzhal	:	Sudhin Shankar
Talam	:	Nirmala Paniker

Troupe

Ammannur Chachu Chakyar Smaraka Gurukulam, Irinjalakuda.

Bali and Sugreeva (Ammannur Madhava Chakyar and Ammannur Parameswaran) in Bali Vadham from Abhisekanatakam Act One; [Guru Ammannur Chachu Chakyar Smarka Gurukulam]

Troanayudham from Abhishekanataka was presented by the Kerala Kala Mandalam on 23 & 24 July 1985 at Sri Chitra Hindu Religious Library Auditorium on the oceasion of 'Kootiyattom Kalotsavam', organised by the Trivandrum Cultural Society.

In 1990, SPIC-MACAY organised some shows of Kudiyattam, the ancient Sanskrit drama form. Ammannur Madhava Chakyar, one of the most renowned exponents of the style, beautifully enacted on excerpt from the Abhisekanatakam by Bhasa in his 90-minutes demonastration. The scene was from the Toranayuddha in which Ravana brags to Narada how he secured the Chandrahasa sword for his unmitigated strength and valour, that helped Shiva to tide over a delicate situation of matrimonial discord. The charming situation was excellently created by this great exponent of Kudiyattam. On an austere stage, seated on a small stool, in the light of a large oil lamp, and to the accompaniment of two Mizhavus large copper drums covered with calfskin, he brought out the importance of Nayanabhi naya (expression through eyes) in this style. This Kerala art has perfected the pantomimic language. The eyes in particular seem remarkably self-sufficient in expressing various moods and forms. It was a treat to watch Parvati's eyes, now filled with love for Siva, now seized with jealous anger, now crying in helpless frustration, while Siva, inspite of his love for Parvati, is unable to control his wandering eye. The face of the artiste, inded his entire being, was suffused with bhava. The artiste also created an amazing illusion of space with the eyes (with minimum aid from hand and body gesture) when he showed the Ganga falling from Siva's locks, when he showed Parvati standing at the peak of Mount Kailasha about to leave Siva for his waywardness. Perched on a small stool, Ammanur Madhava Chakyar effectively conveyed the treamling and unbalancing of Parvati standing at the peak of the mountain as Ravana shakes it. With tremendous economy of movement and dramatic illusion of space, character and mood was created. Ravana is the hero of the piece, the narrative unfolds through him and yet he was not represented, for it is typical of Kudiyattam. Change of character was achieved by a simple device. To show Parvati the actor tucked the lower end of his skirt at the waist. To show Siva he once again lowered the skirt.

Ammannur Chachu Chakyar Smaraka Gurukulam with the help of the Sangeet Nataka Akademi, New Delhi organised its Eighth Kutiyattam Festival from 3 to 14 January 1995 at Natana Kairali, Ammannur Chakyar Madhom, Irinjalakuda, Trichur District, Kerala.

On 5 & 6 January Toranayuddham was performed under the direction of Guru Ammannur Madhava Chakyar.

The Dramatis personae were:-

The First Day

Ravana	:	Sooraj Nambiar
Sankukarnan	:	Ammannur Rajaneesh
Vijaya	:	Aparna Nangiar

The Second Day

Ravana	:	Ranjeeth
Sankukarna	:	Sooraj Nambiar

The Third Day

Ravana	:	Ammannur Parameswaran (Kuttam Chakyar)
Hanuman	:	Kalamandalam Radhakrishnan
Vibhishana	:	Ammannur Rajaneesh

The Accompanists were:-

Mizhavu	:	V.K. Hariharan, C.K. Krishnan Nambiar, Kalamandalam Rajeev, Kalamandalam Narayanan, Ramesh
Idakka	:	Kalanilayam Unnikrishnan
Talam	:	Subhadra Nangiar, Nirmala Paniker etc.
Make up	:	Kalanilayam Parameswaran

'Toranayuddham' is based on the Third Act of Abhisekanatakam to be presented in Kutiyattam style which is regarded as the most prominet survivor among the forms containing some essential elements of content and structural features of the Sanskrit theatre.

This was performed by the Kerala Kalamandalam. Cheruthuruthy at the Ayyappa Temple, Sector-2, Ramakrishna Puram, New Delhi on 29 March 1995 during the Kutiyattam Mahotsavam, sponsored by Sangeet Nataka Akademi, New Delhi. Presented below is an account of the Plot, Text of Peformance, Cast, Accompanists, Make-up and Costumes and the Troupe:-

Toranayuddham (from *Abhisekanataka* (Act Three) of Bhasa) :

Plot: Ravana, receiving the news of the destruction of Asoka Vatika (Asoka's Grove) by a monkey (Hanuman), reflects on his past life, his feats of lifting Mount Kailasa and pleasing Lord Siva, as well as displeasing Parvti and receiving her curse. At the news that the monkey killed many Raksasas, Vibhishana tries to advise Ravana, but the latter disregards his attempts and orders him to bring Hanuman. There is a heated exchange between Ravana and Hanuman, with Vibhishana again offering good advice to Ravana. Angry and upset, Ravana orders to set fire to Hanuman's tail.

***Text of performance*:** The curtain is removed showing Ravana in a reflective mood. He is surprised and even unnerved at the havoc a monkey is capable of, after getting into the impregnable Lanka.

Ravana : Alas, what a pity! Years ago I conquered all the Devas and Asuras and the three worlds. As I stormed the Kailasa (the mountain abode of Lord Siva and his consort Goddess Parvathi), Parvathi got frightened and trembled with fear. However, Siva was pleased with me, but Parvathi and Nandikeswara, irked by the indifference and disrespect shown by me. cursed me, may be those curses have now started taking effect on me.

[Here the actor, going off the text of the play, develops through elaborate *abhinaya* the theme of Kailasodharanam and Parvathi-virabham].

Kailasodharanam is the lifting and tossing of the Kailasa mountain in the air. Parvati-virabham is estrangement of Parvathi with Siva as she grew jealous of her lord's relationship with the Goddess Ganga.

Returning home after a successful battle with Vaisravana, Ravana finds the path of his Pushpakavimana (the flying chariot) obstructed by Mount Kailasa; Ravana gets down from his chariot, uproots the mountain, and throws it up in the air. The *abhinaya* here includes a long description of the mountain, its enormous size, the valleys, peaks, caves, rocks smaller streams trickling down from the top and joining together to make great, meandering rivers, etc.

At that time, Parvathi and Siva are conversing in Kailasa. She is on his lap. She asks him, 'What is that on your head', (suspecting Gangadevi to be there).

Siva : It is water.

Parvathi : But I find a face; how can it be there?

Siva : No,it is a lotus flower.

Parvathi : But how then the curls of hair?

Siva : It is only a row of bees humming and settling down on the flower.

Parvathi : But, then what about the eye-brows?

Siva : They are ripples in the water.

Parvathi : Eyes?

Siva : No, they are two black fishes.

Parvathi : And the two breasts?

Siva : They are Chakravaka birds.

Parvathi : Clearly, you are deceiving me?

[Saying thus, and no longer able to stand the sight of Ganga being borne by her Lord, the jealous Parvathi leaves him. But at this moment Kailasa was being lifted up. The violent tremors caused by Ravana frightens her and she immediately rushes back seeking safety in the loving embrace of Siva. The actor assumes the roles of Siva and Parvathi alternately. As Parvathi, he shows the gradual growth of her jealously towards Ganga and the mixed emotion of "Pranayakopam". Siva, Parvathi and their devoted servant Nandikeswara are pleased with Ravana as his deed led to the happy reconciliation between Siva and Parvathi. They appear before Ravana and offer him boons. But Ravana arrogantly refuses to receive honours from Parvathi as she is a womana and Nandikeswara as he appeared in the form of a monkey. Enraged at the insult, Parvathi and Nandikeswara curse Ravana that monkeys will be the cause of his ruin.]

[Ravana exit]

II

The curtain is held for the *purappad* (entrance) of Vibhishana, the younger brother of Ravana, who is of a gentle disposition. Vibhishana is on his way to Ravana. He is critical of Ravana's action in abducting Sita and in rejecting his repeated advice for returning her to Rama.

Vibhishana : Alas! The king's (Ravana's) mind has turned from the path of virtue. I have told him several times to return Sita to Rama. But he won't listen, to the utter grief of his friends.

[Exit]

III

[Ravana enters, takes his seat and waits for Vibhishana. The latter appears and approaches Ravana.]

Vibhishana : Victory to the king.

Ravana : Vibhishana, come be seated.

Vibhishana : Yes, I am sitting.

Ravana : Vibhishana, why do you look so upset and distraught?

Vibhishana : Distress is the lot of people whose master never listens to their words.

Ravana : Forget it. You just go and bring that monkey.

Vibhishana : As you please.

[Exeunt both]

[Curtain is held for Hanuman. He enters being carried and led by two Raksasa servants of Ravana. Vibhishana also accompanies him. After having been left alone on the stage, Hanuman does some movements characteristic of a monkey.]

Hanuman : [to himself] It is not that I was taken captive by that wicked Raksasa (Ravana). Rather I let myself be captured, so that I can meet Ravana in person.

[In the course of the *abhinaya* of the above lines Hanuman describes in detail how he wanted to leave behind some record his visit to Lanka and meeting Sita; how he, with that object destroyed the garden; how he killed the garden keepers, the army commanders (Panchasenapathi) of Ravana and his son Akshakumara and how he eventually decided to allow himself to be taken captive by Indrajit in order that he might see Ravana himself. He also narrates, giving occasion for much humour and fun, how the guards in the garden were asleep snoring deeply; how he tied the beards and hair together and interchanged their weapons; how they all woke up and ran helter-skelter, shrieking in excitement and terror. Hanuman then leaves the stage.]

[Ravana returns to his seat. Hanuman and Vibhishana appear. Without being asked, Hanuman takes his seat beside Ravana in utter disregard of him. Ravana and Hanuman quarrel and Hanuman, full of confidence, makes fun of Ravana with his pranks and antics.]

Hanuman : Oh, king, how do you do?

Ravana to Vibhishana: Is that handiwork [meeting the destruction of Ravana's garden] done by this one?

Vibhishana : Yes, more than that.

Ravana : Hey, monkey, who are you? Why did you come here disregarding us?

Hanuman : Listen! I am born of Anjana and the wind-God. My name is Hanuman, a monkey, and I am a messenger of Rama.

Vibhishana : King, you hear?

Ravana : Yes, but what for?

Vibhishana : Hanuman, what are Rama's words?

Hanuman : Hear Rama's command.

Ravana : How dare you speak of Rama's command? Finish this monkey off.

Vibhishana : Be pleased, Oh! King. Messengers should not be killed whatever be their crimes and wrongs. You may do what you like after hearing Rama's words.

Ravana : Monkey, what did that 'man' say?

Hanuman : Hear! No matter whether you take refuge under Lord Siva or escape into the inaccessible nether-world I will send you to Death with your body all chopped up with my sharp arrows.

Ravana : I defeated *devas* with divine arrows under my control. Even Vaisravana is in a fix losing his Pushpaka (divine chariot) to me. Then how can Rama, a mere human creature, confront me.

Hanuman : Then why did you choose to steal his wife secretly.

Vibhishana : Well-spoken, Hanuman. Oh, great king, is it not by deceit that you abducted Sita disguising yourself as a mendicant and treacherously drawing Rama away from her?

Ravana : Why do you defect to the enemy side?

Vibhishana : Oh, king, bear with me. My words are for good. Return Sita, the wife of Rama, to him. I wish that you, the great among Raksasas be not the cause of the ruin of this race.

Ravana : Vibhishana, enough of this. How can a deer kill a lion? How can a jackal kill a mighty elephant?

Hanuman : Ravana, is it proper that you speak of Rama this way? You devoid of all virtues. Wicked Ravana, Rama is the hero of heroes. Like Indra, he is without equal. You have lost all virtues. You are of no significance.

Ravana : What, kill this monkey or wait; killing of messengers is reprehensible. Set fire to its tail.

[Hanuman is taken out leaving Ravana alone on the stage]

Ravana : [to himself] Let me make necessary arrangements now for the protection of the city of Lanka.

Cast

Ravana	:	Sivan Namboodiri
Vibhishana	:	Narayana Chakyar

Hanuman	:	Rama Chakyar
Rakshasas	:	Krishna Kumar, Kanaka Kumar

Accompanists

Mizhavu	:	P.V. Iswaranunni, A.N. Hariharan
Edakka	:	M.Narayanan Namboodiri

Make-up & Costumes

P.M. Rammohan, A.S. Rangan, M.Kunjan

Troupe

Kerala Kalamandalam, Cheruthuruthy.

All the performances were recorded by the Sangeet Nataka Akademi, New Delhi for its Archive.

Audio/Vedio Recordings of Kutiyattam available in Sangeet Natak Akademi Archives:

'Toranayuddham' from the Act Three of Abhisekanatakam, performed by artistes of Kerala Kalamandalam led by Painkulam Rama Chakyar was recorded on 2 June 1966 by Sangeet Natak Akademi for its Archive.

Audio - 01 : 50 *Hrs: Mts*

Another recording covers Painkulam Rama Chakyar's depiction of Hanuman in the same play that recorded on 26 June 1966.

Audio - 00 : 45 *Hrs : Mts*

The performance of 'Sutradhara' beloging to Kerala Kalamandalam is available in the Archive that was recorded on 26 June 1966.

Audio - 00 : 45 *Hrs : Mts*

The presentation of Abhisekanatakam in Kutiyattam idiom by Ammannur Madhava Chakyar and Group was recorded on 25 March 1980 for Ashoka-vanikankam taken from the Act - One of Abhisekanatakam was performed by Ammannur Madhava Chakyar and Group from 13 to 26 December 1982 and its video recording is presented in the Akademi's Archive.

Video - 13 : 50 Hrs : Mts

(ii) Avimaraka in Performance

Bhasa's Avimaraka was enacted in Hindi by the Rangaprabhat, Ujjain in the year 1977 under the direction of M.K. Raina. The play was presented at the Kalidasa Festival.

On 11th November 1988, a Japanese troup under the direction of Sumio Murijiri performed Bhasa's romantic play Avimaraka in the second Bhasa Mahotsavam at Trivandrum. A critic observes: The graceful movements, the vigorous gestures, the beautiful sets and fine costumes were pleasing too the eye and I could admire the colourful presentation. But the way the Japanese direction took liberties with the play and added episode after episode introducing a mace of twists and turns in the process was confusing and unwarranted.

The second year students of National School of Drama worked with B.V. Karanth in the production of Bhasa's 'Avimaraka' staged at Little Theatre Group (LTG) Auditorium, New Delhi from 28 to 30 November and 1st December, 1994. The Sanskrit play was adapted in Hindi by Prabhat Kumar Bhattacharya. Set, propeties and lighting were designed by Satyavrat Rout and costume by Dolly Alhuwalia. Shri Shashadar Acharya was the choreographer. A 'Photographic Exhibition of Contemporary Productions of Sanskrit Plays' was also put up at LTG on the occasion.

A scene from 'Avimaraka'; directed by B.V. Karanth for the National School of Drama, New Delhi.

(iii) Balacharitam in Performance

Few countries can boast of a continuing artistic tradition that is over two thousand years old. Kutiyattam, the only surviving example of Sanskrit theatre in India at this time, affords a rare example of such antiquity. Rare even in Kerala, the only state where it exists today, Kutiyattam reflects the principles of Bharata's Natyashastra, which is believed to have been written in the 2nd century, B.C.

A result of the Aryanisation of Kerala's predominantly Dravidian culture, Kutiyattam was nurtured in the temple precinsts for two millennia by 18 families of the Chakyar community. The earliest reference to the art of the Chakyars can be found in the Tamil text 'Silapadikaram' which dates back to the 2nd century A.D.

For the Chakyar's his profession determined his life-style the close association between Bhasa (the playwright) and the Chakyar is reflected in the communities insistence that a Chakyar boy's 'Upanayanam' ceremony should follow his "Arangetram" in which he had to act out the role of the Sutradhara in Bhasa's 'Balacharitam'. This ritual was to be completed before the age of the sixteen or else the boy was excommunicated from the community of Ambalavasis, or temple dwellers. However, things have changed considerably and today this thearical form is faced with a stark future. Its traditional audience has mostly deserted it and its hereditary practitioners are increasingly preferring less compelling and more comfortable way of earning a livelihood. To keep this form alive, gurus are becoming more catholic about taking on students, some of whom do not even belong to traditional Chakyar families.

Die Ambenteuer des Knaben Krischna' (The adventures of boy Krishna); a German translation of the Bhasa's 'Balacharita' was rendered by German Indologist Hermann Weller (1878-1956). It appeared in print in the year 1922. Later it was staged at the Court Theatre of Stockholm in 1925 with grand success.

(iv) Daridracarudatta in Performance

In the summer of 1917, the 'Kalavilasam', a drama troupe of Trivandrum wanted a fresh drama from A.R. Rajaraja Varma who had earlier wrote Kalidasa's classics. This time Rajaraja Varma wanted to give a play which had more action and a wide variety of characters. Sudraka's Mrichhakatikam was first considered for the purpose. But then certain scenes were too long. He also considered Daridracarudattam by Bhasa, which according to the author had inspired his play. So he decided to translate the first four Acts of Charudattam and to give a condensed version of the later portion of

Mrichhakatikam as conclusion. He wrote in his diary : .... "Lived in the imaginative land of poetry from morning. Sudraka's verses had neither the natural beauty of Bhasa nor the artistic perfection and finish of the later poets. Hence I had full scope for improving upon the verses.before they were rendered into Malayalam." This version was quite successfully staged by the Kalavilasam actors.

Daridracarudatta (Adaptation) in Performance:

Veteran Gujarati playwright Sri Rasiklal Chhotolal Parikh's full-length drama 'Sharvilak' is based on the two Sanskrit classics: Daridra Charudatta and Mrichhakatikam. In this five acts drama the author has skilfully drawn on these two sources, he has treated the plot in an entirely new way, thus making it an original creative piece. The playwright has also made use of certain materials from Pratijñayaugandharayana, another Sanskrit play by Bhasa. Critic Utpal Bhayani has stated that the work cannot be labelled as a piece of translation or even transcreation. The craftmanship of the playwright is displayed in turning an original 'shringar' (erotic) play into a socio-political play by efficiently changing the characterisation. At the sametime the original love affair between Charudatta and Vasantasena is not omitted here. But instead of focussing only on this couple, the playwright has given a new dimension of political revolution and coup which has deeply affected the whole city of Ujjain. This is achieved by giving a totally new yet historical context to Sharvilak and a key role to his beloved Madanika. Alongwith this, we witness the fanaticism and political manipulations of Prime Minister Bharata Rohataka, the constant helpless movements of King Palaka from his court to his bedroom events which lead queen Svetapadma to search for her lover and the malice of Shakara, a character who remains as much of a clown as the villain. With the help of these new roles to the original characters, the entire city of the Ujjain is enlivened in different layers before us and we can participate with the people of Ujjain in political changes.

In Gujarati stage, this play has been performed many a times looking at the size and the arrangement of some of the scenes, there is no reason why one should have any doubt about its stagebility. The National School of Drama staged the Hindi version of Rasiklal Parikh's Gujarati play 'Sharvilak' in 1989. The play was rendered in Hindi by Randheer Upadhyaya and Shanti lal Jain and directed by Bansi Kaul. While presenting this play to the Hindi audience Shri Bansi Kaul in his director's note has mentioned that this play for me and the whole cast is a step forward in the search for 'Indian Realism'. I have always felt that we should evolve our own realism, like France or Germany, or any other western nation did, and nor reproduce a watered down misunderstood version of western realism. I find our classical plays provide an interesting example of their own kind of realism; it is like being on the razor's edge where you face the danger of being either naturalistic or completely stylised. Further in our classical tradition lies a fluidity of time and space which is a liberating challenge. Thus Sharvilak for me provided an ample base to launch this search. For though *Sharvilak* is inspired from Bhasa's Charudatta and Shudrak's *Mrichhkatikam* yet it is almost like a new script, in which there are old characters but with added highlights and dimensions as well as some new characters. The basic underlying tone of the play is 'change of power' through a civil uprising. Social and political change is relevant in any period. Thus it has significance and appears new. Even the characters appear as full-fledged human beings with multidimensional personalities. For instance Sharvilak is not just Madanika's lover or a petty thief but the motivating factor in installing Aryak to power through a civil uprising. Vasantsena of *Mrichhkatikam* is not just meant for Shringar and pining for Charudatta but participates in uprising and questions Aryak the new ruler whether 'people like Arya Charudatt will not be murdered'. Similarly Madanika is not just Vasantsena's maid and Sharvilak's lover but contributes to the uprising. Similarly other characters, revolutionaries are not depicted as heroic characters but they have their weak points also like gambling and womanising. Love is seen as an important dimension in the life of revolutionaries, it reinforces and inspires them.

The form of the play is such that actors sometimes extend their voices to play with locales so as to create a sense of time and space that transcends the physical into the cosmic and thus creates an imaginary space in the mind of the audience while being physically present on the stage. This has been done by extension of words or movements, postures or by sounds.

The set is designed in an oval shape similar to an artiste's palette which holds different colours (characters). Light design is such that it adds to the flow of the play. There is never a moment of total darkness on the stage. As one scene fades out another fades in immediately thus imparting its own rhythm.

Music in this play is a protagonist, it has its own individual character. As the story is not linear, but multi-structured, it is the music which knits the episodes together. For example the alaaps are not just musical exercises but represent the voice of the people of Ujjain who have participated in the civil uprising. Property also has a symbolic significance in the play, like the cart in *Mrichhkatikam* or the ring of *Abhigyan Shakuntalam*. Here the rajmudra (state seal) and uttariya (stole) gain a symbolic expression in the play.

"This production initiates us into the search of a new idiom."

The cast of National School of Drama production of 'Sharvilak' (1989) is given below:

ON STAGE

Sharvilak	Shrivallabh Vyas
Nandanak	Bapi Bose
Dardurak	Ashok Lokhande
Charudutt	Vijay Shukla
Maitrak	Anupam Shyam
Palak	Abhijit Lahiri
	Surendra Prasad
Bharat Rohtak	Ravi Khanwilkar
Shakar	Lokendra Trivedi
Vit Shashak	Gajendra Nayak
Vasantsena	Himani Shivpuri
Madanika	Seema Biswas
Shwetpadma	Hema Singh
Madhav, Kapalik,	Motilal Khare
Vardhmanak	
Aryak, Mathur/Man-1	Amit Banerjee
Chatur / Kapalik	Mukesh Saxena
Sthavarak / Citizen	Gautam Chatterjee
Pravahanik / Soldier / Man-4	Aman Gupta
Pravahanik / Soldier / Man-2	Aveg Flora
Man-3 / Citizen	Sandeep Chaudhary
Radanika	Neelima Sharma
Vasantsena's mother,	
Sadhwee	Nutan Surya
Cheti	Kavita Vaid
Dasi	Prem Lata
Rohsen	Kanu Sharma
Main singer	Ram Dayal Sharma

OFF STAGE

Music direction	Bhaskar Chandavarkar
Assistant	Mahendra Sharma
Set design	Bansi Kaul
Assistant	Bapi Bose
Costume design	Dolly Ahluwalia
Assistants	Gajendra Nayak, Neelima Sharma, Bharat Singh Negi
Costume tailoring	Charanjeet Singh
Properties design	Nutan Surya
Assistants	Motilal Khare, Kavita Vaid, Bharat Singh Negi
Set in-charge	Abhijit Lahiri, Surendra Prasad
Assistants	Aveg Flora, Aman, Sandeep, Gautam
Set execution	Abdul Hakim, Bachan Singh, Sant Ram
Panels designed / painted	Ashis Swamy, Sukhvindar Singh
Painter	Rakha Ram
Main singer	Ram Dayal Sharma
Instrumentalists	Om Prakash, Rakesh Prasanna, Afzal Zahoor, Mahendra Sharma Lokendra Trivedi, Gautam Chatterjee

Make-up	Mukesh Saxena, A.P.C. Arackal
Brochure / Exhibition	Himani Shivpuri, Hema Singh, Shrivallabh Vyas, Lokendra Trivedi

Sponsored by 'Kadambari', Bangalore, NSD staged 'Sharvilak' at Chowdiah Memorial Hall, Bangalore on December 22, 1990. Again Maharashtra Kalaupasak sponsored the production on January 3, 1991 and was performed in Tilak Smarak Mandir, Pune. This was followed by another enactment on 10 January, 1991 at the Nehru Centre Auditorium, Bombay, sponsored by the Dynamic Club, Bombay.

Four scenes from NSD production of 'Sharvilak' in Hindi

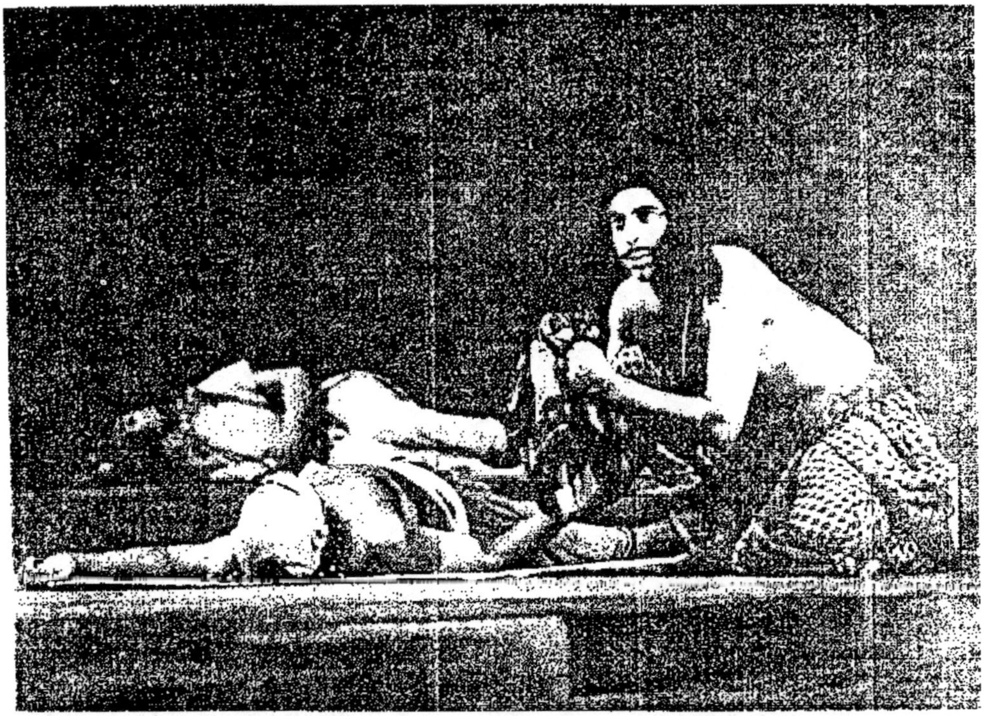

(v) Dutaghatotkacha in Performance

Dutaghatotkacha was staged in Sanskrit by the Harinam Pradayini Sabha, Varanasi in the year 1968.

On the occasion of Sastyabdapurti (61st birthday) of Dr. V. Raghavan, the Samskrita Ranga organised a programme on that auspicious event in the month of August 1968. The students of the Drama Training School of Madras Natya Sangh (of which Dr. Raghavan was the President) staged Dūtaghatotkaca of Bhasa in Tamil, rendered by Dr. Raghavan and Smt. Priyamvada Sankar on 23rd August 1968, at the Museum Theatre, Madras.

In the year 1980, Dutaghatotkacha was again produced in Hindi by M.K.Raina in the Bhasa Festival organised by the Madhya Pradesh Natak Lok Kala Academi at Ujjain. Here the choras recited the verses and main characters entered behind a Rangapati held by two stage hands.

M.K. Raina, Sangeet Natak Akademi Laureate who directed 'Dutaghatotkacha' & 'Karnabharam' of Bhasa in Hindi.

(vi) Dutavakya in Performance

Balraj Pandit

Balraj Pandit directd Dutavakya in Hindi in the year 1976 at Delhi and the venue was Little Theatre Group.

A composite production entitled 'Duryodhana' comprising of Pancharatra, Dutavakya and Urubhanga in Chhatisgarhi was presented by Habib Tanvir's Naya Theatre, New Delhi in 1979. At the Kilidasa Festival, 1980, Shri Dhirendra Kumar presented 'Dutavakyam of Bhasa.

A Bhasa Festival was organised by the Madhya Pradesh Natak Lok Kala Academi at Ujjain in 1980 in which Dutavakyam in Sanskrit by Shrinivas Rath was one of the six plays staged.

The concept of Tanatu Natakavedi, the tradition - based plays of K.N. Panikkar and the steady work done by his theatre group named Sopanam inspired a large number of theatre artists and made tremendous impact on the theatre of Kerala.

K.N. Panikkar

Sri Panikkar produced plays of Bhasa, namely Dutavakya, Karnabharam, Madhyamav-yayogam and Urubhangam, in a style evolved by the re-creation of the theatre practices defined in the Natyasastra on the model of those found in the regional forms of Kerala. These productions were widely recognized as valuable contributions to modern Indian theatre, acknowledgement of the important role that a regional idion could play in revitalizing national theatre.

In the Kalidasa Festival at Ujjain, Kavalam Narayana Panikkar produced Dutavakya in Sanskrit for the Kalidas Akademi in 1980.

Dutavakyam was presented in Sanskrit by Rajendra Upadhyay at Varanasi in the year 1985 under the banner of Abhinaya Bharati.

Govardhan Panchal

Govardhan Panchal, the winner of the Gujarat Government's prestigious Omkar Thakur Award had inmatched zeal for Sanskrit theatre. *The Hindu* on 6 August 1993 issue mentions that under his able guidance, the Gurujara Sanskrit Rangam - an academy of Sanskrit drama and culture bassed in Ahmedabad, of which he was the President, produced Bhasa's Dutavakyam.

At the fall of the century, Pratibha Sanskritik Santhan's presentation Dutavakyam marks the revival of Sanskrit theatre in Delhi. The production was sponsored by the Department of Culture, Ministry of Human Resource Development.

The group produced Bhasa's Dutavakyam in Hindi on 12 April 1998 at Triveni Garden Theatre. Also staged in the Basement Theatre of Shri Ram Centre (SRC), the play was directed and choreographed by Bhumikeshwar Singh. The Sanskrit classic was choreographed in the energetic Seraikella Chhau style. All the actors had gone through rigorous training in order to put up this experimental production. The acting was impressive and their dance movements were generally clean and precise.

A scene from Pratibha Sanskritik Sansthan's Hindi version of 'Dutavakyam' [1998]

In the original text, there are only six actors and characters that appear on stage, while Pratibha Sanskrit Sansthan's production had a lost of actors. Critic Smita Nirula writes about the set design and production in the following words: "A simple set with boundaries defined by the traditional four flag posts signifying the four points of direction, the only 'piece' on stage was a two-tiered circular platform which became a throne or a pedestal as required. Behind this on a black curtain was a white circle effectively lit to highlight certain scenes. A well designed and conceived drama, she adds that technically the production was excellent with effective lighting by Himanshu B-Joshi, costumes by G.S. Bedi and Bhagirath Bhardwaj and set properties and ornaments by Rajendra.

The main Dramatis Personae included:

Bhima: Bhagirath Bhardwaj

Duryodhana: G.S. Bedi

Sudarshana: Bhumikeshwar Singh

Vasudeva: Jitendra

Sutradhar, Kaumodaki Gada & Sahadeva: Jay Ram Mahto.

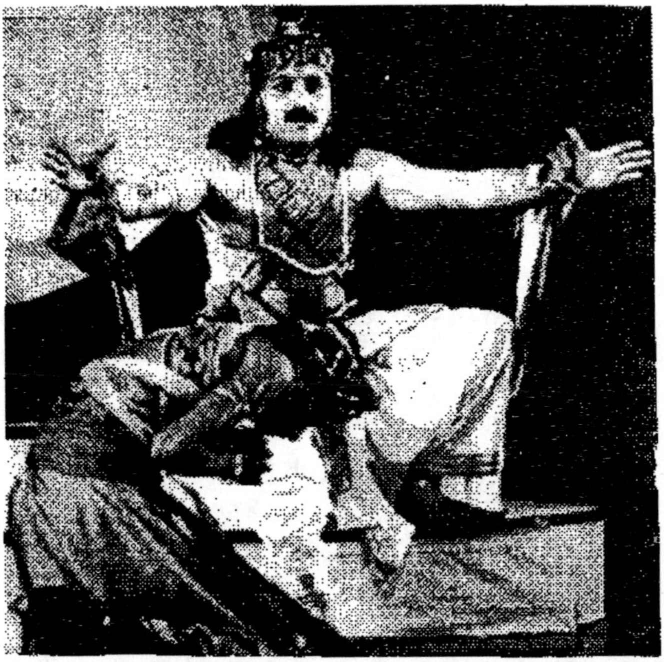

'Dutavakyam' in Hindi; directed and choreographed by Bhumikeshwar Singh [Pratibha Sanskritik Sansthan]

(vii) Karnabharam in Performance

Balodyam of Bombay staged Karnabharam in Sanskrit in the year 1980 under the direction of Shanta Gandhi.

Kalidas Akademi, Ujjain presented Karnabharam in Sanskrit and was directed by Dhirendra Kumar in the year 1981 for the Kalidas Akademi, Ujjain. Karnabharam in Hindi was directed by M.K. Raina in 1980 and was enacted at Ujjain in the Bhasa Festival, organised by the Madhya Pradesh Natak Lok Kala Akademi. The production was comparatively more formal than his other productions such as Svapnavasavadatta, Madhyamavyayoga etc. Karnabhara was more like a long, static monologue with only the Karna-Indra sequence enacted as a flashback.

Kalidasa Festival at Ujjain was founded in 1957 and since then, it had been primarily concerned with academic work, including routine productions of some Sanskrit plays. The Festival was reorganised in 1974 to seek active involvement of serious theatre worker from all parts of the country. Renowned directors were invited to produce a Sanskrit play in the original or in any modern Indian vernacular at Ujjain, or with their own troupe and bring it to the Annaul Kalidasa Festival. In 1984, Kavalam Narayan Pannikar produced Karnabharam in Sanskrit with his own troupe 'Sopanam' in the festival. In this production Panikkar created from a very short text of the play, a two hour absorbing theatre, showing a great warrior, endowed with Supreme human qualities, torn by a shattering inner conflict right at the battle-field. It was a unique enactment of, to use his own words, 'The eternal interactions of the elements of Nature', 'an endless story in which the indomitable will of man struggles for his ultimate liberation.' A classic, thus, became truly contemporary. Visually, the mining of animals in the flashback sequnce with Indra disguised as a Brahmin, the use of small cymbals as weapons in the battle-field scene and many other element were handled with a fascinating theatrical imagination. Shri. K.N. Pannikkar has contributed largely in the revival of Sanskrit dramas. In Bhāsa's Karnabharam he truly embibed the essence of the ancient drama.

Karnabharam was presented by Rajendra Upadhyay in Sanskrit at Varanasi in the year 1986.

Karnabharam in Hindi was produced by Prabhat Kumar Bhattacharya at Ujjain in 1986 for the M.P. Natak Lok Kala Academy.

After Urubhangam in 1981 and followed by Chakravyuha (based on the Drona Parva from the Mahabharata) Chorus Repertory Theatre of Ratan Thiyam completed its Mahabharata trilogy with another Bhasa play. 'Karnabharam' in 1991. Sunil Kothari writes that from the slim text of a few pages by Bhasa, Thiyam created an amazing sub-text, elaborated upon the episodes and developed the play with highly charged visuals, bathed in imaginative lighting which he nimself designed and costomes of arresting colours ... Karna on his way to the battlefield (the horses are suggested by pung players) are scenes one can never forget. Thiyam uses traditional Manipuri forms for spectacular effect.

Ratan Thiyam, the director of 'Karnabharam

(viii) Madhyamavyayoga in Performance

Shanta Gandhi

With the students of the National School of Drama in Delhi, Shant Gandhi (where she was teaching Sanskrit theatre) produced Madhyamavyayoga in Hindi, in the year 1964.

Nemi Chandra Jain observes: With her earlier experience of constructing a wooden model of the Vikrishta Madhyam Natyamandapa according to Natyashastra, and her active involvement in the traditional theatre forms, she attempted now to explore various processes for authentically presenting a Sanskrit play to modern audiences. In her production of Madhyamavyayoga, though staged in the small Studio Theatre in Rabindra Bhavan, she tried to create a feel of the Sanskrita Ranga, of Rangapitha, *Rangashivra*, Mattavarini, etc. There was an elaborate Poorvaranga with music and dance, and in the main play also a judicious inter play of different rasas in the text, a careful mix of the Natyadharmi and Lokadharmi, using rhythmic movement, mime, prose and recitative verse dialogue, straight and mask-like make-up and so on. Since it was an exercise for the trainees, the main emphasis was, naturally, on understanding the staging methods and conventions outlined in the Natyashastra in relation to the play. But it was also, undoubtedly. a satisfying artistic theatre experience even for the ordinary spectators.

The Hindi version was rendered by Panchanan Pathak. The Cast included as follows:-

ON STAGE	
Madhyam Yuvak	G. Kumara Varma
Ma	Pramila Sachdev
Hidimba	Veena Dhar
Nati	Usha Sathe
Nat	Kamlakar Sontakke
Father	Ram Gopal Bajaj
Elder Son	Virendra Sharma
Bheem	B.L. Chopra
Ghatotkacha	V.P. Bali
OFF STAGE	
Lights	G.N. Dasgupta
Costumes	Kokila Mawani
Music	Sushil Dasgupta
Recorded / Played by	J.N. Kaushal

A scene from Bhāsa's 'Madhyam Vyayog'; directed by Shanta Gandhi for the National School of Drama (1966)

Harinam Pradayini Sabha of Varanasi staged Bhasa's Madhyamavyayoga in Sanskrit in the year 1968.

In 1974, Radha Vallabh Tripathi directed Madhyamavyayoga in Sanskrit at Sagar (M.P.) produced by the Natya Parishad, Sanskrit Department. Sagar University.

Since late seventees, Thiruvarang Drama Troupe of Trivandrum has been concentrating its energies in the production of Bhasa plays in the prestine purity and form in which they were conceived. The inspiration for taking up this formidable challenge of presenting the Bhasa plays in their orginal Sanskrit version, in variation from their earlier attempts at presenting Sanskrit plays in the form of adaptation to Malayalam, came from the organisers of Kalidas Samaroh, Ujjain sponsored jointly by the Madhya Pradesh Kala Parishad and the Govenment of Madhya Pradesh. It is only in the fitness of things that the play 'Madhyamavyayoga' of Bhasa was presented at the Kalidas Samaroh in 1979.

Cast

Sutradhara	-	Nedumudy Venu
Brahmana	-	Krishnankutty Nair
Prathama	-	Subramanya Pillai
Madhyama	-	Kaladharan
Thrithiya	-	Jayaraj
Brahmani	-	L.R. Rugmini
Ghatotkacha	-	S. Jagannathan
Bhima	-	Balakrishnan (Sasthamkotta)
Hidimba	-	Gopalakrishnan

Curtain Dancers

Jayanthan

Damodaran Namboothiri

S.Gopinathan Nair

Visakhan

Choreography

M.Parmeswara

Menon (Nattavan)

Chengaarppally Aniyan

Vadithrem

R.Padmanabhan, Kavalam Vasudevan

Music

Sreekumar (Kavalam)

Production

Charge :- K.S. Narayana Pillai

Make-up :- Gopi, Pujappura

Direction :- Kavalam Narayana Panikkar and Aravindan

Ten scenes from Bhasa's 'Madhyamavyayogam'; produced by Sopanam, Thiruvananthapuram and directed by K.N. Panikkar, 1978.

It was at the instance of the Kalidasa Festival that Kavalam Narayana Panikkar agreed to undertake his now widely acclaimed production of Madhyamavyayoga. A drama critic observes that in this production, Panikkar attempted to explore, apart from the 'basic human feelings with all its blemishes, frailities, prejudices, partialities', etc. a deeper meaning of 'madyamatra' or the 'middleness' and the 'tritva' or the 'threeness' in the play. This reveals a very significant philosophical dimension not only of Bhasa's work but also of the director's approach to the theatre. Similarly, his orchestration of 'Karma' 'Hasya' 'Veera' and 'Shrinagara', with sympathy, irony and insight, his treatment of various emotional or structural motifs, his use of rhythm in controlling both Angika and Vachika, the movement and speech and a number of other elements have made his production of Madhyamavyayoga, a memorable theatre experience. It is interesting to find him varying the inner relationship and treatment of these elements in his two versions of this play in 1980 and then again in 1987.

Kavalam Narayana Panikkar established his theatre compnay 'Sopanam' in 1974 at Trivandrum, capital city of Kerala. He is regarded as a major factor in the revival of pan-Indian interest in and understanding of the rich theatrical potential of the Sanskrit classics by producing them in Sanskrit. Philip B. Zarrilli has rightly observed that he interweave dance, music, stylized movement, vibrant vocalization and acting into a unique whole in his dramas. Amongst his sanskrit productions mention could be made of 'Madhyamvyayog' of Bhāsa which he produced in Sanskrit.

Costumes for Madhyamavyayoga

Bhima:- Bhima is a prince in exile - living in forest - he is very strong in physic - seen as engaged in physical exercises. Elements suggesting his princely grandier, superhuman, prowess and wild life are combined; instead of a crown he wears a head gear which befits his present plight. His valour is suggested by a breast plate and the protruding palm sheath ornaments tied on the arms and wrists. The pleated loin cloth (umbralla skirt) worn is in a manner structurally balancing the outfits in the upper portion of the body and representing the 'dhirodatta' quality of Bhima Terra verte green colour suits his life in exile.

Ghatotkacha :- The demon Ghatotkacha who has inherited the qualities of his princely father as well as those of his demonish mother, also wears a breast plate, to indicate his wild strength, made of natural material - the dried grass - his ornaments as well consist of articlesmade of similar materials like tender cocoanut leaves... Ghatotkacha's umbralla skirt in yellow is covered with dried coconut leaves. His long untied hair and the crust made of grass reveal both his way of life and prominance.

Hidimba:- Hidimba is essentially of demonish origin-her basic nature is marked by the canine teeth and by the protruding breasts common for demons in all traditional art forms of Kerala. Her matted hair is tied on the top by a string made of stones and beads. Ornaments also are of similar nature-her umbralla skirt is black in contrast with that of her son who inherit his fathers with that of her son who inherits his fathers qualities also. Her loin cloth also is covered with dried cocoanut leaves.

Brahmin Family:- Elements of Kudiyattom and Kathakali are adopted in the make up of the brahmin and the members of his family who are depicted in the play merely as simple, timid persons who are subjected to great misfortune.The general colour scheme is based on elements of our traiditional and folk art forms to suit the mood in the characters in the play.

[Courtesy:- G. Aravindam]

M.K. Raina presented Madhyamavyayoga of Bhasa in Hindi at the Bhasa Festival organised by the Madhya Pradesh Natak Lok Kala Academi at Ujjain in 1980. In his production. he under lined the Vatsalya or parental love in the Brahmin family as well as between Bhima and Ghatotkacha. Raina attempted to use the elements of folk musical performances in movements. mime. speech, songs, etc with brief Poorvaranga based on Kathak dance and classical music.

(ix) Pancaratra in Performance

A composite production entitled 'Duryodhana' comprising of Pancharatra. Dutavakya and Urubhanga in Chhatisgarhi was presented by Habib Tanvir's Naya Theatre, New Delhi in 1979.

Habib Tanvir, the Fellow of Sangeet Natak Akademi; director of Pancaratra, Dutavakya and Urubhanga a composite production in Chhatisgarhi.

(x) Pratijṇayaugandharayana in Performance

In Kutiyattam idiom, the Act Three of Bhasa's Pratijṇayaugandharayana entitled Mantrankom takes fortyone nights for one performance.

The Act specially chosen for Kutiyattam performances are:-

(i) Manthra

(ii) Mahasena

Every year, the Peruvanam Temple in the village of Cherpu, Trichur District, Kerala presents a performance of Mantrankam, the Act Three of the play 'Pratijṇayaugandharayana' by Bhasa. Susan Oleksiw after witnessing Kudiyattam performance of Mantrãnkam given by the Peruvanam Temple from July 7 to August 16, 1976 remarked: "The performance of Mantrankam at Peluvanam Temple is part of a long tradition that offers to the temple deity the best works of its poets and to its audience an opportunity to hear tales of ancient heroes and obsorb the values of a cultural tradition hundreds of year old..."

Archival Recording (1995):

Kutiyatam Mahotsavam organised by the Sangeet Natak Akademi from 24-29 March 1995 came as an extension of a special project of support to Kutiyattam being implemented by the Akademi since 1991.

The Festival featured eleven performances presenting different acts and scenes from four well-known ancient dramas of Shaktibhadra Bodhyana, Kulasekhara Varman and Abhisekha Natakam of Bhasa.

On this occasion of Kutiyattam Mahotsavam, special archival recordings of the demonstration of Mantrankam by Kitangur Kuttappa Chakyar was done and is available for the theatre-scholars.

(xi) Pratimanatakam in Performance

Mumbai Marathi Sahitya Sangh staged D.G. Godse's Marathi version of Bhasa's 'Pratimanatakam'. Godse himself designed the Natyashastra oriental stage. In 'Dhadila Ram Tine ka vain' deals with the story of Rama and Sita in a new light as interpreted by Bhasa. In his production, the songs played very significant place. The lyrics were written by Raja Badhe and were tuned to classical ragas by Jitendra Abhisheki Daji Bhatwadekar, directed the play and himself portrayed the character 'King Dasharath'.

At Ujjain, Pratimanatakam of Bhasa was presented in Sanskrit in 1978 under the direction of Prabhat Kumr Bhattacharya for the M.P. Natak Lok Kala Academy.

'Pratimanatakam' of Bhasa was enacted in Sanskrit together with Uttararamacarit entitled 'Pratimottra' by the M.P. Natak Lok Kala Academy. Ujjain under the direction of Prabhat Kumar Bhattachary in 1985.

From 'Pratimanatakam', the Acts specially chosen for Kutiyattam performances are:-

(i) Vischinnabhisheka (The Coronation of Rama that did not take place)

(ii) Vilapa (The sorrow and death of King Dasaratha)

(iii) Atavi (Rama and Sita in exile in the forest)

(iv) Asoka Vanika (The King of Lanka and his vain efforts to persuada Sita to accept him)

(v) Bharata (The role of Bharata deputising for Rama during the latter's exile)

(vi) Abhiseka (The coronation of Rama)

Trivandrum Cultural Society's Kutiyattam Kalotsavam's brochure of July 1985 informs us that some decade ago, the Chakyars had combined Bhasa's 'Pratima' and 'Abhisekha' with Saktibhadra's 'Ascaryacudamani' and presented it as Ramayana. This programme comprising of twentyone acts, took a whole year to perform.

(xii) Svapnavasavaatta in Performances

There is evidence to show that Sanskrit dramas were staged in various parts of India in ancient times, but how far they were effective in conveying the several literary attributes and sentiments contemplated by the dramatist, we do not know. It is here that the Kutiyattam type of performance scores over others. On the Kutiyattam stage the performer goes far beyond the ideas of the dramatist. The text of the drama serves, in many cases, only as a nucleus. The actor angments it many fold and brings in all the implied and remok ideas and expresses them in complete form, with definitions, annotations as well as lengthy believable and unbelievable stories of a realistic and unrealistic nature, with sative, obscenities and stinging humour in prose and verse. Philosophy, politics, social behaviour are all covered in the performance. In many, the spirit of the sloka is rendered in gestures, making lengthy excursions into undiscovered and unexpected fields of artistic splendour. The result is that Kutiyattam takes several nights to perform a single drama. That is why usually only one act of a drama is chosen for performance and thus it is the act which has the significance rather than the whole drama. Each act is known by its own name. For instance, Bhasa's Svapnavasavadatta is never known as such, but by the names:-

(i) Brahmacaryankom (The Act One)

(ii) Pandatankom (The Act Second)

(iii) Pootudankom (The Act Third)

and so on. In modern times, Svapnavasavadatta has been staged serveral times.

'Svapnavasavadattam' in Kutiyattam style

A.R. Rajaraja Varma wrote Svapnavasavadatta of Bhasa in Malayalam in the year 1918. The translation and production of a new play became an annual feature of 'Kalavilasam', the most established drama troupe of Trivandrum Keraliya Svapnavasavadatta was a success but there was less of humour in it than in other plays. The clown makes his appearance only in the fourth act. The atmosphere on the whole is less jubilant. The translation was done with ease and delight. A.R. Rajaraja Varma was able to identify himself with the spirit and temper of Bhasa so well that the translation rose to the level of transcreation that explains the excellence of this work which happened to be the last translation of this astute playwright.

Bhasa's 'Vasavadatta' was staged on 15 January 1921 at 'Star Theatre', Calcutta. The play was rendered into Bengali by Apareshchandra Mukhopadhyay.

Amongst the varied functions and entertainments arranged for the distinguished delegates outside India, was a performance of the Svapnavasavadatta in Sanskrit by the Fifth Oriental Conference held at Lahore in November 1928.

The Thirteenth Session of the 'All India Oriental Conference' was held at Nagpur from 19th - 21st October, 1946, under the auspices of the Nagpur University. In this conference. 'Svapnavāsavadatta' of Bhasa was performed in Sanskrit.

In Delhi, the first performance of Bhasa play was in 1956, It was his magnum opus 'Svapnavasavadatta' in Hindi, directed by H.V. Gupte and presented by the Song and Drama Division of the Ministry of Information and Broadcasting, Government of India. It was played on the broad open-air Talkatora Garden Theatre, as a critic puts it, in the more or less mixed heroic realistic style, typical of the earlier Marathi Theatre, it attracted attention as much because of some restrained acting by the performers as the freshness of the play itself.

On 27th December 1957, the Students of Indraparastha College for Women, Delhi staged the drama 'Svapnavāsavadatta' in Sanskrit at the New Convocation Hall, University of Delhi at the 19th Session of the All India Oriental Conference.

Mrinalini Sarabhai; directed Svapnavasavadatta in English (1963)

At the Institute for Advanced Studies in the Theatre Arts, New York, The vision of Vasavadattā was produced in English under the direction of Mrinalini Sarabhai in the year 1963.

The Vision of Vasavadatta, Act Six. Directed by Mrinalini Sarabhai for the Institute for Advanced Studies in the Theatre Arts, New York. King Udayana [Reid Shelton] is remined of his beloved Vasavadatta as he plays the vina, while the jester Vasantaka [Harold Cherry] listens.

South Asian Studies Committee of the Asian Studies Program, University of Hawaii, Honolulu, organised and convened an international conference on Sanskrit drama in performance in the spring of 1974. It was for the first time scholars had met together in the West to discuss this aspect of Sanskrit drama. Seminar papers were read by scholars from the United States, India, and Europe. For participants in the conference, the sense of Sanskrit drama as living theatre was enhanced by the second part of the program. The University of Hawaii, Department of Drama and Theatre, in cooperation with the Department of Music, The College of Continuing Education and Community Services, the Asian Studies Program, The East-

West Center, and The State Foundation on Culture and the Arts (Hawaii), presented Bhasa's magnumopus, 'The vision of Vāsavadatta'. This ancient play was enacted at Kennedy Theatre in Honolulu, from 15-24 March 1974 during the 'International Conference of the Art of Sanskrit Drama in Performance'. The play was directed by Shanta Gandhi, a Senior Fellow at the East-West Center. The Vision of Vāsavadatta' is an example of a play based on the rasa of love and is therefore, a typical Sanskrit drama. It was chosen even though Gandhi feels it is a difficult play for an American audience to appreciate. She had to made specific decisions in the course of rehearsals: how to maintain a balance between prose and sung verses; how to design scenery and costumes; how to place her performers on the stage; what type of curtain to use; the amount and kind of gesture language to strive for; and how to incorporate music and dance into the production. In her own words: A special directing approach is necessary when a cast is non-Indian. For the production. Paul Cravath prepared a new acting version of the play under the director's supervision written in American English for American audiences, it was intended to be actable while remaining faithful in spirit and form to the original. The Sanskrit text and previous English translations were consulted. The verses (śloka) were written and rewritten many times in the attempt to find English to fit Sanskrit metrical patterns. Eleven meters are used: anuṣṭubh, aryḍ, harinī, puṣpitāgrā, śālinī, śārdūlavikrīḍita, śikharinī, upajāti, upendravajra, vaiśvadevī, and vasantatilakā. The meters occuring most frequently are anuṣṭubh (twenty-six times) and vasantatilakā (eleven times). Of the fifty-seven verses used in the Gandhi production, most were sung in English (verses 1, 34, and 57 were sung in both Sanskrit and English; verses 27, 32, 33, 35, 36, 46, 47, 48 and 50 were spoken. Rachel Van M. Baumer, the then Chariman of the South Asia Studies Program at the University of Hawaii comments that in this production, Shanta Gandhi made every effort to achieve an authentically Indian style of performance, utilizing, in so far as they could be known or imagined, the techniques of the classical stage. The Play provided conference members with an intensely interesting laboratory experience, and it commanded the largest public response of the University's Theatre season.

In her production of Svapnavasavadatta in Honolulu she emphasised Veera Rasa (Karmaveera, Dharmaveera) keeping the Vipralambha Shringara as secondary. The treatment was mainly Natyadharmi, using dance like movements, music and recitation in speech. Though the work was with trainees, physically as well as culturally away from the milieu of the play, she found the experience rewarding.

Ten scenes from 'The Vision of Vasavadatta'; produced by the Asian Theatre Program, University Theatre, University of Hawaii, 1974. Directed by Shanta Gandhi; musical direction by M.Y.Kamashastri.

[As part of the invocation ritual of the prologue, the Style Manager carries Indra's Flag staff. The Flag Bearer and the Bearer of the Golden Pitcher raise their hands praying for a successful performance as described in the Natyasastra].

The Vision of Vāsavadattā, Act One. Queen Vāsavadattā is stopped by the Guards of Yaugandharāyaṇa, as Stage Manager, playing the Chamberlain to King Udayana, watches.

The Vision of Vasavadatta, Act Two. Queen Vasavadatta, Padmavati, and Maids are playing ball.

The Vision of Vasavadatta, Act Three. Madhukarikā and Padminika, two maids weave flower garlands with Queen Vasavadatta (using formal hand gestures, as described in the Natyasastra)

The Vision Vāsavadattā, Act Four. Vasantaka, the jester stung by a bee, stands in the central area of the open stage marked by sacred paintings. In keeping with ancient staging practices. Vāsavadattā, Padmāvatī and two Maids are imagined to be peeking out unseen, from a bower on one side of the garden, while the Jester and King Udayana are trying to hide in foliage in another part of the garden.

The Vision Vāsavadattā, Act Five. King Udayana pulling a bow string as he sings the verse, "Our arrows shall fall in waves that crash down upon his ranks. "The Stage Manager, standing to the king's right, takes the role of the Chamberlain who has just announced that the enemy is attacking. The Jester watches.

The Vision Vāsavadattā, Act Five. The scene of the play's title, in which King Udayana, dreaming telles Vāsavadattā of his love for her.

The Vision of Vāsavadattā, Act Six. King Udayana plays the vīṇā and sings, remembering Vāsavadattā. The Jester looks on.

The Vision of Vāsavadattā, Act Six. King Udayana gives Vāsavadattā's portrait to Padmāvatī, as the Nurse, Chamberlain, and Guard look on.

The Vision of Vāsavadattā, Act Six. Queen Vāsavadattā is led into King Udayana's presence by Padmāvatī. Yaugandharāyana, Chamberlain, Nurse, and Guard look on.

Nadira Zaheer Babbar

Nadira Zaheer Babbar directed Svapnavasavadatta in Hindi entitled 'Raja ka sapna' at Delhi in the year 1978 under the banner of Agradoot. This play was staged in Kalidasa Festival at Ujjain.

Svapnavasavadatta was presented in Hindi at the Bhasa Festival organised by the Madhya Pradesh Natak Lok Kala Academi, Ujjain in 1980 under the direction of M.K. Raina. He utilized the folk musical performances in movements, mime, speech, songs, etc. with brief Poorvaranga based on Kathak dance and classical music. In Svapnavasavadatta he made the Vidushaka and Yaugandharayana the central characters and Hasya as the main note ridiculing the consequences of the actions of a weak ruler.

Svapnavasavadatta was produced at Ujjain in Malavi under the title a 'Sapna mein Raani' and was directed by Shrinivas Rath and Sanjeev Dixit in 1981.

Theatre Circle of New Delhi enacted Svapnavasavadatta in Hindi entitled 'Raja ka Sapna' and was directed by Ramesh Manchanda in the year 1985.

Shri Sanakhya Ebotombi directed Bhasa's Svapnavasavadatta in Shri B.V. Karanth's Hindi translation for second - year students of National School of Drama employing some traditional performing arts of Manipur like Thabalchombi and Nat Sankintara. The play was performed from 11-16 November, 1992.

A scene from the play Svapnavasavadatta. Directed by S. Ebotombi.

(xiii) Urubhangam in Performance

Bhasa's Urubhangama was enacted by National School of Drama in the years 1966-67 under the direction of Shanta Gandhi.

Ranga Shivir, Bhopal presented 'Urubhanga' in Hindi under the direction of M.K. Raina in 1976. This version was expressive and moving even without boldness and inventiveness in form and style. He emphasized the horrors of was and the resulting pathos of the situation, and created an atmosphere of the battle field by a careful and well-designed choreography of the movements of the three warriors.

'Urubhangam' of Bhasa was directed by M.K. Raina for the Ranga Shivir, Bhopal at the Kalidasa Festival of 1976.

At Ujjain, in the Kalidasa Festival, Shanta Gandhi presented Urubhanga both in Sanskrit and Hindi in 1979 for the Kalidas Akademi. Enacted on the same evening, one after another, the Sanskrit version followed by the Hindi one with a specially written Prastavana in Hindi to link them together. The Poorvaranga was only in the Sanskrit version with rhythm controlled movement and recitation of the verses. In Hindi, both the movement and speech were straight without the use of rhythm or recitation. The general theme of both was the meaninglessness of war, but in Hindi the three warriors of the Vishkambhaka were made representatives of the three main political trends of contemporary times - a radical, a religious fanatic and a supporter of the establishment. They were identified by different suggestive bands on their head dresses, and the entire Hindi production was in modern costumes with some use of masks also.

This Mahabharata play was also directed by Sri G. Kumara Varma.

G. Kumara Varma

A composite production entitled 'Duryodhana' comprising of Pancaratra, Dutavakya and Urubhanga in Chhatisgarhi was presented by Habib Tanvir's Naya Theatre, New Delhi in 1979.

In the Bhasa Festival organised by the Madhya Pradesh Lqk Kala Academi at Ujjain in 1980, Urubhangam in Hindi was presented by Raj Kumud.

Shamushang Uku is about five kilometers from Imphal. Here the director of the 'Chorus Repertory Theatre', Sri Ratan Thiyam has produced some remarkable plays based on Mahabharata epic. It was in the year 1981 with the Bhasa play 'Urubhangam' (the slaying of Duryodhana) that Thiyan left his idelible mark as an outstanding director. A critic observes with a deep and innate sense of aesthetics, he creates the perfect backdrop against which epic heroes and heroines comes alive. The fierce battles of the Mahabharata sounds of a chariot driving through, the clanging of swords, the blowing of the conch, the crescendo of Manipuri Meitei pung, the drum and the high pitched singing - fill the air as his play unfolds. Employing the Natyasastra as a premise, blending it with traditional Manipuri forms of dance, music, costumes, martial arts and a distinct body language, Thiyam took his audiences by surprise with his professional sophistication.

His theatre stood out for its chaged visuals, integrity of forms and contemporary flavour. Above all, his play succeeded in breathing the language barrier as 'Meitei' is the tongue that was employed for this classical drama.

Urubhangam is one of the most popular of Bhasa's plays and has been produced by a number of well known directors with imaginative variations in emphasis in its meaning, formal innovations and visual treatment. Thiyam took this production to the Kalidasa Festival at Ujjain. He truly suggested a close paralled with contemporary political situation in which there is very little truth on any side. The three soldiers were almost like present day camp-followers who blidnly glorify their own leaders. His Suyodhana was a sort of tragic figure who failed to achieve what he sought and ultimately persons like Ashwatthama took over.

A drama critic writes that Ratan made a very creative use of the rich traditions of Manipuri dance and movement, tunes and musical instruments, colours and designs in costumes and stage properties etc. The performance was inventively choreographed and had a fascinating lyrical quality, making it an unforgettable and moving theatrical experience.

An extension of tradition with contemporary sensibilities occur in the final scene of Karnabharam, when Karna drives off in his chariot to the battlefield. The horses are suggested by four pung cholom dancers playing drums (while dancing), their beats creating the sound of the hoofs of the galloping horses, and four dancers on the sides taking circular movements with drums in their hands suggest the rotation of the wheels. The understanding of traditional forms and their creative usage set Ratan Thiyam apart from others who had been inserting dance into theatre.

In his production of Urubhangam in Hindi with the students of the National school of Drama in 1983, Kavalam Narayana Panikkar not only underlined the meaninglessness of war, but also related it to the inner conflict of Duryodhana. He created three different images of Duryodhana - as a representative of the Kaurava might, as an ordinary human being tormented at the moment of his death by his own ego and failures in life, and the third, as his conscience or soul in the form of a Theyyam realising and contemplating the pointlessness of war. Nemi Chand Jain states that Urubhanga has a long narrative Vishkambhaka and Panikkar gave an inventive visual form to some of its descriptive verses. As a result, the various individual and group combats, divine nymphs welcoming the dead heroes, or vultures descending upon their dead bodies, and above all, the final duel between Duryodhana and Bhima became theatrically very vibrant, exciting and gripping.

Six scenes from 'Urubhangam'; produced by Drama

King Dhritarashtra on the battlefield; A National School of Drama Presentation of Bhasa's 'Urubhangam'

Duryodhana on the battlefield

The wounded Duryodhana being visited by his family on the battlefield

Ashvatthama in a belligerent mood

Two more sequences from 'Urubhangam'

In Urubhangam, Kavalam used the huge masks and costumes of Theyyam with sensitivity and imagination which made the character of Duryodhana acquire a new dimension.

Kavalam Narayana Panikkar and Phillip B. Zarilli produced Urubhanga in Sanskrit at the University of Wisconsin - Madison. Chicago in 1985.

The first great Mahotsava in Kerala on the great Sanskrit playwright of ancient times. Bhasa was held in 1987.

This was followed by another theatre festival on Bhasa at Trivandrum from 11 to 13 November 1988. As earlier, this Mahotsavam was organised by Sopanam, the wellknown theatre Group formed and led by the veteran theatre personality K.N. Panikkar, and Sangeet Natak Academi, Kerala University and various other organisations as its co-sponsors. After the inaugural session, Bhasa's 'Urubhangam' was produced by Sopanam under Panikkar's direction. Commenting on the production, critic Kironmory Raha said: what impressed me most was the absence of super fluity in the different components of the production, of a near-austerity in Panikkar's directional control.

Fringe Performances

Repertory Company of the National School of Drama launched a new programme of 'Fringe Performances' in the year 1994. The programme consist of among other activities, the play reading sessions of world classics as well as contemporary plays. The first set of presentations under the 'Fringe Performances' was the dramatic reading of two classics: Bhasa's Urubhangam in N.C. Jains Hindi translation and Bodhyan's Bhagavadajjukiyam in Bharat Bhusan Aggarwal's Hindi translation from 21 to 23 October in Studio Theatre of the Repertory Company.

Play Reading: Urubhangam (NSD)

'Urubhangam' in Hindi; directed by Satyabrat Raut and produced by Rangvasundhara, New Delhi.

'Urubhangam' of Bhasa was well staged by 'Rangvasundhara', a theatre group of Delhi under the design and direction of National School of Drama alumni Satyabrata Raut at the Shri Ram Centre in 1996. The play was chosen by the Sahitya Kala Parishad for its Bharatendu Theatre Festival. The production was worth seeing for those interested in classical theatre. Sponsored by the Sangeet Natak Akademi, the play was staged repeatedly because of the encouraging response from the audience. Rendered into Hindi by Bharat Bhusan Aggarwal, this play received applause from theatre critic that conformed to the basic format of classical theatre-poetic narration, speech rhythm, exaggerated gesturing, music and dance. Chhau dance based choreography by Bhumikeshwar Singh and Parag Chapekar's sound direction (particularly the noise of the vultures) enriched the production above all, the acting was impressive that called for heavy emoting.

On 5 March 1995, The Repertary Company of the National School of Drama staged Bhasa's Urubhangam for the participants of the National Theatre Workshop organised by Sangeet Natak Akademi in Delhi.

Costume Design for Urubhangam:

Aśvatthama: [Top knot with a halmet (Śiraṣakaṭāha) from Vogel, "La Sculpture de Mathura" Mat. p. xxxvi. Also from Dr. Motichandra. Costumes, Textiles, Cosmetics, Coiffure in Ancient and Mediaval India.- Delhi: Oriental Publishers, 1973.] p. 76, fig. 64 (Sanchi) and p. 85, Fig. 110 (for footwear).

Duryodhana: [Ajanta Cave 2. Ceiling detail of first aisle. Zimmer, Henrich. The Art of Indian Asia/ed. by Joseph Campbell crois. IXII.- Princeton University Press, 1955. Bollington series. pl. 159. Also from Dr. Motichandra, op. cit., p. 85, fig. 108 (Sanchi)

Baladeva: [Ajanta Cave 1. From line drawing in the Prince of Wales Museum, Bombay. Also from Dr. Motichandra, op. cit., p. 98, fig. 127 (Gandhara)]

Bibliography

PRINCIPAL WORKS

TEXT

Abhisekanāṭakam by Bhasa; ed. by C.R. Devadhar - Poona: Oriental Book Agency, 1937.

Poona Oriental seires.

Abhiṣekanāṭaka by Bhasa; ed. by T. Gaṇpati Sāstri:- Trivandrum: Government of Travancore, 1913.

iv, 76, [4]p; 24cm.- (Trivandrum Sanskrit series; 26)

Includes Index.

Based on the Ramayana, the play begins with the story of the slaying of Vālin and the consequence of Sugriva and ends with the ordeal of Sītā and the consecration of Rāma.

Abhiṣekanāṭakam by Bhasa; ed. [with a comm.] by V. Venkatarama Sastri - Lahore: Motilal Banarsidass, 1930.

83, 40p.

Includes English translation and notes.

Avimāraka/by Bhasa; ed. by T. Ganapati Sāstri.- Trivandrum: Government of Travancore, 1912.

vi, 112 [4]p; 24 cm.- (Trivandrum Sanskrit series: 207).

Includes index.

Drama portrays the love adventure of Avimāraka, Prince of Sauvīrakas, in disguise, whom a curse turned, for the time being into an out caste.

Balacharitam / by Bhasa; ed. with a Hindi tr. by S.R. Sehgal.- Delhi:

Munshiram Manoharlal, 1959.

106, 179p. 522 cm.

Bālacaritam/by Bhasa; ed. with notes by T. Ganapati Sāstri.- Trivandrum: Government of Travancore, 1912.

iv, 68 [2]p.; 24 cm.- (Trivandrum Sanskrit series; 217.)

Includes index.

Play that exhibits the feats of young Kṛṣna.

Bhāsanāṭakacakram/by Bhasa; ed. by C.R. Devadhar.- Poona: Oriental Book Agency, 1937.

xiv, 583p.; 18cm.- (Poona Oriental series; 54)

Includes Index and Appendices.

Contains thirteen plays ascribed to Bhasa. These are:- Svapnavāsavadattam, Pratijṇāyaugandharāyanam, Avimārakam, Cārudattam, Pratima, Abhiṣekanāṭ-akam, Paṇcarātram, Madhyamavyāyoga, Dūtavākyam, Dūtaghaṭotkacam, Karṇabhāram, Urubhaṇgam, Bālacaritam.

---------------: Delhi: Motilal Banarasidass, 1987.

x,2, 583 p.; 18cm.

Original thirteen texts in Devanagari.

---------------: 2nd ed.- Poona: Oriental Book Agency, 1951.

16,583 p; 18cm.

The Bhasanatakachakram: thirteen Trivandrum plays of Bhasa/ by Bhasa; ed. by Sudhakar Malaviya and others. - Varanasi: Krishnadas Academy, 1987.

2 vols; 18.5 cm.

Cārudatta/by Bhasa; ed. with notes by T. Ganapati Sāstri.- Trivandrum: Govt. of Travancore, 1914.

iv, 86 [2] p; 24 cm. - (Trivandrum Sanskrit series; 39).

Includes index.

Four acts play based on the theme of Sūdraka's Mṛcchakaṭika.

Complete Plays of Bhasa ed. by K.P.A. Menon in three volumes--Delhi; Nag Publishers, 1996 3 vol.

Dūtavākyam/by Bhāsa.- 3rd ed. - Trichur: Kerala Sahitya Akademi, 1989.

68 p.; 22 cm.

Dutavakyam/ by Bhasa; tr. into Hindi by Harivamsha Ancja - New Delhi: Kadambari Prakashan, 1977.

56 p; 21.5 cm

Includes Sanskrit text.

Madhyamavyāyoga and Paṇcarātra by Bhasa; ed. with an English translation and critical notes by Sivarām Mahādev Parāṇjpe. - Poona: The editor, 1917.

29.9 p; 21 cm.

Madhyamavyāyoga, Dutavākya, Dutaghaṭotkaca, Karṇabhara and Urubhanga/ by Bhasa; ed. with notes by T. Ganapati Sāstri. - Trivandrum: Govt. of Travancore, 1912.

iv, 114 [6] p; 24 cm. - (Trivandrum Sanskrit series, 227).

Includes Index.

The volume covers five plays based on some incidents from the epic Mahābharta.

Pancaratra/ by Bhasa; ed. by Dileep Kumar Kanjilal.- Modern Book Agency, 1973.

11, 186 p.

Paṇcarātra / by Bhasa; ed. with notes by T. Ganapati Sāstri.- Trivandrum: Govt. of Travancore, 1912.

iv, 52, [4] p; 24 cm.- (Trivandrum Sanskrit series; 170).

Includes index.

Play centres on the story of the Pāṇḍavas in disguise narrated in the Virāṭaparva of Mahābharata.

Pratijṇāyaugandharāyaṇa / by Bhasa; ed. by T. Ganapati Sāstri. - Trivandrum: Govt. of Travancore, 1912.

vi, 74, [24] p; 24 cm. - (Trivandrum Sanskrit series, 16).

Includes Index and Appendices.

Drama in four acts based on the legend of Udayana and Vāsavadattā.

Pratimānāṭkam/ by Bhasa; ed. and tr. into English by Paranjape.

Includes 'Prakāsa' commentary.

Pratimānāṭakam/ by Bhasa; ed. and tr. into English by S. Rangachar. - Bangalore: Samskrita Sahitya Sadana, 1950.

Pratimānāṭakam/ by Bhāsa; ed. tr. into English by V. Raghavan and S.S. Janaki.- Madras: Kuppuswami Sastri Research Institute, 1986.

90,61 p.

Pratimānāṭakam/ by Bhasa; ed. by C.R. Devadhar. - Poona: Oriental Book Agency, 1937.

Poona Oriental series

Pratimanatakam/ by Bhasa; ed. with Hindi and English tr. and notes in Hindi. by Kapildeva Dvivedi Acharya - Allahabad: Ramnarayanlal, 1953.

34, 498 p; 18cm.

Pratimanataka/ by Bhasa.; text with English translation by M.R. Kale.- Delhi: MLBD, 1983.

234 p.

Classical Sanskrit play on the exile of Rama, Hindu deity.

Pratimānāṭakam/ by Bhasa; ed. by T. Ganapati Sastri.- Trivandrum: [s.n.], 1915.

(Trivandrum Sanskrit series; 40,42)

Pratimānāṭakam/ by Bhasa; ed. critical, with introduction, notes, translation and appendices by C.R. Devadhar.- Poona: Sri Ganesh Priting Press, 1927.

xv, [157] p.; 21 cm.

Seven acts play on the story of the Rāmāyaṇa with special reference to the character of Bharata and Kaikeyi.

Pratimānāṭakam/ by Bhasa; ed. with Engish tr. by C.Shankara Rama Sastri.- Madras: Balamanorama Press.

Pratimānāṭaka/ by Bhasa; ed. with English translation, notes and introduction by R.P. Kāṇgle and F.C. Trivedi.- Ahmedabad: Vasanta Printing Press, 1927.

[284]; 21 cm.

Pratimānāṭakam/ by Bhasa; ed. with introduction, critical notes and appendices by Sivarām Mahādev Parāṇjpe. - Poona: Goverdhan Press, 1927.

xliv, [260] p.; 22cm.

Pratimānāṭaka/ by Bhasa; ed. with introduction in English and Sanskrit by T.Ganapati Sāstri.- Trivandrum: Govt. of Travancore, 1915.

lxxii, 116, [20] p; 24 cm.- (Trivandrum Sanskrit series; 42).

Includes Index and Appendices.

Svapnavasavadattam / by Bhasa; comm. 'Abhirava Rajalaxmi' and 'Kalabhashini' by Guruprasad Sastri and Sitaram Sastri.- Benaras: Bhargava Pustakalya, 1951.

11, 362 p; 18cm.

Svapnavasavadatta/ by Bhasa; text with English tr. by M.R. Kale.-Delhi: MLBD, 1980.

Classical Sanskrit play on Udayana and Vasavadatta legendary characters.

Svapnavāsavadattam/ by Bhasa; ed. by T. Ganapati Sastri.- 2nd ed. Trivandrum: [s.n.], 1915.

(Trivandrum Sanskrit series; 15)

Svapnavāsavadattam/by Bhasa; ed. with a commentary '*Sanjīvanī* and a Hindi translation by Vijayānanda Tripāṭhī.- Benaras: Lakṣmīnārāyaṇ Press, 1925.

viii, [184] p; 18cm.- (Sanskrit Granthamālā ; 5.)

Svapnavāsavadattam/ by Bhasa; ed. with a Sanskrit parapharase, English translation and notes by Banārasidās Jain and Madangopal Sāstrī. Lahore: Panjab Printing Works, 1920.

xxviii, [117] p; 21 cm.

Six acts play on the legend of Udayana and Vāsavadatta.

Svapnavāsavadattam/by Bhasa; ed. with introduction in English and Sanskrit by T. Ganapati Sāstrī.- Trivandrum: Govt. of Travancore, 1912.

xcviii, 78, [16] p; 24cm. - (Trivandrum Sanskrit series; 15)

Includes Index and Appendix.

Svapnavāsavadattam/ by Bhasa; ed. with introduction notes and appendices by C.R.Devadhar.- Poona: Oriental Book Agency, 1926.

xviii, [134] p; 23cm.

Svapnavāsavadattam/ by Bhasa; ed. with short Sanskrit commentary, English translation and critical notes by M.R. Kāle.- Bombay: Bombay Vaibhava Press, 1929.

xxxiv, [168] p; 22 cm.

TRANSLATIONS

ASSAMESE

[Pratimānāṭakam] Pratimā/ tr. by Khagendranāth Sāstri.- Tezpur: The translator, 1948. xii, 81 p; 19 cm.

BENGALI

Basavadatta/ by Bhasa; tr. into Bengali by Aparesh Chandra Mukhopadhyay.- Calcutta: [s.n.], [n.d.].

Staged in 1921.

Sanskrita Sahitya Sambhar / ed. by Gaurinath Sastri and... et. al. [vol.9].- Calcutta: Navpatra Prakashan, [n.d.]

Includes Bengali rendering of Bhasa's 'Abhiśeka', 'Dutavakya', 'Dutagatotkacha' and 'Urubhanga'.

Sanskrita Sahitya Sambhar / ed. by Gaurinath Sastri and... et. al. [vol.10]. Calcutta: Navpatra Prakashan, [n.d.]

Includes Bengali rendering of 'Pratijṇayaugandharāyaṇa' and 'Madhyamvyayoga' of Bhasa.

Sanskrita Sahitya Sambhar / ed. by Gaurinath Sastri and... et.al. [vol.11]. - Calcutta: Navpatra Prakashan, [n.d.]

Includes Bengali rendering of Bhasa's 'Charudatta' and 'Balacarita'.

DOGRI

Bhāsa raṇga / tr. by Rāmnāth Sastri.- Jammu: Jammu University, 1974.

xliv, 144 p; 18.5 cm.

Volume contains four plays of Bhasa.

Chanāṭ / ed. by Lālchand Prārthi and ... et.al.- Shimla: Himachal Kalā Sanskriti Bhāsā Academy, 1975. 167 p; 24cm.

Contains six dramas of Bhasa, i.e. Svapnavāsavadatta, Pancarati, Bālacarit, Abhiṣeknaṭak, Dūtaghaṭotkaca, Dūtavākya.

Pratimānatak / tr. by Dīnubhai Pant.- Jammu: Jammu and Kashmir Academy of Art, Culture and Languages, 1968.

60 p; 22 cm.

ENGLISH

Abhiṣekanāṭakam / by Bhasa; tr. into English by C.R. Devadhar. - Poona: Oriental Book Agency, 1937.

Abhiṣekanāṭakam / by Bhasa; tr. into English by S. Rangachar. - Mysore: Sanskrita Sahitya Sadana, 1961.

Abhiṣekanāṭakam / by Bhasa; tr. into English by V.S.Venkatarama Sastri.- Lahore: Motilal Banarsidass, 1930. 90 p. Includes notes.

Avimraka = Loves enchanted world / by Bhasa; tr. into English by J.L. Masson and D.D. Kosambi.- Delhi: Motilal Banarsidass, 1970.

151 p; 22 cm.

A.S.P. Ayyar

(Fellow of the Royal Society of Literature of the U.K.; known for his English rendering of all XII Trivandrum Plays of Bhasa)

Bhasa / by A.S.P. Ayyar.- Madras: V. Ramaswamy Sastrulu & Sons; 1957, 583, [7]p.; 18 c.m.- (Indian Men of Letters Includes English version of all the Series plays of Bhasa.)

Bhāsanāṭakacakram / tr. by A.C. Woolner and Lakṣmaṇ Svarup. - Lahore: Punjab University, 1930.

Thirteen plays ascribed to Bhasa.

'Bhasa's Pratimā Nāṭaka: Act 1' / by Bhasa; tr. with critical and explanatory notes by K. Rama Pisharoti. *Quarterly Journal of Mythic Society*; 1921, vo. 11.; p. 355-66.

Complete Plays of Bhasa / by Bhasa; ed. & tr. into English by K.P.A. Menon in three volumes-Delhi; Nag Publishers 1996 3 Vols.

The Envoy: a dramatic fragment/ by Bhasa; tr. from Sanskrit into English by A.N.D. Haksar. *National Herald;* December 3, 1989. p.3.

Excerpts from '*Dutavakyam*'

'Karṇabhāram' / by Bhasa, tr. into English by A.N.D. Haksar. *In* Glimpses of Sanskrit literature / ed. by A.N.D. Haksar.- New Delhi: ICCR, 1995. pp. 203-209.

Madhyamavyayogam/by Bhasa; tr. into English by A.C. Woolner and Lakshman Sarup. *In Thiṇvarang Sauvenir*; 1979 (Trivandrum) pp. 8-16.

Pratimanaṭaka of Bhasa / ed. by M.R. Kale - Delhi: Motilal Banarsidass.

Text with English translation, notes, introduction etc.

Pratimanatakam / by Bhasa; ed. with Hindi and English tr. and notes in Hindi. by Kapildeva Dvivedi Acharya - Allahabad: Ramnarayanlal, 1953.

34, 498 P; 18 cm.

Pratimānāṭakam / by Bhasa; ed. and tr. by Paranjape. Includes 'Prakāśa' commentary.

Pratimānāṭakam / by Bhāsa; ed. and tr. by S. Rangachar. - Bangalore: Samskrita Sahitya Sadana, 1950.

Pratimānāṭakam/by Bhasa; ed. and tr. into English by V. Raghavan and S.S. Janaki. Madras: Kuppuswami Sastri Research Institute, 1986. 61p.

Pratimānāṭakam / by Bhasa; tr. into English by C.R. Devadhar. - Poona: Poona Oriental Book Agency, 1937.

Pratimānāṭakam / by Bhāsa; tr. into English by Sankara Rama Sastri.- Madras: Balamanorama Press.

Sanskrit plays from epic sources / tr. into English verse by Henry W. Wells. - Baroda: Maharaja Sayajirao University, 1968.

xi, 258 p. ; 22.5 cm. Includes Fratricidal war by Bhasa.

The Shatered thigh: a heroic tragedy / by Bhasa; tr. into English by A.N.D. Haksar. *National Herald;* Sept. 3, 1989. p-4.

Excerpts from *Urubhangam*.

The Shattered thigh and the other Mahabharata plays / by Bhasa; tr. from the original Sanskrit into English with an introducltion by A.N.D. Haksar. - Penguin: [s.n.] 1993. 115 p; 18.5 cm.

[Svapnavasavadatta] Vasavadatta/tr. into English by Aurobindo Ghose Pondicherry: Aurobindo Ashram; 1915.

Reproduced below is the excerpts from Act I, Scene I of Vasavadatta, rendered into English by Sri Aurobindo Ghose This play was written between 18th and 30th October 1915. Completed 30th October:-

Act I

Scene I

An inner room of the palace in Avunthy
Chunda Mahasegn, seated; Gopalaca

Mahasegn

(2) Our strengths retire from our luxurious boy;[F]
(1) Vatsa Udayan drives my fortunes back
Defeated.

Gopalaca

I have seen him in the ~~battle~~ fight
And I have lived to wonder. O, he ranges
As lightly through the passages of war
As might the moonbeam feet of some bright laughing girl,
Her skill concealing in her reckless grace,
The measures of a rapid dance.

Mahasegn

If this dawn
Brings its portentous morning to our gates,
Our aims are ended. Yet I had great dreams,
Oudh and Cowsamby crowd my high carved doors;
Ganges, Godavery and Narmada
In her race besprayed with sacred dew
The moonlit jasmines in my pleasure grounds.
All this great sunlit continent lay sleeping
At peace beneath the shadow of my brows.
But they were dreams.

Gopalaca

Art thou not great enough
To live them?

Mahasegn

O my son, many high hearts
Must first have striven, many must have failed
Before a great thing can be done on earth;
(2) For one age sing the dreams another lives!
(1) And who shall say then that he is the man?

Svapnavasavadatta of Bhasa / ed. by M.R. Kale.- Delhi: Motilal Banarsidass.

Text with English translation, notes, introduction etc.

Six Sanskrit plays / by Henry Wells. - London: Asia Publishing House, 1964.

xxxi, 487 p.: plates; 21 cm.

Includes "The Vision of Vasavadatta" by Bhasa.

Thirteen plays of Bhasa/ by Bhasa; tr. into English by A.C. Woolner and Lakshman Svarup.- Delhi.: Motilal Banarsidass, 1930.

viii, 181 p; 22.5 cm.

2 Vols. in One

Reprint.

Thirteen Trivandrum plays attributed to Bhasa / tr. into English by A.C. Woolner and Lakshman Sarup. - London: Oxford University Press for Punjab University, 1930-31.

2 Vols.; 24.5 cm. - (Punjab University Oriental Publications; 13)

This translation is of thirteen plays discovered in south India by the Late Paṇḍit T. Gaṇapati Sāstri and edited by him in the Trivandrum Sanskrit series.

Three plays of Bhasa / by Bhasa; tr. by Amiya Rao and B.G. Rao.- New Delhi: Oriental Longman, 1971.

165 p; 18 cm.

Includes 'Karna' 'The Five Nights,' and 'Image'.

Two plays of Bhasa / by Bhasa; tr. into English by A.S.P. Ayyar.- Madras: V. Ramaswamy Sastrulu, 1959.

222 p; 18.5 cm.

Vasavadattā / by V.S. Sukhantankar.- Bombay: Oxford University Press, 1923.

v, 94 p; 21.5 cm. Includes Appendices and Bibliography.

The Vision of Vāsavadattā / by Bhasa; an acting version in English by Paul Cravath. *In* Sanskrit drama in performance / ed. by Racnel Van M. Baumer and James R. Branden. - Honolulu: The University Press of Hawaii, 1981 pp. 167-207.

GERMAN

[Awimaraka]/by Bhasa; tr into German by Hermann Weller.- Leipzig: [s.n.], 1924.

Work includes in the series "Indische Dichtung" (Indian Poetry); edited General Editor: Herman Weller.

Die Abenteur des Knaben Krischna = The Balacharita/by Bhasa; tr. into German by Hermann Weller. 1922.

Svapnavasavadatta/by Bhasa; tr. into German by Hermann Weller. Leipzig: [s.n.], 1926.

HERMANN WELLER (1878-1956)

Herman Weller *was born on 4.2.1878 in Schwaebisch-Gmuend, the son of merchant. He qualified as a university teacher in Tuebingen where he chose Sanskrit and Avesta as his subjects. He lectured on Indian literature and culture till 1954. Weller died on 9.12.1956 in Tuebingen. Hermann Weller translated several Indian texts. He also wrote extensively on Vedic metre. Weller studied the dramas of Bhasa, a pre-classical poet, whose work had then been discovered in South India. Weller translated plays of Bhasa into German: Balacharita, Die Abenteuer des Knaben Krischna ("The adventures of boy Krishna"), 1922 (the play was performed at the court-theatre of Stockholm in 1925); Awimaraka, Leipzig, 1924, in the series Indische Dichtung ("Indian Poetry") of which Weller was the general editor; Wasawadatta, a translation of the play Svapnavasavadatta, Leipzig, 1926 and Durjodhans Ende. Eine indische Tragoedie? ("Durjodhanas end. An Indian tragedy?), Tuebingen, 1933. He also wrote Ein Beitrag zur Bhasa-Frage ("A contribution to the Bhasa Problem") in the commemoration volume for H.Jacobi, 1926.*

GUJARATI

Bhasa-natakchakra / by Bhasa; tr. into Gujarati by Keshavram K. Shastri. - Ahmedabad: Navachetan Sahitya Mandir, [n.d.]

iv, 30, 210 p.; 18.5 cm.

[Madhyamavyāyoga] Madhyam nāṭāk / tr. by Keśavalāl H. Dhruv. - Baroda: Luhāṇā Mitra Press, 1921. xxxii, 46. p; 18 cm.

Pāṇḍavguptanivās athvā Pancaratra/tr. by Iśvarlāl Vīmāvālā. - Surat: Natvor M. Vimāvelā, [n.d.] 1920. xvi, 78 p; 16.5 cm.

[Pratijṇayaugandharāyaṇa] Pradhānni pratijṇā/ tr. by Kesavalal H. Dhruv.- 2nd ed.- Ahmedabad: Aditya Mudraṇalay, 1923.

xliii, 148 p; 18.5 cm. First published in 1915.

Pratimā nāṭak / tr. by Manilāl Chabārām Bhaṭṭ. - Ahmedabad: The translator, 1916. x, 80 p; 21.5 cm.

[Svapnavāsavadatta] Sācum svapna / tr. by Keśavalāl Harṣadrāy Dhruv. - Ahmedabad: The translator, 1916. xliv, 102 p; 22 cm.

Republished in 1923 under the title Svapna-ni Sundari.

Prof. Rasik Lal Parikh

The author of 'Sharvilak', based on the Sanskrit classics 'Daridracarudatta' & 'Mṛchhakatikam'.

Sharvilak / by Rasiklal C. Parekh.- Ahmedabad: Gujar Grantharatna Karyalaya, 1957.

xx, 216 p.

The play is based on Sanskrit classics '*Darida Carudatta* by *Bhasa and Mrichhakatikam* of *Sudraka* and even certain portions of this play is nothing but the direct translation of the above two plays. The playwright has also made use of certain materials from '*Pratijṇayaugandharayana*' *of Bhasa*.

The book received the prestigious 'Sahitya Akademi Award' of 1960 in Gujarati language.

HINDI

Abhiṣeka/by Bhāsa; commentary by Rāmcandra Miśra.- Varanasī: Caukhamba Vidyabhavan, 1962.

Abhiṣeka/by Bhāsa; tr. by Maithilīśarana Gupta. - Ciragaon, Jhansi: Sahitya Sadan, [n.d.]

Abhiṣcka/by Bhāsa; tr. by Thākurdatta Miśra.- Allahbad: Kitab Mahal, [n.d.]

Hindi rendering of 'Abhiṣekanātakam'.

Avimārakam/by Bhāsa; commentary by Rāmacandra Miśra. - Varanasi: Caukhamba Vidyabhavan, 1962.

Bālacaritam/by Bhāsa; commentary by Rāmajī Miśra.- Varanasī: Caukhamba Vidyabhavan, 1961.

Balacharitam/by Bhasa; ed. with a Hindi tr. by S.R. Sehgal.- Delhi: Munshiram Manoharlal, 1959.

106,179 p; 22 cm.

Bhāsanātakāvalī/by Bhāsa;tr.by Vrijajīvanadāsa.- Varanasi: Vani Sanjivan Granthamala Karyalay, 1929.

Bhāsa granthavalī / by Bhāsa; by Hardayalu Simha.- Agra: Gayaprasad & Sons, [n.d.]

Bhasa ke natak / by Bhasa; tr. into Hindi by Manoharlal Gaud. - Kanpur: Grantham, 1967. 10, 437 p; 22cm.

Bhāsa ke tin nātak / by Bhāsa; tr. by Hardayālu Simha.- Allahbad: Hindi Sahitya Sammelan, [n.d.]

Bhāsanātakamcakram / by Bhāsa; ed. and tr. by Baladev Upādhyaya.- Varanasī: Caukhamba Vidyabhavan, 1963.

Bhasanatakacakram / by Bhasa; ed. by C.R. Devadhar. - Delhi: Motilal Banarsidass, 1987.

x,2, 583 p; 18 cm.

Original thirteen texts in Devanagari.

Bhāsanātakāvali / by Bhāsa; tr. by Hardayālu Simha.- Varanasi: Hindi Pracharak Pustakalan, [n.d.]

Cārudattam / by Bhāsa; tr. by Kapiladevagiri.- Varanasi:Caukhamba Vidyabhavan, 1956.

Tr. of 'Daridracarudattam'.

Cārudatam / by Bhasa; tr. into by Vinod Godre. - Bombay: C. Mehta & Sons, [n.d.]

Dūtaghatotkacam/ by Bhāsa; commentary. by Rāmcandra Miśra.- Varanasi: Chaukhamba Vidyabhavan, [n.d.]

Dutāvākyam / by Bhāsa; commentary by Rāmjī Miśra.- Varanasi: Caukhamba Vidyabhavan, 1903.

Dūtavākyam / by Bhasa; ed. with 'Jyotsnā', 'Sarala' Sanskrit and Hindi commentaries by Sudhakar Malaviya.- Varanasi: Krishnadas Akademi, 1987, viii, 84 p; 18 cm. (Krishnadās Sanskrit series: 95)

Dutavakyam / by Bhasa; tr. into Hindi by Harivamsha Aneja.- New Delhi: Kadambari Prakashan, 1977.

56 p; 21.5 cm.

Includes original text in Sanskrit.

Dūtavākyam/ by Bhāsa; tr. into Hindi by Kṛṣṇakumar Dhavan.- Jullandhar: Standard Publishing Co., 1958.

Dūtavākyam/ by Bhāsa; tr. into Hindi by Sudarshan Sarmā.- Delhi: Raj Publishers, 1963.

Karṇabhāram / by Bhāsa; commentary by Rāmji Miśra.- Varanasi: Caukhamba Vidyabhavan, 1960.

Madhyamavyāyoga / by Bhāsa.- Gazipur: Ashokashram, 1928.

Madhyamavyāyoga / Bhāsa.- Lucknow: Ganga Pustakmala Karyalay, [n.d.]

Mādhyamavyāyoga / by Bhāsa; commentary by Ramjī Miśra.- Caukhamba Vidyabhavan, 1960.

Madhyamavyāyoga / by Bhāsa; tr. by R. Narayan Ayyar.- Trivandrum: Hindi Pustak Bhandar, 1955.

Pancarāg / by Bhāsa; commentary by Nigamananda.- Lahore: Motilal Banarsidass, [n.d.]

Pancarāg / by Bhasa; commentary by Rāmacandra Miśra.-Varanasi: Caukhamba Vidyabhavan, 1958.

Pancarāg / by Bhāsa.- New Delhi: Sastra Sahitya Mandal, [n.d.]

Pancarāg / by Bhāsa; tr. into Hindi by Baldevaprasād Sāstri.- Lahore: Meharcand Lakśmaṇdās, 1938.

Pancarāg / by Bhāsa; tr. into by Rāmadāsa Rāya. - Gazipur: Aśokashram, 1931.

Pancarāg / by Bhāsa; tr. into Hindi by Thakurdatta Miśra.-Allahabad: Kitab Mahal, [n.d.]

Pratijṇāyaugandharāyaṇa / by Bhāsa.-New Delhi: Sastra Sahitya Mandal, [n.d.]

Pratijṇāyaugandharāyaṇa / by Bhāsa; tr. into by Hardayalu Simha.- Allahabad: Hindi Sahitya Sammelan, 1946.

Pratijṇāyaugandharmanām / by Bhāsa; tr. into Hindi by Kapildeva Giri.- 2nd ed. - Varanasi: Caukhamba Vidyabhavan, 1965.

Pratijṇā / by Bhāsa; tr. into Hindi by Thakurdatta Miśra.- Allahabad: Kitab Mahal, [n.d.]

Pratimānātakam / by Bhāsa; commentary by Rāmcandra Miśra.- 3rd ed. - Varanasi: Chaukhamba Vidyabhavan, 1958.

Pratimanatakam / by Bhasa; ed. with Hindi and English tr. and notes in Hindi.- by Kapildeva Dvivedi Acharya Allahabad: Ramnarayanlal, 1953, 34, 498 p; 18cm.

Pratimānātakam / by Bhāsa; tr. into Hindi by Baladeva Prasāda Sāstrī.- Delhi: Meharchand Lakshmandas, 1947.

Pratimā / by Bhāsa; tr. into Hindi by Devarṣī Sanādaya.- New Delhi: Sastra Sahitya Mandal, 1958.

Pratimānātakam: samkśiptam / by Bhāsa; tr. into Hindi by Dhīrajalāla Sāstri.- Delhi: Haryana Prakashan Griha, [n.d.]

Pratimā / by Bhāsa; tr. into Hindi by Maithilīśaraṇa Gupta.- Chiragaon, Jhansi: Sahitya Sadan, [n.d.]

Pratimānātakam / by Bhāsa; tr. into Hindi by Srīdharānanda Sāstrī.- Delhi: Motilal Banarsidass, 1963.

Pratimanātakam / by Bhāsa; tr. into Hindi by Vijayānanda Sāstrī.- 3rd ed.- Lahore: Meharchand Lakshmandas, 1939.

Pratima aur Pancarāg / by Bhāsa.- Lahore: Antarchand Kapoor & Sons, 1930.

Hindi rendering of 'Pratimanātākam' and 'Pancarāgam'.

Pratimā nāṭak aur Pancarātra / tr. by Sūryakānt. - Lahore: Attarchand Kapūr, 1930. v, 192 p; 18.5 cm.

Sarala vupakamanjarī / by Bhāsa; tr. and ed. by Virāj.- Delhi: National Publishing House, [n.d.]

Play of Bhāsa in Hindi translation.

Svapnasundarī / by Bhāsa; tr. by Rāmavacana Dvivedī 'Aravinda'. - Delhi: Rajarajeshwari Book Depot, [n.d.]

Tr. of 'Svapnavāsavadattam' into Hindi.

Svapnasundari / by Bhasa; tr. into Hindi by Ramvacana Dvivedi 'Aravind'. - Goya: Rājrājeśvari Pustakalay, 1927.

76 p; 18 cm.

Svapnavāsavadattā / by Bhāsa.- Allahabad: Indian Press, 1931

Svapnavāsavadatta / by Bhāsa.- New Delhi: Sastra Sahitya Mandal, [n.d.]

Svapnavāsavadatta / by Bhāsa; commentary by Guruprasad Sāstrī.- 3rd ed. - Varanasī: Bhargav Pustakalay, 1951.

Svapnavāsavadatta / by Bhāsa; commentary by Vijayananda Sāstrī.- Lahore: Meharchand Lakshmandass, 1939.

Svapnavasavadatta / by Bhasa; ed. with notes by Dharmendra Kumar Gupta.- Delhi: Meharchand Lachhmandas, 1975.

192 p; 21.5 cm.

Svapnabāsavadattā / by Bhāsa; tr. by Brijabihārīlāla Sarmā. - Delhi: Lakshmi Pustak Sadan, 1969.

Svapnavāsavadattā / by Bhāsa; tr. by Haradayāla Simha.- Allahabad: Hindi Sahitya Sammelan, 1946.

Svapnavāsavadatta / by Bhāsa. tr. by Jagadis Sāstrī.- 3rd ed. - Patna: Motilal Banarsidass, [n.d.]

Svapnavāsavadatta / by Bhāsa; tr. by Jagannatha Sāstrī Hośing.- Varanasi: Chaukhamba Sanskrit Series, 1971.

Svapnavāsavadattā / by Bhasa; tr. by Maithiliśaran Gupta.- Chirgaon: Sahitya Sadan, 1929.

vi, 124 p; 16 cm.

Svapnavāsavadattā / by Bhāsa; tr. by Māyāsankara Dūbey.- Rajanandgaon. Bastar: [s.n.], 1914.

Svapnavāsavadattā / by Bhāsa; tr. by Samsāracandra.- Delhi: Meharcand Lakshmandās, 1951.

Svapnavāsavadattā / by Bhāsa; to by Satyajivan Varmā.- Allahabad: Indian Press, 1930.

xix, 115 p; 16 cm.

Svapnavāsavadatta / by Bhāsa; tr. by Tāriniś Jhā.- Varanasi: Ramnarayanlal Benimadhav, 1961.

Svapnavāsavadatta / by Bhāsa; tr. by Upendranārāyana Miśra.- Varanasi: Rāmnarayanlal Beniprasad, 1962.

Svapnavāsavadata tathā Pratijṇayaudandharāyāṇa / by Bhāsa; tr. by Bhagavatśaraṇ Upadhyaya.- 3rd ed. - Delhi: Rajpal & Sons, [n.d.]

Urubhangam / by Bhāsa; tr. into Hindi by Kapildevagiri.- Varanasi: Caukhamba Vidyabhavan, [n.d.]

Urubhanga / by Bhāsa; tr. tr. into Hindi by Raghunāthacandra-vaśiṣṭha.- Delhi: Lakshmi Pustak Sadan, [n.d.]

KANNADA

Abhiṣeka-nāṭakam / by Bhasa.- Mysore: Samskrita Sahitya Sadana, 1961.

Abhiṣeka-nāṭakam / by Bhasa; tr. by B. Nanjunda Svami.- Udupi: Pavanje Guru Rao, 1934,

Prose and verse.

Abhiṣeka nāṭaka / by Bhasa; tr. into Kannada by B. Nanjuṇḍa Svāmi.- 3rd ed. - Udipi: Hindi Pustaka Bhaṇḍāra. 1947.

iv, 60 [6] p; 18 cm.

Includes index.

First published in 1928.

'Abhiṣeka-nāṭakam' / by Bhasa; tr. into Kannada by B. Nanjunda Sastri. *Kannada Sāhitya Parisat Patrike*; 14: 3 (1929), pp. 182-194; 15:1,4 (1930-31), pp. 12-26, 347-397; 16:1,4 (1931-32) pp. 31-36, 334-342

Bhasana ekanka natakagalu / by Bhasa; tr. into Kannada by L. Gundappa.- Bangalore: Satyashodhara Prakatanamandiva, 1947.

xii, 110 p; 18cm.

Bhāsa - mahāsamputa / by Bhasa.- tr. into Kannada by S.V. Paramesvara Bhatta. Mangalore: [s.n.], 1975

Includes Abhiṣeka-nātakam; Pratima-natakam, etc. of Bhasa in prose and verse.

Bhāsa - Rāmāyaṇa - nāṭaka - triveṇi / by Bhasa; tr. into Kannada by L. Basavaraju.- [s.l.]: Gaurishankara Book Depot, 1958.

Contains three plays of Bhasa entitled ' Yajṇaphala, Abhiṣeka and Pratimā - knit together and organised in twentyone scenes.

2nd ed. - Mysore: D.V.K. Murthy, 1966.

Bhārata cakra / tr. by L. Guṇdappa—2nd ed. - Bangalore: Satya Sodhana Prakaṭana Mandira, 1945.

xi, 164 p; 18 cm.

First published in 1933.

Anthology of six plays: Madhyamavyāyoga, Dūtavākya; Dūta Ghaṭotkaca; Karṇabhāra; Urubhaṇga; and Paṇcorātra.

Dutavakyavu / by Bhasa; tr. into Kannada by Kadabada Nanjunda Sastri.- Bangalore: Kannada Sahitya Parishat, 1922.

18 p; 22 cm.

Karṇāṭaka Paṇcarātravu / tr. by Pānyam Sundara Sāstri.- Bangalore: Satya Sodhana Prakaṭana Mandira, 1933.

xvi, 56 p; 18 cm.

Mūru ekāṇkagalu / tr. by Moleyara Saṇkaranārayaṇa Bhaṭṭa.- Mangalore; U.R. Seṇai Sons, 1947.

iv, 105 p; 18 cm.

Three one-act plays Madhyamavyāyoga; Dūtta Ghaṭotkaca; and Karṇabhāra.

Nāṭakāmṛta - bindugalu / by Bhasa; tr. from Sanskrit into Kannada by L. Basavaraju.- Mysore: Gaurishankara Book Depot, 1958.

Includes some portions of Bhasa's Pratimā naṭakam; also incudes Uttararāmacarita of Bhavabhuti.

Paṇcarātra rūpakam / tr. by Devaśikhāmaṇi Alasiṇgarācārya.- Madras: Karnāṭ ak Book Depot, 1942.

iv, 64 p; 18 cm.

Pratimā-nāṭakam / by Bhasa; tr. into Kannada by H.G. Sannaguddayya.-

Tumkur: Sirigannada Prakashana, 1967.

Pratimā-nāṭakam / by Bhasa; tr. into Kannada by K. Krishnamoorthy.- Mysore: Sharada Mandira, 1954.

In prose and verse.

Pratimā-nāṭakam / by Bhasa; ed. and tr. into Kannada by S. Rangachar. - Mysore: Samskrita Sahitya Sadana, 1959.

Prose with introduction.

Pratimā-nāṭakam / by Bhasa, tr. into Kannada by T.S. Krishnamurthy.- Bangalore: Bangalore University, 1979.

Edited with explanatory notes and introduction.

Pratimā-nāṭakam / by Bhāsa; tr. into Kannada by M. Vasudeva Bhatta.- Mangalore: Ratnakara Prakashana, [n.d.].

Pratimā-nāṭakam / by Bhasa; tr. into Kannada by Sitarama Sastri. - Mysore: Sharada Mandira, 1962.

In prose and verse.

Pratinjṇa Yaugandharāyaṇa / by Bhasa; tr. by L. Guṇḍappa.- Bangalore: The translator, 1937.

xviii, 54, 14 p; 18 cm.

Svapnavāsavadatta.- / by Bhasa; tr. into Kannada by Devaśikhāmani Alasiṇgarācarya. 2nd ed. - Madras: Karṇāṭaka Book Depot, 1953.

xli, 62 p; 18 cm.

First Published in 1938.

Critical introduction by A.R. Kṛṣṇa Sāstri.

Svapnavasavadatta / by Bhasa; tr. into Kannada by L. Gundappa. - Bangalore: Satyashodhana Prakatana Mandira, 1947.

xi, 52 p; 17 cm.

Yajṇaphalam / by Bhāsa; tr. into Kannada by K. Krishnamoorthy.- Mysore: Sharada Mandira, 1958.

Tr. in prose and verse.

MAITHILI

Abhishek natak / by Bhasa; tr. into Maithili by Jivanand Thakur.- Darbhanga: Raj Darbhanga Press, 1945. viii, 52 p; 22 cm.

Bhasa nāṭakāvalī / by Bhasa; tr. by Jivānanda Thākur. - Darabhanga: Darabhanga: Darbhangā Press, 1945-67. 4 Vols. 22 cm.

Vol. 1 has viii, 52 p; 22 cm and published in 1945.

Vol. 2 has iv, 92 p; 22 cm. and published in 1947.

Vol. 3 has viii, 24, 48 p; 22 cm. and published in 1948

Vol. 4 has iv, 14 p; 27 cm and published in 1967.

Contents:- Vol. 1: Abhiṣek nātak.

Vol. 2: Dūtavākya, Madhyamavyāyoga, Pancarātra.

Vol. 3: Urubhanga and Bālacarit.

MALAYALAM

Abhishekanatakam / by Bhasa; tr. into Malayalam by Vallattol Narayana Menon.- 8th ed. - Trivandrum: Kamalaya Book Depot, 1954

31, 62 p; 18 cm.

Avimārakam / by Bhasa's; tr. by Aruvikkara R. Nārāyanan Poṭṭi.- Trivandrum: Ananta Rāmvarma Press, 1925. 98 p; 23 cm.

Bhasa - Rāmāyanam-nāṭakam / by Bhasa; tr. into Malayalam by Attupurathu Govinda Pillai.

Charudattam / by Bhasa; tr. into Malayalam by Raja Raja Verma. 1917

Madhyamavyāyogam / by Bhasa; tr. by C.R. Nārāyana Pillai.- Trivandrum: V.V. Press, 1928. 22 p; 23 cm.

Introduction by Ullūr S. Parameśsvarayyar.

Madhyamavyayogam / by Bhasa; tr. into Malayalam by Vallattol Narayana Menon.- 4th ed. - Charuthuruthy: Vaallatol Ganthalayam, 1951.

30 p; 18 cm.

Paṇcarātram / by Bhasa; tr. by M. Rāja Rāja Varma.- Trivandrum: B.V. Book Depot, 1918. 58 p.

Paṇcarātram / by Bhasa; tr. by Vaallatol Nārāyana Menon.- Kunnamkulom: Akṣararatnaprakāśika Press, 1923.

6th ed.- Cheruthuruthy: Vaallatol Granthalayam, 1948.

74 p; 18 cm.

Pratima natakam / by Bhasa; tr. into Malayalam by A.P.P. Namputiri.- Kozhikode: P.K. Brothers, 1985.

93 p; 18 cm.

Pratimā nāṭakam / by Bhasa; tr. by Kuṭṭippurāttu Keśāvan Nāyar.- Cheruthuruthy: Vaallatol Granthālayam, 1948. 26, 94 p; 19 cm.

Pratima nāṭakam/ by Bhasa; tr. by M. Rājarāja Varma. - Trivandrum: B.V. Book Depot, 1945. 106 p; 19 cm.

Rāmāyanam - Bhāsa-nāṭakam / by Bhasa; tr. into Malayalam by Nalukettil Krishna Menon.

Svapnavasavadatta / by Bhasa.- Kottayam: D.C. Books, 1985.

156 p; 18 cm. Malayalam rendering

Svapnavāsavadatta / by Bhasa; tr. by Aruvikkara R. Varayanan Potti.- Trivandrum: Bhāskara Press, 1914.

50 p; 23 cm.

Raja Raja Varma, known for his Malayalam versions of Carudattam and Svapnavasavadattam

Svapnavāsavadatta / by Bhasa; tr. by A.R. Rāja Rāja Varma.- 8th ed.- Trivandrum: Kamalālaya Printing Works, 1954.

55 p; 19 cm.

First published in 1918.

10th ed.- Trivandrum: Kamalalaya Book Depot, 1955.

46, 50 p; 18 cm.

Svapnavāsavadata / by Bhasa; tr. by Vaallatol Nārāyana Menon.- 5th ed.- Cheruthuruthy: Vaallatol. Granthaloyam, 1925.

`70 p; 23 cm.

Cheruthuruthy:, Vallattol Granthalayam, 1949.

70 p; 18 cm.

Urubhangam / by Bhasa; tr. into Malayalam by Vaallatol Narayana Menon. - 5th ed.- Cheruthuruthy: Vaallatol Granthalayam, 1949.

36 p; 18 cm.

MANIPURI

Pratimā nāṭak / by Bhasa; tr. from Sanskrit by Laurembam Iboyāima Simha.- Imphal: The translator, 1974.

117 p; 22 cm.

Svapna Vasavadattam / by Bhasa; tr. from Sanskrit original by Laurembem Iboyaima Simha.- Imphal: The translator, 1965.

146p.; 18 cm.

MARATHI

Bhāsa kavicīm nāṭakam / by Bhasa; tr. by Balavanta Rāmcandra Hivargāmvkar.- Ahmedanagar: The translator, 1926-31.

2 Vols ; 18 cm.

Vol. 1 includes a critical introduction on the plays of Bhāsa by the translation.

Vol. 2 furnishes an introduction by J.S. Karandīkar and a brief biographical sketch of the translator.

Bhāsacīm nāṭakam arthāt Bhāsakavica Marāṭhīnta avtār / by Bhasa; tr. by Krṣṇāji Lakṣmaṇ Somaṇ 'Kirāt'- Poona: Citraśaṭa Press, 1927

ii, 394 p; plate; 18 cm.

Sanskrit plays of Bhasa, presented in three parts.

Contents: Part - 1: Pratima, Abhiṣeka, Bālacarita:

Part - 2: Madhyama - Vyāyoga, Pañcarātra, Dūtavakya, Dūtaghaṭotkaca, Karnabhāra, Urubhaṇga;

Part - 3: Pratijñāyaugandharāyana, Svapnavāsavadatta, Avimāraka, Cārudatta.

MARATHI ADAPTATION:

Apte, Hari Nārāyan. Bhāsakavīcyā nāṭak kathā / by Hari Nārāyan Apṭe.- Poona: Aryabhūṣaṇ Press, 1917.

xii, 115 p; 21 cm.

Stories based on the plays of Bhasa.

NEPALI

Carudatta / by Bhasa; tr. into Nepali by Harinarayan Upadhyay.

POLISH

Legation / by Bhasa; tr. into Polish by M.K. Byrski. *Przeglad Orientalistyczny*; 1968, No.2.

The Shattered thighs / by Bhasa; tr. into Polish by M.K. Byrski. *Dialog;* 1969, No. 2; pp. 72-87.

RAJASTHANI

Sapano / by Bhasa; tr. and ed. by Devadatt Nag. - Jalor: Kala Prakashan, 1974.

72 p; 18 cm.

Tr. of Svapnavasavadatta.

Sahitya Akademi Translation Prize of 1990.

TAMIL

Bhāsamalākaviyin iraṭṭai nāṭakankal / by Bhasa; tr. by T.A. Svāminātha Ayyar.- 2nd ed.- Madras: Teachers' Publishing House, 1949.

171 p; 18 cm.

First published in 1944.

Collected plays of Bhasa, tr. from the English version of A.S. Pañcāpakeśa.

Dūtaghaṭotkacam / by Bhasa; tr. by K. Seṣādri Ayyar.- Madras: A. Gopāla Ayyar, 1922.

vii, 40 p; 17 cm.

Dutaghatotkaca / by Bhasa; tr. into Tamil by V. Raghavan and Priyamvada Sankar.

The play was staged at the Museum Theatre, Madras on 23rd August 1968 by the students of Madras Natya Sangh.

Svapnavāsavadattam / by Bhasa; tr. by G. Harihara Sāstrī.- Madras: Kalaimagal Kāryālayam, 1949.

vi, 51 p; 18 cm.

Svapna Vasavadattam / by Bhasa. - Madras: Kalaimagal K, 1948.

56 p; 18 cm.

Tamil rendering.

TELUGU

Abhiṣekanāṭakamu / by Bhasa; tr. by Bulusu Veṇkaṭaramaṇayya; introduction by N. Venkaṭarāvu.- Madras: R. Veṇkaṭeśvara & Co., 1948.

xii, 89 p; 18 cm.

Abhiṣekanāṭakamu / by Bhasa; tr. by Bulusu Venkaṭeśvarulu. - Kakinada: The translator, 1952.

xxiv, 91 p; 18 cm.

Abhiṣeka-nāṭakam / by Bhasa; tr. into Telugu by Bharatula Markandeya Sarma.

Abhiṣeka-nāṭakam / by Bhasa; tr. into Telugu by Chilakamarthi Lakshminarasimham.

Karṇabhāramu / by Bhasa; tr. by Veṭūri Prabhākara Sāstri. - Madras: K. Venkaṭ aśeṣayya, 1913.

16 p; 18 cm.

Madhyamavyāyogamu / by Bhasa; tr. into by Telugu Cilakamarti Lakṣ mīnarasimhamu.- Rajahmundry: Telikicarla Venkaṭasubbārāvu, 1915.

iv, 24 p; 19 cm.

Madhyamavyayogamu / by Bhasa; tr. by Veturi Prabhakarasastri. - Madras: K. Venkate.- / tr. by Veturi se sayya, 1913.

24p.; 18 cm.

Madhyamudu / by Bhasa; tr. into Telugu by Bhamudiputi Kamesvara Rao.- Rajahmundry: K. Veeravenkatayya [sic] & Sons, 1963.

88 p; 17.5 cm.

Pratijñāyaugandharāyaṇamu / by Bhasa; tr. by Dharaṇikoṭa Venkaṭasubbayya.- Nellore: The translator, 1953.

xxxiv, 116 p; 18 cm.

---------; /tr. by Kāṭūri Venkaṭeśvararāvu.- Vijayawada: Gūḍūri Namaśśivaya, 1945.

86 p; 16 cm.

---------; / tr. by Palle Pūrnaprajñācāryulu.- Guntur: M. Hanumantarāvu, 1947.

iv, 64 p; 20.5 cm.

Pratimānāṭakamu / by Bhasa; tr. into Telugu by B. Mārkaṇḍeyaśarma. - Ongole: The translator, 1934.

iv, 106 p; 21 cm.

Pratimānāṭakamu / by Bhasa; tr. by Jandhyala Lakṣmīnārāyanaśāstri.- Guntur: Karunaśrī Kāvyamālā, [n.d.]

viii, 80 p; 18 cm.

--------; / tr. by Veṭuri Prabhākaraśāstri.- 2nd ed.- Madras: The translator, 1934.

vi, 164 p; 21 cm.

Pratimā-nāṭakam / by Bhāsa; tr. into Telugu by Bhamidipati Kameswara Rao.

Pratimā - nāṭakam / by Bhāsa; tr. into Telugu by Bharatula Markandeya Sarma.

Pratimā - nāṭakamu / by Bhasa; tr. into Telugu Chilakamarthi Lakshminarasimham.

Pratimā - nāṭakamu / by Bhāsa; tr. into Telugu by Edavalli Adinarayana.

Pratima natakamu / by Bhasa; tr. into Telugu by Jeereddi Chennareddi and Jendhyala Lakshmi Narayana Sastri.- Guntur: The translator, [n.d.]

97 p; 18 cm.

Pratimā - nāṭakamu / by Bhāsa; tr. into Telugu by Kodanda Rama Sastry.

Pratima natakamu / by Bhasa; tr. into Telugu by M. Khasim Khan.-Madras: Orient Publishing Company, 1953.

40 p; 17.5 cm.

Pratima natakamu / by Bhasa; tr. into Telugu by Veturi Prabhakara Sastri.- Madras: The translator, 1953. 150 p; 17 cm.

Svapnavāsavadatta / by Bhasa; tr. by Kāṭūri Venkaṭeśvararāvu.- Madras: Yuva Book Depot, 1946.

60 p; 18 cm.

Svapnavāsavadattamu / by Bhasa; tr. by Dharaṇikoṭa Venkatasubhayya.- Nellore: The translator, 1951.

xi, 125 p; 18 cm.

Svapnavāsavadattanāṭakamu / by Bhasa; tr. by Cilakamarti Lakṣminarasimham.- Rajahmundry: [s.n.], 1930.

60 p; 21 cm.

Urubhangamu / by Bhasa; tr. by Vedamu Venkaṭakṛṣṇa Sarma. -Madras: The translator, 1951.

40 p; 18 cm.

Vatsarāju / by Bhasa; tr. by Sthānāpati Rukmiṇamma. - 2nd ed.- Visakhapatnam: Kavisamiti, 1952.

x, 17 p; 18 cm.

Tr. of 'Pratijṇāyaugandharāyaṇa'.

Yajṇaphalamu / by Bhasa; tr. into Telugu by Bulusu Venkateswaralu.

---------; Kakinada: The translator, 1952.

xx, 120 p; 18 cm.

Yajṇaphalamu / by Bhāsa; tr. into Telugu by Svipada Krishnamurthy Sastry.

TELUGU ADAPTATION

Kṛṣṇamācāryulu, Kapiṣṭhalam. Bhāsamahākavi kṛtanāṭaka kathāsāramu/ by Kapiṣṭhalam Kṛṣṇamācāryulu.- Madras: Macmillan & Co., 1919.

viii, 67 p; 17 cm.

Eight stories from Bhāsa's dramas.

Suryaṇarāyaṇaśāstri, Mallādi. Bhāsa nāṭaka kathalu /by Mallādi Sūryanārāyaṇaśāstri. - Rajahmundry: Aryan Book Depot, 1929.

107 p; 18 cm.

Stories from Bhāsa's dramas.

THAI

[Svapnavāsavadatta] / by Bhasa; tr. into Thai by Dusdie Malakun.

BIO-CRITICAL NOTICES

Adya Rangacharya. Drama in Sanskrit literature. -Bombay: Popular Prakashan, 1967.

Pp. 45,63,64,68,72,78,95,96,106,128,140,200,205,-212

Aggarwal, H.R. A short history of Sanskrit literature. - 2nd rev. ed.- Delhi: Munshiram Manohartal, 1963.

Contents: Bhasa Pp. 45-55.

'Alekhya nāṭaka: a new drama'. *Annals of the Bhandarkar Oriental Research Institute;* 1929; Vol.x, Nos. I-II.

'The Ancient Indian stage' .../by P.V. Rajamannar. *Cultural Souvenir, Madras Cosmopolitan Club*; 1956.

'Ancient play well staged'. *The Statesman*, 8 January 1996. P. 13.

'Appukuttan Nair, D. Kutiyattam and Bhasa'. *Malyalam Literary Survey*; July - December, 1987; Pp. 34-39.

Aravindan. 'Aharyam in Madhyamavyayogam production'. *In Thiruvarang Souvenir* (Trivandrum), 1979. p.21.

Aufrecht, Theodor. Catalogus catalogorum.- Weisbaden: Franz Steiner Verlag Gmb. H, 1962.

2 Vols. 26 cm.

[Authenticity of Bhāsa plays]: Symposium organised by the XII Oriental Conference held at Benaras from the 31st December 1943 to 2nd January 1944.

Ayyar, A.S.P. Bhasa.- Madras: V. Ramaswamy Sastrulu & Sons, 1957.

583, 11 p; 18.5 cm.

Awasthi, Sudha Rani. Comparative study of the dramatic technique of Bhasa and Kalidasa / by Sudha Rani Awasthi.

Ph.D thesis in Hindi approved by the Kanpur University in 1979.

Balivadhankom from Abhisheka nataka of Bhasa'. *In Trivandrum Cultural Society Souvenir*, July 1985.

Sypnosis:

Banerji, A. The play of Bhasa. *JRAS*; 1921. Pp. 317-382.

Banerji, Suresh Chandra. A Companion to Sanskrit literature.-Delhi: Motilal Banarsidass, 1971.

----------.- Sanskrit sahityer itihas. - Calcutta: The Dacca Students LIbrary, [1907?]

In Bengali.

Barnett, L.D. The plays ascribed to Bhasa and the Mattavilasa.- *JRAS*, 1919; Pp. 233-234.

--------. *JRAS*, 1921, Pp. 587-589.

--------. *BSOS*, Vol. I, Part III; Pp. 35-38.

Belvalkar, S.K. The Relation of Sūdraka's Mṛcchakaṭika to the Carudatta of Bhasa. *All India Oriental Conference* I, Vol.2, Pp. 189-204.

Belvalkar, S.K. 'The Relation of Sūdraka's Mṛcchakaṭika to the Cārudatta of Bhāsa' *Proceedings and Transactions of the First Oriental Conference* at Poona, held on the 5th, 6th and 7th of November, 1919.

Benegal, Som. A Panorama of theatre in India / by Som Benegal.-Bombay: Popular Prakashan, 1967. Pp. 26-28.

Published for Indian Council For Cultural Relations.

Bhartiya, Kanti Kishore. Sanskrit natakkar.- Uttar Pradesh: Prakashan Sakha, Suchana Vibhag, 1959.

(Hindi-Samiti granthamala; 25)

Contents: Bhasa Pp. 51-62.

The Bhasa festival: a brief recall / by Kironmoy Raha. *Sangeet Natak Akademi Journal*; January - March 1989; Vol. 91 Pp. 58-59.

Bhāsa's Abhiṣekanāṭaka / by Ganesan Ratnam. *18th All India Oriental Conference*.

Bhāsa's affiliation with epic poet's / by U. Venkatakrishna Rao. *Journal of Oriental Institute*; 1953-54, Vol. 3 Pp. 370-79.

Bhāsa's Rāma dramas / by U. Venkatakrishna Rao. *Poona Orientalist*; 1950, Vol. 15-16. Pp. 112-119

Bhāsa's Urubhangam in the light of Bharata's Natyasastra./ by Vimala Rama Rao. *Literary Criterion* 1988. Vol. 23, No. 4; Pp 80-83.

Bhat, G.K. Bana's tribute to Bhasa. *OT*; VI; Pp. 18-26.

---------. Bhasa and the problem of tragedy. *Bharatiya Vidya;* 1975; Vol. 35, Nos. 1-4; Pp. 82-91.

Bhat, G.K. Dramatic themes of Bhasa and their treatment

Ph.D. thesis approved by the University of Bombay in 1950.

[Bhat, G.K.?]. The problems of Mahabharata play of Bhasa. *ABI*, I, XXXV; Pp. 73-83.

Bhat, G.K. Prologues in the Bhāsa's plays'. *19th All India Oriental Conference.*

Bhat, G.K. Sanskrit drama: problems and perspectives.-Delhi: Ajanta Publications, 1985.

Bhatt, S.C. Drama in ancient India.- New Delhi: Amrit Book Co., 1961.

Bhattacharya, Bimanchandra. Sanskrit sahitya ruprekha.- 5th ed.-

Calcutta: Vidyodaya Library Pvt. Ltd.; 1972. *Contents Bhasa* Pp. 78-86.

In Bengali.

Bhattacharya, Biswanath. A Critical survey of Bhasa's Mahabharata dramas.- Calcutta: Sanskrit Pustak Bhandar, 1991.

v, 182 p; 22 cm.

Bibliography: Pp. 175-182.

Bhattacharya, Biswanath. Critical survey of Bhasa's Mahabharta dramas/ by Biswanath Bhattacharya.

Ph.D. thesis approved by the University of Calcutta in 1985.

Bhattacharya, Biswanath. Sanskrit drama and dramaturgy / by Biswanath Bhattacharya. - Delhi: Sharada Publishing House, 1994.

Pp. 190-203, 333, 382-386, 393-400, 411-415.

Bhattacharya, D. [Vision of Vasavadatta]. *Indian Historical Quarterly*; March 1926; Vol. 2, No. 1; Pp. 209-210.

Review of book published from Lahore in 1925.

Bhattacharya, D.C. Bhasa and his alleged works. *Proc. A.S.B.*; 1917. P- CC XIV.

Bhattacharya, Sukhamayee. Survey of Bhasa / by Sukhamayee Bhattacharya

Ph.D. thesis in Hindi approved by the University of Calcutta in 1974.

Briar, Asha. Cultural study of the plays of Bhasa / by Asha Briar.

Ph.D. thesis in Hindi approved by the Patna Unniversity in 1976.

The Cambridge guide to Asian Theatre / ed. by James R. Brandon.- Cambridge: Cambridge University Press, 1993.

The Cambridge guide to world theatre / ed. by Martin Bannam.- Cambridge:

Cambridge University Press, 1988.

Chaturvedi, Sudamsu. Bhasan: oru pathanam.- Thrissur: Sudha Publication, 1986.

188 p; 18 cm.

Critical study in Malayalam.

Chaudhury, Robin. Mahakavi Bhasa aru Svapnavasavadatta.- Guwahati: Granthapith, 1988.

80 p; 20 cm.

Chawla, Soraj. Sources of the plots of the dramas of Bhasa / by Soraj Chawla.

Ph.D. thesis in Hindi approved by the Meerutt University in 1976.

Chennareddi, J. Bhasuni. Ramanataka moolamalu.- Tirupati: The author, 1962.

390 p; 22 cm.

In Telugu

Comparative Indian literature / ed. by K.M. George.-Trichur: Kerala Sahitya Akademi, 1994. Pp. 562-564.

Cultural heritages of India [Vol. V] / ed. by Suniti Kumar Chatterji.- rev. ed.- Calcutta: The Ramakrishna Mission Institute of Culture, 1978.

p.242.

Dakshinamurthy, N.M. Bhāsa kā nātyaloka / by N.B. Dakshinamurthy.- Najgud: Srīprakāśun, 1971.

In Hindi.

Dalal, Minakshi L. Conflict in Sanskrit drama.-Bombay: Somaiya Publications Pvt. Ltd., 1973.

Contents: Bhasa Pp. 161-183.

Dange, Sadashiv A. An Order of Duryodhana plays by Bhasa. *All India Oriental* Conference XVII (Summary); P. 29.

----------. *Journal of the University of Bombay*; September, 1954; Vol. XXIII; No. 11, Pp. 49-59.

Dange, Sadashiv A and Dange, Sindhu S. Critiques on Sanskrit dramas. - 2nd rev. ed. - New Delhi: Aryan Books International, 1994.

Das, Manoj Svapnavasavadatta. *Indian and Foreign Review*; 15 April, 1980; Vol. 17 No. 13, p-35.

Das, Sarbeshwar. The comic and romantic in Sanskrit dramas with special reference to Bhāsa, Kālidāsa, Harṣa and Bhavabhūti. *Summary of Papers: All India Oriental Conference (Bhubaneshwar);* 1959; Vol. XX.

De, S.K. Dramas ascribed to Bhasa. *Indian Historical Quarterly*; December. 1941; 17 (4); Pp. 415-429.

Deep Shikha. Comparative study of the dramas of Bhasa based on the Mahabharata and Venisamhara of Bhattanarayana from the angle of skills of dramatics / by Deep Shikha.

Ph.D. thesis in Hindi approved by the Meerut University in 1986.

Deolia, Asha. Comparative study of the heros of the Sanskrit dramas: from Bhasa upto Jayadeva / by Asha Deolia.

Ph.D. thesis approved by the Rajasthan University in 1972.

Devadhar, C.R. Plays ascribed to Bhasa: their authenticity and merits.*ABORI*; Vol. VII, Pts I & II.

---------. Plays ascribed to Bhasa. - Poona: [s.n.] 1937.

(Poona Oriental series; no. 54)

2nd ed. published in 1951.

---------. 'The Svapnavāsavadatta of Bhāsa' *Annals of the Bhandarkar Institute; 1925;* Vol. VI, Nos. I-II. Pp. 55-57.

Devasthali, G.V. The Viṣkambhakas and the praveśakas of Bhāsa. *All India Oriental Conference* XV. (Summary); p.190.

----------. *Journal of University of Bombay*; September 1950; Vol. XIX, No. 2, Pp. 71-79.

Dictionary of oriental literatures (Vol. II): South and South - East Asia.- Delhi: Vikas Publishing, 1975.

Dikshit, Jagadish Datta. Bhasa ki bhasa sambandhi tatha natakiya visheshtayen.- New Delhi: Arya Book Depot., 1967.

xiii, 305 p; 21.5 cm.

---------. Specialities of language and dramaturgy of Bhasa / by Jagadish Datta Dikshit.

Ph.D. thesis in Hindi approved by the Agra University in 1962.

'Dramatic perspective in the plays of Bhasa and Aeschylus'/ by M.S. Pati. *Indian Literature*; 1978, Vol. XXI Pp. 46-77.

Weller, Hermann. Duryodhans Ende, Eine indische Tragoedie ?/ by Hermann Weller. - Tuebingen: [s.n.], 1933.

'Duryodhana in theatre' / by M.L. Varadpande. *The Hindustan Times*; 23 March 1996; P.4.

On Bhasa's characterization of Duryodhana in his Mahabharatan plays.

Ein Beitrag zur Bhasa - Frage / by Hermann Weller. *In* H. Jacobi Commemoration Volume. 1926.

A paper on 'A contribution to the Bhasa problem'.

'Encounter between Ravana and Hanuman'. *Trivandrum Cultural Society Souvenir*, July 1985.

Excerpt from the Act Three 'Thoranayudham' of Abhishekanatakam of Bhasa in English.

Encyclopaedia of Indian literature.- New Delhi: Sahitya Akademi, 1987-1994. 6 Vols.

Contents: Bhasa: Pp. 463, 464, 645, 1102, 1103, 1105, 1108, 1109, 1206, 2434, 3061, 3331, 3570, 4660.

'The First dramalist in Sanskrit: Aśvaghoṣa or Bhasa?'/by D.G. Joshi.

Paper presented at the *All India Oriental Conference* (22nd Session) held at Gauhati, Assam in January 1965.

Garg, Ganga Ram. An Encyclopaedia of Indian literature.-Delhi: Mittal Publishers, 1982.

Pp. 5, 31, 34, 46-47, 76, 107, 176, 216, 285, 305, 428-29, 457.

Ghatak, Jyotish Chandra. The Dramas of Bhasa. *JDL*; 1925; XII. Pp. 1-4 and *BK*-I. Pp. 1-46.

Ghosh, Suparna. Comparative study of the dramas based on Ramacarita: the Pratimānatakam of Bhasa and the Mahaviracharitam of Bhavabhuti / by Suparna Ghosh.

Ph.D. thesis approved by the Patna University in 1979.

Glimpses of Sanskrit literature / ed. by A.N.D. Haksar.- New Delhi: Indian Council for Cultural Relations, 1995.

Contents: Bhasa: Pp. 37, 51-59, 100-110, 113, 132.

Gopalakrishnan, Sudha. From the comic to the comedic: The traditions of comedy of Bhasa and Shakeshpeare.- New Delhi: Bibliotheca Orientalia, 1990.

viii, 169 p; 22 cm.

'Grace of gestures' / by Ranjini Rajagopal. *Indian Express (Magazine)*; 9 April. 1995. P.7.

On Kuttiyattam Festival organised by Sangeet Natak Akademi: includes performance of 'Bali Vadam' from Act One of 'Abhiṣ ekanaṭakam'.

Gupta, Mridula. Bhasa's characters: a psychological study / by mridula Gupta.

Ph.D. thesis in Hindi approved by the Agra University in 1978.

Hajela, Pushpa. Treatment of nature in Sanskrit drama from Bhasa to Bhavabhuti. / by Pushpa Hajela.

Ph.D. thesis approved by the Aligarh Muslim University in 1961.

Harihara G. Sastri. The Bhasa problem: a reply. *IHQ*; Vol. I. Pp. 370-378.

Indian theatre: traditions of performance / ed. by Farley P. Richmond, Darius L. Swann and Philip B. Zarrill.- Delhi: Motilal Banarsidass, 1993.

Iyengar, M.B. Narasimha. The words 'devalaya and garbhagrha' in Bhasa; a reply. *JOI*, V. Pp. 193-195.

Iyer, K.G. Sesha. The Bhasa problem. *IHQ*. P - 361.

Jagirdar, R.V. A Note on the ten plays of Bhasa. *IA*; 1931. Pp. 41-45.

Jain, Nemi Chandra. 'Contemporary productions of Bhasa plays'. *Sangeet Natak Akademi Journal*; Jan - March 1988, Vol-87. Pp. 21-36.

---------. Indian theatre: tradition, continuity and change. - New Delhi: Vikas Publishing House, 1992.

Jayaswal, K.P. The plays of Bhasa and King Darsaka of Magadha. *JASB*, 1913. Pp. 259-269.

Jhala, G.C. 'Cārudattam and Mṛchhakaṭikam'. *JBBRAS;* December 1952. Vol. 27. Supplementary.

---------. A note on Karṇabhara. *Journal of the Asiatic Society* (Vol. 28)

Jhala. 'The Problem of the Yajnaphalam'. *JBBRA*; 1954; Vol. XXIX, Part I.

Kavi. M. Ramakrishna. Two more dramas of Bhāsa: [Dāmaka and Traivikrama]. *All India Oriental Conference III*, Pp. 80-84.

Keith, A. Berriedale. Notes on the Sanskrit drama (1-Bhasa). *BSOS*; III. Pp. 259-297.

----------. The Sanskrit drama in its origin, development, theory and practice.- Oxford: OUP, 1924.

405 p; 22 cm.

---------. Sanskrit - natak: udbhav aur vikas: siddhanta aur prayog/ tr. into Hindi by Udaybhanu Singh.- Delhi: Motilal Banarsidass, 1965.

Kṛshnamachariar, M and Srinivasachariar. History of classical Sanskrit literature.- Delhi: Motilal Banarsidass, 1989. Pp. 552-567.

Krishnamoorthy, K. Bhasa as a Prakrit poet: miscellany. *Indian Historical Quarterly;* June 1946, Vol. 22, No.1, Pp. 73-74.

Krishna Sāstri, A.R. Bhāsa kavi / by A.R. Kṛṣṇa Sāstri.- 2nd ed. - Mysore: Kannada Kavikāvyamāle, 1950.

viii, 173 p; plate; 18 cm.

First Published in 1933.

Critical estimate of Bhasa, the Sanskrit playwright.

Kulshreshtha, R.B. 'Urubhange as a tragedy'. *Vishveshvaranand Indological Journal*; March - September, 1972; Vol. 10, Nos. 1-2; Pp. 36-46.

Lakshmi Kutti. Bhasa and his plays / by Lakshmi Kutti.

Ph.D. thesis approved by the Bangalore University in 1987.

Lesny, V. Die Entwicklungss tufe des Prakrits in Bhasa's dramas and Zeitaltern Bhasa's. *ZDMG*; Vol. 72. Pp. 203-208.

Lisney, V. The stage of development of Prakrit of Bhasa's drama and his age / tr. from original German by S.N. Ghosal. *Journal of Oriental Institute*; September 1963; Vol. 13, No. 1; Pp. 48-53.

Levi, Sulvain. The theatre of India / tr. from the French by Narayan Mukherji. - Calcutta: Writers Workshop, 1978.

2 Vols.

Contents: Bhasa. Pp. 136-139, 162; (II) 40, 75.

Lindonau, M. Bhasa: studies.- Leipzig: [s.n.], 1918.

'Linguistic structure of Sanskrit drama'. In Three-day Seminar on Sanskrit Drama held at Ranchi University from 24th 26th March, 1982.

Paper presented on Rasa, Plot Dialogue with special reference to Bhāsa, Kālidasa and Sūdraka.

Macdonell, A.A. India's past: a survey of her literatures, religious, languages and antiquities.- Varanasi: Motilal Banarsidass, 1956.

[Macdonell A.A.?]. Three plays of Bhasa in the TSS. *JRAS*; 1913: Pp. 186-190.

Majumdar, G.N. Bhāsa and music. *All India Oriental Conference XV*: P. 36.

Mankad, D.R. 'Pratima and Kundamālā' *Annals of the Bhandarkar Oriental Research Institute; 1930;* Vol. XII, No. 1, Pp. 97-98.

Marasinghe, E.W. The Sanskrit theatre and stagecraft. - Delhi: Sri. Satguru Publications, 1989.

(Sri Garib Dass Oriental series; no. 78)

Masterpieces of Indian literature [Vol.2].- New Delhi: National Book Trust, 1997.

Contents: Svapnavasavadattam - Bhasa. Pp. 1224-1226.

Masterpieces of Indian literature (Vol.3) / ed. by K.M. George.- New Delhi: National Book Trust, 1997.

Meerwarth, A.M. The Dramas of Bhasa: a literary study. *JASRB*; Vol. XIII. Pp. 261-280.

Merriam - Webster's Enoyclopedia of literature. - Springfield, Massachusetts: Merriam - Webster Inc, 1995. p. 136.

Nanavati, Rajendra I. 'A Note on Carudattam'. *Proceedings of the All India Oriental Conference (25 Session)* held at Jadavpur University, Calcutta in October, 1969.- Poona: *BORI*, 1972. Pp. 257-260.

Narang, Manju. Critical study of the development of stories of the dramas of Kalidasa and Bhasa / by Manju Narang.

Ph.D. thesis in Hindi, approved by the Garhwal University in 1980.

'New Problems in Bhasa plays'. *Vishveshvaranand Indological Journal*; 1979, Vol. 17; Pp. 312-313.

Book review.

'Old wine in new bottle'. *The Statesman*: 20 April 1998. p 12.

On Hindi adaptation of Bhasa's Dutavakyam; includes brief synopsis of the play alongwith an insight into the production.

Oleksiw, Susan ' Mantrankam at Peruvanam'. *Sangeet Natak Akademi Journal* July; September 1977; Vol. 45. Pp. 43-46.

'On the authorship of Yajnaphala'/ by R.N. Dandekar. *ABORI*; 1950.

Otto, Stein. Contribution to Bhasa question. *IHQ* 1938; Vol. XIV. Pp. 633-659.

Panchapakesa Aiyer, A.S. Bhasa / by A.S. Panchapakesa Aiyar.- Madras: Madras Law Journal Office, 1942.

viii, 294 p. 21.5 cm. - (Indian Men of Letters series; 1)

A short study on the life and works of Bhasa, the Sanskrit dramatist to the English - speaking world.

[Pancaratram of Bhasa]. *Vishveshvaranand Indological Journal*; 136-137.

Book review.

Panikkar, Kavalam Narayan. Natyaprakaram of Madhyamavyayogam production'. *Thiruvarang Souvenir* (Trivandrum), 1979. Pp. 17-20.

Pathak, M.C. Sanskrit nāṭaka men atiprākṛta tattva.- Jaipur: Devanagar Prakashan, [n.d.]

18, 468 p.

Pati, Madhusudan. 'Dramatic perspective in the plays of Bhasa and Aeschylus'. *Indian Literature*; May - June 1978; Vol. 21, No.3; Pp. 46-71. ft-n.

----------. Sanskrit drama: essays in revaluation / by Madhusudan Pati. - Delhi: Amar Prakashan, [1991].

Contents: 'Urubhangam: metamorphosis of the tragic muse'. Pp. 87-112.

Phadke, S.S. Analysis of figures of speech in Bhasa's dramas. - Goa: Rajhans Vitaran, 1990.

138 p; 23 cm. - (Publication; 83)

Phadke, Sridhr. Analysis of figures of speech in Bhasa's plays / by Sridhar Phadke.

Ph.D. thesis approved by the Bombay University in 1977.

Pisharoti, K.R. Bhasa's work: a criticism. - Trivandrum: [s.n.], 1925.

Pisharoti, K.R. Bhasa problem I. *Indian Historical Quarterly*, March, 1925; Vol. 1, No. 1, Pp. 103-11.

----------. Bhasa problem II *Indian Historical Quarterly* ; June

1925, Vol. 1, No. 2, Pp. 330-340.

---------. The Bhāsa problem: a criticsm. *All India Oriental Conference* III (Summaries), 13-14.

---------. *Indian Historical Quarterly*, Vol. I, Pp. 103-11. 330-40.

---------. Bhasa theory again: a reply to Prof. Keith. *Indian Historical Quarterly*; Sept. 1929; Vol. 5, No. 3; Pp. 552-558.

---------. Bhasa's works: are they genuine ? *BSOS*; Vol. III. Pp. 107-117.

'Plays ascribed to Bhāsa: their authenticity and merits'/ by Prof. Devadhar.- Poona: 1927.

(V.N. Mandlik Gold Medalist Essay, 1922.)

Printa, Withlem. Bhasa's Prakrit.- Frankfurt: [s.n.], 1921.

'A probable Malayalam word in Bhāsa and doubtful authenticity of the Abhiṣekanāṭaka as a play of Bhāsa'. *20th All India Oriental Conference*.

--------. *Journal of Oriental Institute*; 1957-58; Vol. 27. Pp. 122-25.

Pusalkar, A.D. Are there two Bālacaritas: [of Bhāsa]? *All India Oriental Conference* IX (Summaries, 14).

---------. *In* P.V. Kane Commemoration Volume; Pp. 339-344.

----------. Bhasa: a study / by A.D. Pusalkar; foreward by A Berriedale Keith. - Lahore: Lachhimandas, 1940.

xix, 472,29, xlp; 24 cm. - (Meharchand Lachhmandas Sanskrit and Prakrit seires; 7)

Includes bibliography, appendix and index.

--------. Bhasa: a study.- 2nd rev. ed. - New Delhi: Munshiram Manoharlal, 1968.

xxiii, 613 p; 21.5 cm.

-------. Bhasa: a study / by Achyuth Dattatreya Pusalkar.

Ph.D. thesis approved by the University of Bombay in 1941.

--------. Two seventeenth century works on Bhāsa: [Padyaracanā and Sabhyālankara]. *All India Oriental Conference* XII (Summaries; pt.i); Pp. 65-66.

---------. Yajnaphalam: a newly discovered drama by Bhāsa. *All India Oriental Conference* XI, pt. i, P. 45.

---------. *Journal of the Bombay Branch of the Royal Asiatic Society* Vol. XVIII; Pp. 23-29.

Raja, C.E. Bhasa: another side. *ZII*; Vol. II. Pp. 247-264.

Raja, C.E. The Bhasa - problem. *JOR*; Vol. I. Pp. 217-245.

Raja, C. Kunhan. A New drama of Bhāsa ?: [Vīnāvāsavadattam]. *All India Oriental Conference* VI. 593.

Ramabhadur. Comparative study of Pratimanatakam and Mahaviracharitam.

Ph.D. thesis in Hindi approved by the Rohilkhand University in 1982.

Rāman Nampūtiri, E.V. Bhāsānāṭakacakra carca / by E.V. Rāman Nampūtiri.- Trivandrum: B.V. Book Depot, 1929.

275 p; 19 cm.

Critical studies of Bhāsā.

Ramanathan, C. The tragic parts in the plays of Bhāsa. *In.* Studies in Indian culture / ed. by G. Ramakrishna.- Bangalore: Prof. S. Ramachandra Rao Felicitation Committee, 1986.

Pp. 263-267.

Ramesh Chand. Humour and satire in Sanskrit dramas: Bhasa to Rajasekhara / by Ramesh Chand.

Ph.D. thesis approved by the Punjab University in 1985.

Rawat, Usha. Imagery of Bhasa / by Usha Rawat.

Ph.D. thesis in Hindi approved by the Awadesh Pratap Singh University in 1983.

Roy, Ashim Kumar and Gidwani, N.N. A Dictionary of Indology (Vol.1).- New Delhi: Oxford & IBH Publishing Co., 1983.

Contents: Bhasa. Pp. 211-212.

Sahitya Akademi - New Delhi.: The National bibliography of Indian literature.- New Delhi: The author, 1962 - 1990.

5 Vols.

Sankar, K.G. The Problems of Bhasa. *In* Sir Asutosh Memorial Volume - Part II.- 1926. Pp. 51-64.

Sanskrit drama in performance / ed. by Rachel Van M. Banner and James R. Brandon.- Honolulu: The University Press of Hawaii, 1981.

Sarup, L. Poems and plays of Bhasa. *HR*; 1927. Pp. 116-121.

Satyavrat. 'The Cārudatta and Mṛcchakaṭika: a reappraisal of their relationship'. *Visveshvaranand Indological Journal* / ed. by K.V. Sarma; September, 1976; Vol. XIV, No. II.

Sethi, Atmaram. Anudit Hindi sahitya: vishishta granthasuchi / by Atmaram Sethi.- Gurgaon: Indian Documentation Service, 1981.

Contents: Sanskrit (Pp. 1-624)

Sharma, Chitra. Sanskrit natakam mein samaj-chitran.- Delhi: Meherchand Lachhmandass, 1969.

In Hindi.

Sharma, D.D. 'Vāsavadattā: the most popular and multi - dimensional woman character of Sanskrit drama'. *Vishveshvaranand Indological Journal*; March - September, 1979; Vol. XVII, Nos.I-II. Pp. 39-48.

Sharma, K.V. New problems in Bhāsa plays by N.P. Unni'. *Vishveshvaranand Indological Journal*; March - September, 1979; Vol. XVII; Nos. I-II. P. 312-313.

Book review by K.V. Sharma.

Sharma, Shiva Dutta. A Summary of the 5th Act of Svapnavāsavadatta of Bhāsa in Hindi. *All India Oriental Conference X* (Summaries); p.35.

Sharma, Soma. Sanskrit mein vyayog = Vyāyogas in Sanskrit.- Delhi: Nirman Prakashan, 1992.

Sharma, Sudarshan Kumar. 'Svapnavasavadattam of Bhasa: a reap- praisal'. *Journal of Oriental Institute;* March - June 1980; Vol. 29, Nos. 3-4; Pp. 198-208. ft-n.

Sharma, Ujjwala. Study of metres in Sanskrit dramas: Bhasa to Bhavabhuti / by Ujjwala Sharma.

Ph.D. thesis approved by the University of Delhi in 1974.

Sharma, Virbala. Sanskrit mein ekanki rupak. - Bhopal: Madhya Pradesh Hindi Granth Akademi, 1972.

Sastri, Gaurinath. Sanskrit sahitya itihas.- Calcutta: Sarasvata Library, 1969? [Aśvin 1376]

In Bengali.

---------. Bhasa and the authorship of the thirteen Trivandrum plays / by Hirananda Sastri - Calcutta: Govt. of India Central Publication Branch, 1926.

V, 36 p; 33 cm.- (Memories: Archaeological Survey of India; 28)

---------. Bhasa and the authorship of the thirteen Trivandrum plays. *MASI* (Calcutta); No. 28.

Shastri, Nemichandra. Mahakavi Bhasa. - Bhopal: Madhya Pradesh Hindi Granth Akademi, 1972. 565 p; 22 cm.

Shastri, T. Bhāsa's plays: a critical study.- Trivandrum: [s.n.] 1925.

124 p.

---------. Bhasa's works: a critical study.- Trivandrum: [s.n.], 1925.

----------. *BSOS*; Vol. III. Pp. 627-637.

---------. The Svapnavasavadatta of Bhasa. *JRAS* 1924. Pp. 668-669.

Shekhar, I. Sanskrit drama: its origin and decline.- Leiden: E.J. Brill. 1960.

Pp. 55, 64, 65, 75, 79n, 80n, 85, 115, 130, 135-137, 148, 150, 155, 156, 174, 176, 179.

Shukla, Sarala. Comparative study of the life in the dramas of Bhasa and Kalidasa / by Sarala Shukla.

Ph.D. thesis approved by the Jiwaji University in 1978.

Singh, Inder Mohan. Dramatic craft of Bhasa in the light of Natya Sastra / by Inder Mohan Singh.

Ph.D. thesis in Hindi approved by Saugar (H.S. Gaur) University in 1979.

Social life as revealed in Bhāsa's Rāmāyana and Mahābhārata plays' / by P.M. Upadhya. *Bharatiya Vidya*, 1975, Vol. 35. Pp. 108-12.

Sreekantaiya, T.N. Imagination in Indian poetics and other literary studies. - Mysore: Geetha Book House, 1980.

Sud, Suman. Karuna rasa: from the view point of Valmiki, Bhasa, Asvaghosa, Kalidasa and Bhavabhuti / by Suman Sud.

Ph.D. thesis in Hindi, approved by the Kurukshetra University in 1969.

Sukthankar, V.S.? The Date of Svpna. *JRAS*, 1928. Pp. 877-88.

----------. Studies in Bhasa: on certain archaisms in the Prakrit of these dramas. *JAOS*; Vol. XLI. Pp. 107-130.

---------. Studies in Bhasa: on the Prakrit of the drama. *JBRAS*; 1925. Pp. 103-117.

[Symposium on Bhasa]. *Proceedings and Translations of the All - India Oriental Conference* 1943-44. (12th session) held at Benaras Hindu University.

Dr. Pusalkar presented a paper in favour of the authenticity of the thirteen Trivandrum plays.

Thomas, F. W. The Plays of Bhasa. *JRAS*; 1922. Pp. 79-83.

---------. Svapnavasavadatta. *JRAS*; 1928.

Tirtha: the treasury of Indian expressions / ed. by Vijaya Ghose.- New Delhi: CMC Ltd., 1992. Pp. 131-132, 203,210.

Treatment of pathos in Sanskrit drama / ed. by Pushpendra Kumar.-

Delhi: Nag Publishers, 1981.

Trivedi, Chandra Bhusan. Gleanings from the dramas of Bhasa and Kalidasa: critical and comparative study / by Chandra Bhusan Trivedi.

Ph.D. thesis approved by the Bhagalpur University in 1981.

Unni, N.P. New problems in Bhasa plays.- [s.l.] College Book House, 1978. 338 p.

---------. 'The Trivandrum plays and the Abhijṇanśākuntala - carcā. *Vishveshvaranand Indological Journal;* March - September 1975. Vol. XIII, Nos. I-II. Pp. 376-84.

Veera Bala. Art and mind of Bhasa / by Veera Bala.

Ph.D. thesis approved by the University of Delhi in 1972.

Venkatakrishna Rao, U. Bhasa. *Indian Historical Quarterly;* June 1958; Vol. 34, No. 2; Pp. 96-113.

Venkatarama Sarma, V. Svapnanataka and Svapnavasavadatta.*Indian Historical Quarterly* December, 1929; Vol. 5, No. 4; Pp. 721-728.

Venkaṭarāmayya, C.K. Bhāsa mahakavi / by C.K. Venkatarāmayya. - Bangalore: The author, 1937.

xii, 534 p; plate; 18 cm.

Critical study of the writings of Bhāsa in Kannada.

Venkatacalam, V. Bhāsudu / by V. Venkatacalam; tr. from English by Pullela Srīrāmacandrudu.- New Delhi: Sahitya Akademi, 1991.

203 p; 21 cm.

Critical study of Bhasa in Telugu.

Verma, Mahendra Kumar. Critical and comparative study of Sudraka's Mricchakatika and Bhasa's Charudatta / by Mahendra Kumar Verma.

Ph.D. thesis approved by the Agra University in 1970.

Walimbe, Y.S. 'Pancaratram and Madyamavyayoga of Bhasa'. *Bharatiya Vidya*; 1975, Vol. 35, Nos. 1-4; Pp. 92-103.

Winternitz, M. Bhasa: what do we really knows of him and his work? *In* Wc. Iner Commemoration Volume. Pp. 297-308.

---------. "Bhāsa and the Mahābhārata and Kṛṣṇa play". *Bulletin of the Ramavarma Research Institute*, 1974. Vol. 5, Pp. 1-15.

---------. History of Indian Literature (Vol.3)/ tr. from German into English by Subhadra Jha. - Delhi: Motilal Banarsidass, 1985.

INDEX

B

E

F

G

H

I

J

N

P

T

U

V

W

Y

Z